A SHORT HISTORY OF THE BRITISH INDUSTRIAL REVOLUTION

A SHORT HISTORY OF THE BRITISH INDUSTRIAL REVOLUTION

Emma Griffin

palgrave
macmillan

First published 2010 by
PALGRAVE MACMILLAN

Palgrave Macmillan in the UK is an imprint of Macmillan Publishers Limited,
registered in England, company number 785998, of Houndmills, Basingstoke,
Hampshire RG21 6XS.

Palgrave Macmillan in the US is a division of St Martin's Press LLC,
175 Fifth Avenue, New York, NY 10010.

Palgrave Macmillan is the global academic imprint of the above companies
and has companies and representatives throughout the world.

Palgrave® and Macmillan® are registered trademarks in the United States,
the United Kingdom, Europe and other countries.

ISBN-13: 978–0–230–57925–5 hardback
ISBN-13: 978–0–230–57926–2 paperback

This book is printed on paper suitable for recycling and made from fully
managed and sustained forest sources. Logging, pulping and manufacturing
processes are expected to conform to the environmental regulations of the
country of origin.

A catalogue record for this book is available from the British Library.

Library of Congress Cataloging-in-Publication Data
Griffin, Emma.
    A short history of the British Industrial Revolution / Emma Griffin.
      p.   cm.
    ISBN 978–0–230–57926–2 (pbk.)
    1. Industrial revolution—Great Britain.   2. Great Britain—Social
conditions—19th century.   3. Great Britain—Economic conditions—
19th century.   I. Title.
    HC255.G84 2010
    330.941′081—dc22   2010032626

10   9   8   7   6   5   4   3   2   1
19   18   17   16   15   14   13   12   11   10

Printed in China

For David, Benedict and Anna.

Contents

List of Figures

List of Illustrations

List of Maps

Acknowledgements

I first began thinking about the industrial revolution when asked to teach the Social and Economic History Paper from 1700 to 1914 to Cambridge undergraduates in the late 1990s. I felt the need to establish for myself exactly what the industrial revolution was before supervising my young charges, but there were so many conflicting interpretations out there, and few signposts to help me decide among them. The problem was further exacerbated when discussions with Leigh Shaw-Taylor got me worrying about the statistical basis on which much of our understanding of economic change is grounded. I have been pondering the nature of industrialisation and have been looking for ways to render economic history intelligible to undergraduates ever since. Students at the universities of Cambridge, Paris, Sheffield and East Anglia have been on the receiving end of these efforts, and this dialogue over the years provided the inspiration for this book as well as its basic outline and much of its content. The original proposal was subjected to careful critical scrutiny by three anonymous readers at Palgrave and by Andy Wood, and these comments helped to refocus and extend my initial plan for the book considerably. Kind friends and colleagues have assisted me in many ways, by discussing elements of the book, commenting upon draft chapters or passing on references or unpublished work. I would like to thank Lawrence Cole, Tony Howe, Craig Muldrew, Matthias Neumann, Sarah Pearsall, Leigh Shaw-Taylor, Paul Warde and Samantha Williams. Tony Howe has also lent illustrations for reproduction. Especial thanks are owing to Martin Daunton, whose own work towers over anyone thinking about British industrialisation, but who nevertheless spared the time to read over draft chapters. His comments led to the addition of significant new material elsewhere in the book. I am also grateful to Peter Kitson, whose extremely careful reading of draft chapters on work and population substantially improved both sections. It goes without saying that any errors remaining are all my own. Mostly, however, I should like to thank my husband, David Milne, for taking so much interest in both the general idea and the fine detail of this research: his love and support has made the writing of this book possible. I can't claim that our two small children, Benedict and Anna, have provided much useful assistance, except to make me focussed when working and happy when not. I dedicate this book to the three of them with all my love.

The author and publisher wish to thank the following for permission to reproduce the following copyright material:

University of Nottingham Manuscripts and Special Collection for 'A New Plan of the Town of Nottingham' by J. Badder and T. Peat (1744); 'Plan of the Town and Country of the Town of Nottingham by E. Staveley and H. M. Wood (1831); and for 'Plan of the Town and County of the Town of Nottingham by Frederick Jackson (1861).

The *Illustrated London News* for 'The Manufacture of Steel Pens in Birmingham, Messrs Hinks Wells and Co, The Pen Grinding Room' (22 February 1851); 'Welding the Gun-Barrels, Birmingham' (1 February 1851); 'Grinding the Gun-Barrels, Birmingham' (1 February, 1851); 'Birmingham New Street Station' (3 June 1854); and for 'Indian Spinning' (20 October 1855).

Routledge for 'Woman Spinning on the One Thread Wheel', 'Mule Spinning' and 'Calico Printing' by Edward Baines in *History of the Cotton Manufacture in Great Britain* (1835).

Longman for 'Arkwright, Hargreaves and Crompton's Spinning Machines' by John James in *History of the Worsted Manufacture in England* (1857).

Ironbridge Gorge Museum Trust for 'A Forge Near Dolgellau, Gwynedd' by Paul Sandby (1776).

Cyfarthfa Castle Museum and Art Gallery, Merthyr Tydfil for 'Cyfarthfa Rolling Mills at Night' by Penny Williams (1825).

Newcastle University Library for 'The Archaeology of the coal trade' and 'Early Steam Engine and Double Water Wheel' by Whim Gin. T. John Taylor in *Memoirs Chiefly Illustrative of the History and Antiquities of Northumberland* (London: Archaeological Institute of Great Britain and Ireland, 1858).

Manchester Public Library for 'Bridgewater Canal, Manchester'.

Glasgow University Library for 'Close, No. 80 High Street, plate 13' by Thomas Annan in *Old Closes and Streets of Glasgow*.

Wiley Blackwell for 'Map of the Historic Counties of England' adapted from E. A. Wrigley 'English County Populations in the Later Eighteenth Century' in *The Economic History Review* 60/1 (2007).

Cambridge University Press for 'Map of Britain's Thirty Largest Towns in 1871' adapted from B. R. Mitchell and Phyllis Deane in the *Abstract of British Historical Statistics* (1962); and for 'Distribution of Household Budgets by County' adapted from S. Horrell and J. Humphries, 'Old Questions, new data, and alternative perspectives: Families' living standards during the industrial revolution' in the *Journal of Economic History* 52/4 (1992).

Taylor and Francis for 'Distribution of British Coalfields' adapted from John Langton and R. J. Morris eds., *Atlas of Industrialising Britain* (1986).

Every effort has been made to trace rights holders, but if any have been inadvertently overlooked the publishers would be pleased to make the necessary arrangements at the first opportunity.

Map 0.1 Map of the historic counties of England. Adapted from E. A. Wrigley, 'English county populations in the later eighteenth century', *Economic History Review*, 60/1 (2007), p. 57.

Introduction

In 2008, the *Guardian* newspaper ran a series of articles about a problem they labelled the 'Global Food Crisis'. The fourth of these featured Zhang Xiuwen, a Chinese worker who in the 1990s abandoned a life of farming in Yunnan province to become a tennis coach in Beijing. For Xiuwen, the contrast between these two lives was epitomised above all by the vastly improved diet that followed his migration to the city. As a child in the 1970s, Xiuwen and his family had subsisted on a largely vegetarian diet; we 'children looked forward to spring festival,' he recalled, 'partly because it was fun, but also because it was a chance to eat meat.' And not only was eating meat something of a rarity, having too little to eat altogether was something that Xiuwen knew only too well: 'In my childhood I sometimes went hungry. During July and August, just before harvest, we usually did not have enough to eat.' How different this was to his life in Beijing: beef, chicken, pork and fish are a part of his and his family's daily diet the year round; 'in the past we couldn't imagine [meals] like this . . . now we can eat meat every day if we want. It has become part of our lives.'[1]

Industrialisation in Britain was considerably less rapid than it has been in China in recent years, and it was also considerably slower to bring measurable benefits to working people. Nonetheless it is possible to find echoes of Xiuwen's experiences in the autobiographical writings of many nineteenth-century workers. Joseph Arch, for example, an agricultural labourer and the first president of the farm workers' union, recalled that during his childhood in the 1820s and 1830s, 'the food we could get was of very poor quality, and there was far too little of it. Meat was rarely, if ever to be seen on the labourer's table . . . in many a household even a morsel of bacon was considered a luxury.' For Arch, the contrast with the diets that his own children and grandchildren could enjoy was every bit as striking as it would be for Xiuwen a century later. 'If fresh meat is still scarcer than it should be in the labourer's cottage today, he can at any rate get good wheaten bread and plenty of potatoes.'[2] Zhang Xiuwen and Joseph Arch were separated by over a hundred years and by many thousands of miles. But both lived through an industrial revolution, and both used remarkably similar language when comparing their children's lives with that of their own childhood.

Lack of food remains the most poignant aspect of life for the labouring poor in early nineteenth-century England, but nineteenth-century autobiographical literature abounds with other examples of material hardship. There is Robert Anderson, for example, who recalled the time he fell in the river and soaked his clothes: his mother sent him to bed 'for such was the poverty of the family I could not reckon more than one suit at a time.'[3] Or Alexander Somerville, who remembered his parents being the proud owners of one small pane of glass – a window which they took with them and had fixed 'in each hovel' they tenanted.[4] At the close of the nineteenth century, James Hawker could only marvel at the fact that some men now travelled to work on bicycles that cost £12. 'The only Ride I can Remember was to Push a Gate wide open and then step on it and Bang against a Gate post. If you Had any Food inside of you, it would Shake out.'[5] Indeed, everywhere in the working-class literature of the nineteenth century we find writers describing a paucity of material possessions that is hard to comprehend in today's affluent Britain.

These reflections on food, clothing, windows and bicycles may seem tangential to a study of the industrial revolution, but they, in fact, provide a potent reminder of the pivotal place of industrialisation in the history of human life. The threat of hunger that Xiuwen and Arch experienced has been the scourge of humanity since the beginning of time. *Homo sapiens* emerged as a sub-species around 200,000 years ago. Yet throughout this very long period no human society succeeded in decisively and permanently protecting every one of its members from the threat of an empty belly prior to our own industrial era, beginning in Britain just 200 years ago.[6] As such, the onset of Britain's industrial revolution inaugurated an extraordinary divergence from the established parameters of past experience. Little wonder, therefore, that the industrial revolution has been the focus of so much scholarly attention throughout the twentieth century, marking as it does a true, and quite remarkable, turning point in human history.

In pre-industrial societies, large numbers of the population were typically engaged in agriculture, their lives devoted to procuring the food, shelter, heating and clothing necessary to sustain human life.[7] Life was thus an endlessly repeating cycle of ploughing, sowing, harvesting and consuming, a cycle repeated year in year out, but without much hope of a sustained increase in living standards, without the expectation that the lives of the next generation would differ in any substantial way from that of their parents. Studies of calorie consumption in early modern Europe tell some depressing tales about the scant rewards that this round of labour produced. In late eighteenth-century France, for example, it has been calculated that the bottom 30 per cent of the population subsisted on around 1574 calories a day (today's recommendations are between 2000 and 2500 calories per day); many therefore lacked the energy to perform more than a few hours of sustained work each day.[8] Analyses of calorie consumption in some of the least industrially developed parts of present-day Africa tell a similar woeful tale. In the Congo, for example, the World Food Programme estimates the consumption of calories at around 1500 per person per day, substantially below that required for optimal nutrition.[9]

Alongside inadequate nutrition, other measurable indicators of quality of life such as morbidity and mortality testify to a very depressed standard of living in pre-industrial societies. In Sweden, life expectancy at birth rose no higher than 37 years throughout the eighteenth and nineteenth centuries, but by the early twenty-first century that had more than doubled to 80 years.[10] Once again, it is not difficult to find non-industrialised parts of the world which have not shared these gains in longevity. In Angola, for example, life expectancy hovered around 38 years (37 for men, 39 for women) in 2008.[11] Low standards of living have ever characterised pre-industrial societies, and they remain the hallmark of non-industrialised parts of the world today.

Of course, not all pre-industrial societies were agricultural. Ancient Rome provides an early and particularly vivid example of a pre-industrial, yet urban and relatively wealthy, society; northern Italy during the Renaissance and the Dutch Republic during its 'Golden Age' in the seventeenth century provide other more recent examples. Indeed, so impressive was growth in the Dutch Republic during this period that Jan de Vries and Ad van der Woude have argued that Holland deserves the title of the 'first modern economy'.[12] In each of these societies, the combination of a successful, thriving economy and relatively efficient agriculture enabled large numbers to move away from farming to find work in towns and cities. But although this shift was often associated with impressive gains in living standards, these gains tended to be rather meagre, and still left large numbers living perilously close to the margins of existence. In even the most urbanised and developed pre-industrial economies, most of the population in fact remained heavily dependent upon the land. Town-dwellers relied on the surrounding rural areas for their food and fuel; and much of their trade and industry was also derived from the soil.

Consider, for example, two of the industries upon which Holland's prosperous Golden Age was founded: ship-building and textiles. Seventeenth-century ships were constructed from timber; thus the entire industry was dependent on reserving large areas of land as managed forests in order to produce the oak trees necessary for construction – which, of course, left less land available to provide the population with food and firewood. In a similar vein, the highly successful woollen textiles industry required setting land aside for sheep-grazing, and although sheep-grazing could help serve the population's food needs, it was a far less efficient use of the land than putting it under the plough. These industries provided work and wages for a growing urban population, but by making land more scarce also helped to raise the price of food. There was, therefore, a constant tension between providing employment and providing the food and fuel necessary for a comfortable existence. The consequence was that large numbers of men and women did not escape the threat of hunger, which leaves the suggestion that there was something 'modern' about the economy problematic.

This tension between manufacturing and agriculture was widely recognised by early modern political economists, who gloomily concluded that while some economic gains were always possible through improved techniques, the extent of those gains was strictly limited. Consider, for example, the French economist Richard Cantillon who opened his *Essai sur la nature du commerce en général* with the statement: 'The land is the source or matter whence all wealth is produced.'[13] For Cantillon, the land provided both food and all the raw materials needed for manufacturing, effectively placing a cap on the amount of economic growth that could ever be achieved. These ideas may seem strange in the twenty-first century given our expectation of long term, continuous economic growth – growth derived in large part from items such as mobile phones, pop music, designer trainers and other goods that bear no obvious relation to the land. Yet Cantillon's scheme would not have sounded so strange to his own generation. At the time that he wrote in the early eighteenth century, despite the considerable economic diversification and urbanisation achieved in some nations, none had managed to break free from the constraints imposed by the land. Throughout the pre-industrial world, a life of unremitting labour, inadequate food, housing and clothing, and chronic ill health remained the unenviable lot of many.

The contrast with present-day Britain is clear. No matter what rosy prelapsarian tales anti-Capitalists have sometimes constructed about Britain before the industrial revolution, no serious historian today supports the claim that living standards in the eighteenth century or earlier equalled or surpassed those of the present day.[14] This is not of course to deny the problems of poverty and inequality in our own society but as poverty is usually defined in terms of a proportion of average incomes, steadily rising incomes in the past century and a half have also meant material improvements in real terms for those defined as living in poverty. And of course, a moment's reflection upon our own experience of modern life quickly confirms this. The gnawing hunger that Xiuwen and Arch describe is not something that we, our parents, our grandparents or even (for most) our great-grandparents have ever experienced. Poverty remains with us, but is now a matter of having to eat frozen, canned and processed foods rather than eating too little altogether; of owning few, cheap or second-hand clothes, not of possessing just one outfit; and of adult life expectancies cut to the late sixties rather than somewhere in the thirties.[15] Windows and bikes are no longer valued luxuries, but everyday items within the reach of all. Indeed, one of the most critical health problems to have emerged in the western world in the past few decades has been the rise of obesity, a development that is now being mirrored in China as that country continues to industrialise at a galloping pace. It simply was not possible for a large part of the British population to put on excess weight in the eighteenth or early nineteenth centuries: they could not afford to buy the calorie-dense food to gorge on. Or, to describe the situation in another, perhaps more telling, way – the economy was unable to produce calorie-rich food in sufficiently abundant quantities and to provide the general population with the relatively high incomes needed to purchase it.

Recognising that economic change in the period 1700–1870 in some way involved the untapping of far greater levels of material well-being for far greater numbers provides a starting point for our analysis of the industrial revolution, but of course it swiftly raises many more questions: exactly *how* did the industrial revolution raise material well-being in Britain? *When* precisely during this long period did it happen? *Why* did it occur? It is with these questions that this book is centrally concerned. The following eight chapters seek to provide some answers by analysing different aspects of the British economy during the years 1700–1870. Changing levels of national income, population growth and movement, working patterns, technological change and the emergence of a new supply of energy in the form of coal are the themes considered in greatest detail. By looking at each of these topics in turn, the book aims to make sense of the ways in which these factors interacted to create the world's first industrial revolution.

It must be admitted at the outset that answers and analyses to these questions already abound – there can, in fact, be few areas of British history that have attracted quite so much scholarly attention. And inevitably, not only have opinions differed, but interpretative fashions have changed with the generations.[16] Indeed, while this book, in line with many recent historians, uses the expression 'industrial revolution', it is helpful to recognise that at no point during the period considered here did contemporaries use that term to describe the dramatic economic and industrial developments that encircled them. Through most of the nineteenth century, the expression the 'industrial revolution' was largely confined to European languages[17] and was used only occasionally and rather inconsistently by English-speaking commentators.[18]

It was not until the end of the nineteenth century, with the work of the social reformer and historian Arnold Toynbee, that the term an 'industrial revolution' decisively entered the English language, and within a few decades it had entered the vocabulary of historians, undergraduates and even members of the chattering classes and workers' educational movements.[19] But no sooner had the expression begun to gain a degree of popular currency, than the academic community began to query the existence of this supposed 'industrial revolution'. A new generation of scholars began asking whether the industrial revolution was really so 'revolutionary', or indeed so located in 'industry', as the ebullient Toynbee had declared, and throughout the first half of the twentieth century the emphasis was firmly on the gradual rather than on the revolutionary nature of nineteenth-century economic change.[20]

Yet the writing of history rarely stands still. No sooner had scholars shaped a process of gradual and piecemeal industrialisation, than interpretative fashions changed once again, and the fast-paced 'revolution' that Toynbee had postulated seemed to be back in vogue once more. The Yale-educated economic theorist Walt Rostow's *The Stages of Economic Growth* was hugely influential on post-war conceptions of industrialisation. Rostow not only held that an industrial revolution, the world's first, had occurred in Britain somewhere between 1790 and 1850, but he even argued that it represented the lynchpin of modern history: the economic step-change that all nations had to emulate in order to thrive. Rostow defined the industrial revolution as a period of rapid economic growth, or 'take off' – he dated 'take-off' in Britain between 1783 and 1802 – followed by sustained higher levels of economic growth.[21] This model formed a sharp contrast to the more gradualist models that had held sway in the inter-war period. Here was an altogether punchier story, with the industrial revolution marking a watershed not just in British but in world history.

Rostow's account was not of course simply swallowed wholesale by British historians, but it did provide them with a meaningful framework for the study of industrialisation, and in the years that followed, the focus switched from downplaying the significance of change during the period to identifying the moment of 'take-off'. The most influential work in this vein was produced by the economic historians Phyllis Deane and W. A. Cole, who returned to the economic records collected at the time in order to provide ground-breaking estimates for the size and rate of growth of the economy between the late seventeenth and the mid-twentieth centuries. While considering the concept of take-off to be a 'dramatic simplification' and taking great care to stress the deep roots of economic change, Deane and Cole nonetheless spoke of a 'crucial breakthrough', and it was this theme that seemed to resonate most widely among scholars.[22] Throughout the 1960s and 1970s, the existence of an 'industrial revolution' was widely held as an article of faith. One of the leading historians of the 1960s, Eric Hobsbawm, saw fit to declare that the 'Industrial Revolution marks the most fundamental transformation of human life in the history of the world recorded in written document.'[23] Elsewhere, the nation's pre-eminent historians spoke of 'one of the great watersheds in the history of human society'; a 'great upheaval'; and a 'great discontinuity'.[24] It all amounted to a total revision of the pre-war generation's understanding of industrialisation.

But as should already be clear, historical interpretations rarely stand still for long, and so proved the case for this dramatic account of industrialisation. No sooner had the ink dried on the latest accounts of the revolutionary social changes wrought by industrialisation, than a new challenge to the concept was made. In the late 1970s, A. E. Musson's textbook, *The Growth of British Industry*, declared that the notion of a short and cataclysmic industrial revolution was 'clearly no longer tenable'.[25] This suggestion was led further, highly influential, support in the 1980s by a new breed of economic historians, preoccupied with measuring the various parameters of the national economy – industrial output, gross domestic product, productivity and so forth – and armed with an impressive command of economic theory and complex statistical methods. First, C. Knick Harley provided a critique of Deane and Cole's estimates for economic growth, suggesting they had overestimated gains during the crucial years 1770–1815.[26] The revision was completed shortly after by Nick Crafts, an economist then based in

Oxford, who reworked growth rates in the period 1700–1830, indicating much slower gains than the concept of rapid take-off permitted.[27]

This research inevitably had a profound impact on the existing literature, for by this point the industrial revolution was not simply an economic event, it was also, to quote Hobsbawm once more, 'the most fundamental transformation of human life in the history of the world'. If there had, in fact, been no great upsurge in industrial growth, where did this leave all those social transformations, watersheds and discontinuities that two decades of social, as well as economic, history had described? The re-emergence of a gradualist interpretation of the period roughly spanning 1760 to 1830 raised a certain degree of alarm among the historical profession. Patrick O'Brien observed that 'the British Industrial Revolution is once again under attack as a "misnomer", a "myth" ... and dismissed as one among a "spurious list of revolutions".'[28] And in their highly influential response to Crafts' work, Maxine Berg and Pat Hudson declared that 'the notion of an industrial revolution has been dethroned almost entirely.'[29]

But the consequences of these new estimates for economic growth were more complicated than the notion of a 'dethroning' of the industrial revolution admits. It is certainly true that one or two maverick voices questioned the use of the term, but in reality one needs to search the literature long and hard to find scholars who used Crafts' new statistics to argue that the concept of an industrial revolution was no longer valid.[30] In fact, what Crafts did was not dethrone the industrial revolution, but force scholars to question more deeply what exactly the 'industrial revolution' was. It was a problem with no easy answers, and we are arguably still witnessing the full unfolding of responses to this question.

The historians' initial response was to challenge the validity of the new statistics. Looking in detail at every element of these figures, critics sought to demonstrate not only that Crafts' figures were subject to a considerable margin of error but also that many of these errors were likely to underestimate, rather than exaggerate, the overall rate of growth. Yet for all the dissatisfaction that historians expressed with the new estimates, this critique ultimately resulted in a modification, rather than an outright rejection, of the new estimates provided, and it soon became clear that there was no desire to return to the older idea of a short period of dramatic economic advance. Instead, within less than a decade, most economic historians had begrudgingly accepted that during the classic period of the industrial revolution, economic growth, if not quite so slow as Crafts argued, was nonetheless considerably slower than an earlier generation had imagined.

For most historians, however, evidence of slow economic growth simply did not provide compelling grounds for dismissing the concept of an industrial revolution. The general consensus was that growth rates were no way to measure the existence (or otherwise) of something so complex as the industrial revolution. In this line of argument, the growth rates were not so much inaccurate as simply irrelevant, since they measured phenomena that had little do with the industrial revolution. Yet in pursuing this line of argument the ground between Crafts and his critics was much narrower than was sometimes implied. Though Crafts never described his figures as 'irrelevant', he certainly did use them to argue it was time to redefine the 'industrial revolution'. Crafts found evidence of both slow economic growth *and* a significant restructuring of the workforce – marked above all by the transfer of workers from agriculture to new industrial occupations – a restructuring that he considered to be amply sufficient to justify the continued use of the term 'industrial revolution'. In the event, however, Crafts' new definition received very much less attention than his statistics had. With a new found consensus that national growth rates were not pivotal to understanding the industrial revolution, the ground was levelled for fresh interpretations and assessments.

Specialists of different areas of the early industrial economy were quick to re-emphasise the significance of their particular area of interest. The role of inventions, for example, once again received critical attention. New technologies had long held a central position in interpretations of the industrial revolution. They had lain at the heart of French and German definitions in the nineteenth century and had also been integral to English uses of the expression, once it became commonplace in the early twentieth century. The 1926 edition of the *Oxford English Dictionary* (the earliest to include a definition of the industrial revolution) described it as 'rapid development of industry owing to the employment of machinery'. In the late 1940s, T. S. Ashton memorably equated the industrial revolution with a 'wave of gadgets' and David Landes' influential work of the 1960s echoed the view that technological change had played a vital role in powering industrialisation. In true revisionist fashion, the stress that previous generations of historians had placed upon technology was out of fashion by the 1980s. The highly respected French historian Fernand Braudel, for example, considered that 'if there is one factor which has lost ground as a key explanation of the Industrial Revolution, it is technology.'[31] Yet Crafts' new estimates for national growth coincided with renewed interest in the role of technology, innovation and creativity in powering economic change.[32] Although Crafts rejected the significance of new technologies, slower growth rates did not in themselves disprove their importance, since the large investments required to purchase new machines may result in many years elapsing before significant gains are realised, and several historians consequently sought to demonstrate the breathtaking range and extent of inventive creativity that lay beneath Crafts' rather flat growth curves. So pivotal was inventive activity in the century after 1750 that Joel Mokyr has concluded, 'it is appropriate to think about the Industrial Revolution primarily in terms of accelerating and unprecedented technological change.'[33]

As historians have noted, moreover, explaining the industrial revolution in terms of new technology quickly raises a further question: why did Britain prove such a fertile environment for technological innovation at this time? What factors – cultural, religious, educational and so forth – predisposed Britain to so much, and such successful, inventive activity? Margaret C. Jacob has highlighted the cultural forces that helped aid the diffusion of scientific knowledge from the academy to the workshop. By putting abstract scientific concepts to practical use, she argues, British entrepreneurs and inventors gained a clear advantage over their continental neighbours; the nation's fertile scientific culture was thus a key cause of its rapid industrial progress in the eighteenth century.[34]

Scientific culture was one element of British society which helped produce the right environment for industrialisation, but historians have also drawn attention to many other ways in which British politics and culture promoted prosperity. Patrick O'Brien, for example, has repeatedly stressed the role of the state in providing the necessary preconditions for a successful market economy, placing emphasis on its foreign policies in particular.[35] William J. Ashworth has also focused on the state, arguing that the institutions of taxation led to the development of governmental involvement in the broader economic sphere, with important ramifications for the expansion of manufacturing.[36] A particularly detailed and nuanced account of some of the wider cultural and political forces promoting industrialisation has been provided by Martin Daunton. Daunton has demonstrated how developments in finance, a reduction in transport costs, and public policy all helped to create the integrated market economy that formed a necessary precondition to industrialisation.[37]

In a more unorthodox strain, Gregory Clark has even suggested that Britain attained the cultural qualities required for capitalism to take root by the process of evolution by natural selection.[38] Using evidence from wills, Clark has argued that the upper classes had more surviving children than the poor had. Consequently they passed on more of their personality traits and cultural values – most significantly those that embodied modern economic attitudes – through their genes, which over time had a lasting impact on the genetics of English society. These traits included a preference for non-violence and literacy, a readiness to trade leisure for long working hours (and therefore higher income) and a willingness to put aside income for future possible needs. In this way, Clark concludes, 'man was becoming biologically better adapted to the modern economic world.'[39] This is, needless to say, a bold and provocative thesis, and one which has failed to gain universal assent.

On more familiar territory, Maxine Berg, one of Crafts' foremost critics, focussed on areas of the industrial economy that had traditionally received rather little consideration: the worlds of female and child labour, of domestic work and artisan workshops, handheld tools, small machines and skilled labour – what she called 'the other Industrial Revolution'.[40] Despite looking beyond the steam engines and factories that long formed the mainstay of industrial history, Berg found evidence of a 'transformation of production processes and regions ... and restructuring of industry over the course of the eighteenth and nineteenth centuries' and was left in no doubt that these changes amounted to an industrial revolution.[41]

Meanwhile, Tony Wrigley placed critical emphasis on the emergence of a new source of fuel: coal. Prior to the industrial revolution the economy was dependent upon the power provided by wood, wind, water, horses and humans, and only limited growth was achievable by these means. Wind power was unreliable and water power could only be provided by fast-flowing rivers, which effectively restricted its use to a finite number of locations. The power provided by horses and wood could be more actively expanded, but increasing power from either of these sources required land, either to grow the fodder for the horses or to grow woodlands to provide the timber. Yet, as Wrigley points out, the landmass of Britain was fixed, so extending the amount of land to be put to industrial purposes effectively required taking it out of cultivation for human consumption, and that in turn would restrict the possibilities of demographic growth. You could, therefore, have either industrial growth or population growth: you could not have both. Yet we know that at some point during the period 1700–1870, Britain entered a new era of sustained economic advance combined with population growth, breaking free from this centuries' old pattern of limited progress. According to Wrigley, the switch to coal provides the key to understanding this process. Switching to coal tapped a massive new source of energy that enabled industry to grow to a previously unimaginable extent, growth moreover which did not occur at the expense of feeding and housing the population. This process, he argued, provides the key to understanding the British industrial revolution.[42]

Placing the emphasis upon coal positions Britain's industrialisation in the context of the nation's resource endowments. Other historians, however, have been more interested by the way in which Britain exploited foreign resources in order to fund its industrial revolution. In the 1940s, the historian (and future prime minister of Trinidad and Tobago) Eric Williams argued that Britain's industrial revolution had been based upon the profits of slavery and the slave trade.[43] In the decades that followed, most historians rejected this thesis, arguing that slavery was a rather unprofitable system of production and therefore unlikely to have been able to provide anywhere near the capital required for industrialisation. Yet Crafts' figures provided the Williams thesis with a new lease of life. Robin Blackburn has noted that with British growth occurring more slowly, the contribution of the triangular trade in slaves, crops and manufactures between West Africa, New England and Britain begins to appear more significant.[44] Crafts' downward revisions of British growth, coupled with upward revisions of the profitability of the slave trade, have made the suggestion that Britain's involvement in slavery and the slave trade was an important trigger for industrialisation considerably more plausible. This argument has recently been taken yet further by Joseph E. Inikori, who has attempted to provide a detailed account of the 'role of Africans in England's industrialization'.[45] Highlighting the benefits England accrued through slave-based production and the slave trade, along with the development of shipping and financial services which flowed from the institution of slavery, and the emergence of

Atlantic markets for English manufactures, Inikori has concluded that the slave economy was a critical factor in England's transformation to industrial economy.

Despite the great variety of these analyses of the British industrial revolution, all effectively focus upon supply, that is, they focus upon how improvements in technology or increases in capital, energy or raw material enabled the economy to grow. Yet some historians have always maintained that the forces of consumer demand were a major driver of growth. Neil McKendrick, for example, argued that the eighteenth century witnessed a 'consumer revolution' – an increasing appetite for items such as furniture, fabrics and pottery which formed a 'demand side analogue to the supply-side industrial revolution'.[46] More recently, the role of consumer demand in promoting economic growth has been reformulated by Jan de Vries, who has argued that it is necessary to consider rising demand alongside changes in supply in order to understand British industrialisation.[47] According to de Vries, this rise in demand stemmed from a twofold change in the way in which families earned and spent their income. Firstly, workers had traditionally exhibited a preference for leisure over goods, that is, they had worked just so long as was necessary in order to procure life's essentials – housing, food and clothing – and then abandoned work (and the possibility of buying small luxuries with those extra wages) for leisure. In the second half of the seventeenth century, this traditional working pattern gave way to a more recognisably 'modern' pattern, in which individuals worked longer hours in order to earn the wherewithal to purchase a few luxuries – tea, sugar, new cotton clothing, a decorative plate or whatever else the consumer desired. Secondly, early modern workers had tended to produce much of what they consumed within the home rather than buying it at the market place. So a household got by by growing a few potatoes in the garden, baking their own bread, brewing their own beer and making their own clothes – cheaper alternatives to buying such goods from others. At the same time as families began to work harder in order to purchase small consumer goods, they also abandoned this domestic production in favour of buying goods readymade at the market, or even in one of the nation's rapidly growing number of shops. Although this change in household behaviour proceeded slowly, it gradually led to a rise in demand over the eighteenth century, which helped in turn to stimulate industrial growth. It constituted, de Vries argued, an '"industrious revolution" ... which preceded and prepared the way for the industrial revolution'.[48]

It is clearly not the case, therefore, that the concept of an industrial revolution was 'dethroned' following the publication of Crafts' new figures. To the contrary, by the end of the 1990s, we had far more industrial revolutions than ever before. By the same token, however, by the time the historians had finished 'rehabilitating' the industrial revolution, confusion over the term was also far greater. While most agreed that an industrial revolution had taken place, none could agree over exactly what it was. The possibilities of 'take-off', or rapid economic growth, had been safely ruled out, but this still left plenty of possibilities. Was it, as Crafts had suggested, a switch of economic activity from agriculture to industry and services? What was the role of those great inventors and their inventions – the steam engine, the power loom and the railways? How did the switch from wood to coal fit into the picture? Was the focus on the more dramatic technological innovations misplaced; should the industrial revolution be located instead in the sphere of domestic industry and female and child labour? And how did changes in household demand over the eighteenth century feed into the process of industrialisation? By the close of the twentieth century, the centrality of the industrial revolution to Britain's history was firmly established, but an embarrassment of definitions undermined its value as a concept more powerfully than any of the more overt attacks it had had to endure in the preceding 100 years.

Clearly, Crafts' research has had a profound impact on the reconceptualisation of the industrial revolution over the past 20 years, and given its far-reaching influence it provides a natural starting point for our analysis. In Chapter 2, we review Crafts' figures in detail, explaining what they measure and how they have been calculated. According to Crafts, economic growth was relatively slow throughout most of the eighteenth century and then picked up speed considerably in the early nineteenth century. This is a pattern of change that we will frequently encounter in the course of this book and will be important in helping to understand exactly what the industrial revolution was, and when it occurred. Before accepting Crafts' account, however, it is necessary to look at the criticisms that historians have levelled against his estimates and at possible margins of error, and the remaining part of Chapter 2 accordingly does this.

The following three chapters – Chapters 3–5 – seek to provide a fuller sketch of economic change over the period 1700–1870 by analysing the population from various perspectives. In Chapter 3 we look at the absolute numbers of people living in Britain throughout the period. We sketch a two-step pattern of growth, with population expanding relatively slowly and steadily through most of the eighteenth century, and then growing considerably more quickly in the following 70 years. As ever we consider how historians have sought to derive these measures and review the criticisms of these estimates before accepting them. This analysis is taken a step further in Chapter 4, where the distribution of population across Britain is explored more fully. This chapter illustrates how migration served to redistribute population growth across Britain in an uneven pattern, with people draining away from the countryside and clustering around the emerging industrial and coalmining districts. We observe the related process of urbanisation and note once more that two-part process of change, with steady urban growth over the eighteenth century followed by a shorter period of more dramatic change in the nineteenth. We also look briefly at agriculture, in order to assess how a dwindling proportion of the workforce nonetheless succeeded in feeding a fast-growing population. Finally in Chapter 5 we look at the employment that this steadily expanding and highly mobile population performed. Clearly urbanisation was accompanied by a drift of labour out of agriculture, but how did these workers earn their living once they had left the land? We describe and assess recent endeavours by historians to address this question and notice that their answers sketch a by now familiar pattern of change in two stages, with employment patterns changing quite modestly throughout most of the eighteenth century and then changing more rapidly in the final 50 years of our period.

In Chapters 6 and 7, we turn away from studying the broad contours of the economy and look instead at two of the factors that historians have used to explain the timing and causes of Britain's industrial revolution: technology and coal. In Chapter 6, we investigate Joel Mokyr's recent suggestion that the industrial revolution should be thought of primarily in terms of unprecedented technological change. We discover that although technology did have a revolutionary impact in some spheres of the economy, in other areas the relationship between technology and economic change was considerably more complex. As impressive economic growth and change also occurred in sectors of the economy that experienced only very limited technological change; we conclude that technology is not in itself sufficient to explain the pattern and timing of Britain's industrialisation. In Chapter 7, we consider the second possibility, advanced most consistently in recent years by Tony Wrigley, that the switch from wood to coal underpinned the industrial revolution. We look carefully at the mechanisms and timing at which coal was introduced to a number of key industries and suggest that although coal most certainly did have the power to unleash unprecedented economic growth, that potential was often unlocked only when new technologies that permitted manufacturers to switch from wood to coal came on stream. We conclude that although the switch to coal should be given primacy in our explanations for Britain's industrial revolution, the twin forces of coal and technology should also be viewed as complementary, not opposing, forces. Defining the industrial revolution in terms of the harnessing of new sources of energy also permits us to pinpoint the moment of its happening more precisely. Most manufacturing only successfully switched from wood, water and wind power to coal in the nineteenth century, which suggests that the industrial revolution should not be confused with the steady growth that occurred throughout the eighteenth century, but should instead be identified as the shorter period of more dynamic change that occurred somewhere between 1800 and 1870.

These ideas are pursued more fully in Chapter 8, which extends the discussion to a number of European and Asian nations, some of which industrialised during the nineteenth century, and some of which did not. Here we find that the success with which different nations discovered and exploited new sources of fuel correlates closely with their transition to industrial society, which lends considerable support for the argument that the harnessing of new forms of power should lie at the core of our understanding of the process. At the same time, however, this comparative perspective raises the question: why did some nations switch to new sources of fuel while others so signally did not? This in turn forces attention back to the two stages of change that have been delineated in several areas of the British economy during the period 1700–1870 and underscores the importance of the century of slow steady growth that preceded the industrial revolution. By the end of the eighteenth century, the avenues for further growth in the British economy were closing down. This century of growth should not be confused with the industrial revolution, but it did provide a vital spur for it.

The book ends where it began – by thinking about the living standards of the men, women and children who lived through Britain's industrial revolution. In Chapter 9 we explore the many different ways in which historians have attempted to measure 'living standards' and, as ever, scrutinise the reliability of their measurements. We also record for the first time a divergence from the general two-stage pattern of change that we have repeatedly observed in different areas of the economy. Through most of the eighteenth century, living standards stagnated and in the nineteenth century some measures suggest that living standards improved modestly, while others suggest they actually went into decline. We conclude that despite the undoubted long-term material gains that industrialisation has repeatedly been shown to usher in, the reality of living through Britain's industrial revolution was very different indeed. The first half of the nineteenth century witnessed the most rapid and profound economic restructuring in British history, yet it brought few tangible improvements to the society at large. The sustained rises in living standards that are ever the hallmark of industrialisation were delayed until the world's first industrial revolution was largely complete.

Counting Growth: Measuring the Economy

THOMAS GRADGRIND, sir. A man of realities. A man of facts and calculations. A man who proceeds upon the principle that two and two are four, and nothing over, and who is not to be talked into allowing for anything over.... With a rule and a pair of scales, and the multiplication table always in his pocket, sir, ready to weigh and measure any parcel of human nature, and tell you exactly what it comes to. It is a mere question of figures, a case of simple arithmetic.

(Dickens, *Hard Times*, 1854)[1]

During most of the second half of the twentieth century, the industrial revolution was regarded as a period of sustained economic growth, and many analyses of industrialisation have therefore been centred on attempts to count and measure the pace, extent and timing of this growth. The imperative to put some figures to the exact dimensions of economic change is self-evident. The problem, however, is that few systematic records for industrial production – or indeed for any other part of the economy – were kept, and growth rates must therefore be constructed from the most fragmentary of evidence.

There are many different ways of trying to measure growth in the economy and in this chapter we shall survey the so-called 'macroeconomic' or national accounting approach. Macroeconomics seeks to analyse the structure and performance of the national economy as a whole, in contrast to microeconomics, where the focus is upon the individual businessman or firm and the impact their actions have upon specific markets. The study of macroeconomics developed slowly from the 1930s, in part as economists sought ways of understanding, and remedying, the Great Depression – the worldwide economic downturn which followed the Wall Street Crash of 1929. The first attempt to use these techniques to measure the economy in a historical rather than contemporary context was made by W. G. Hoffmann in the 1950s, though his estimates were swiftly revised by the two economic historians, Phyllis Deane and W. A. Cole.[2] Since that time, macroeconomics has remained an important tool for studying and analysing the British industrial revolution.

Deane and Cole's estimates for economic growth suggested that, despite some deeper taproots, a new phase of rapid gains had begun in the 1780s. Their account of the onset of a period of sustained growth between then and about 1830 formed the backbone of most historians' conceptualisations of the industrial revolution for the best part of two decades, until C. Knick Harley revisited their calculations for manufacturing output in the early 1980s and suggested they had significantly overestimated the rate of growth in this sector.[3] Shortly afterwards, Nick Crafts independently reworked the figures for industrial output and then incorporated these estimates into a new set of national accounts.[4] Crafts, Harley and others continued to refine their estimates for growth both within the industrial sector and across the economy as a whole over the next decade, and a final set of figures was presented by Crafts and Harley in 1992.[5] Together, this series of revisions forcefully argued that economic growth during the classic period of the industrial revolution was considerably slower than Deane and Cole had envisaged.

In this chapter, we shall consider the macroeconomic approach to understanding the British industrial revolution. We shall begin by describing in some detail Crafts and Harley's results, and the ways in which they differ from Deane and Cole's earlier accounts. We shall then explain how they were calculated and review some of the criticisms that historians have levelled against them. We shall close by appraising more generally these attempts to put some figures to the industrial revolution, to conceptualise British industrialisation as (borrowing Dickens' words) 'a mere question of figures, a case of simple arithmetic'.

To begin, then, let us look at the figures that successive generations of economic historians have put to the industrial revolution in a little more detail. Deane and Cole had reported minimal gains in industry and commerce in the first half of the eighteenth century, followed by an upturn in the 1740s which slackened in the 1770s. This was then followed by the onset of more rapid growth of 3.4 per cent per year between 1780 and 1801, rising to almost 4 per cent in the next three decades.[6] Deane and Cole rejected the then highly influential idea of a Rostovian 'take-off' – a period of slow growth, followed by a short period of more dynamic growth launching the industrial revolution and a new era of sustained economic advance – owing to the upturn they identified at mid-century and argued instead that the deeper origins of growth needed to be recognised.

In Harley's calculations a much more sober account of industrial progress was provided. Rather than a burst of intensive growth in the half century after 1780, Harley's estimates suggested slow and steady improvement throughout the period. He reported the industrial growth rate hovering around 1.6 per cent per year from 1770 rising to 3.1 per cent per year in the three decades following 1815.[7] Crafts' subsequent estimates yielded broadly similar results: his calculations produced a growth rate of 1.5 per cent per year in the period 1760–80; 2 per cent per year in the next two decades; and 3 per cent per year in the three decades after 1801.[8] These figures were

Deane and Cole (1962)	Industry and Commerce
1700–60	0.98
1760–80	0.49
1780–1800	3.43
1801–31	3.97
Harley (1982)	Industry
1770–1815	1.6
1815–41	3.1
Crafts (1985)	Industry
1700–60	0.71
1760–80	1.15
1780–1800	2.11
1801–31	3.00
Crafts and Harley (1992)	Industry
1700–60	0.7
1760–80	1.29
1780–1800	1.96
1801–31	2.78

Figure 2.1 *Estimates of industrial output growth in Britain (per cent per year), 1700–1831.* Sources: Deane and Cole, *British Economic Growth*, p. 78; Harley, 'British industrialisation', table 5, p. 276; Crafts, *British Economic Growth*, table 2.7, p. 32; Crafts and Harley, 'Output growth', table 2, p. 711; table 4, p. 715.

subsequently revised downwards (a summary of all of these estimates is contained in Figure 2.1). The relatively small differences between Crafts and Harley's estimates and those of Deane and Cole nonetheless had a significant cumulative impact on the overall growth of industry over the period. Deane and Cole's estimates implied that industrial production had increased sixfold between 1780 and 1830: Crafts' estimates indicated a more modest (though nonetheless sizeable) increase of less than fourfold.[9]

This downward revision of the growth of industrial output led in turn to a downward revision in the rate of growth of the economy as a whole. Economists commonly use gross domestic product or GDP, which is defined as the market value of all the goods and services produced within the country in a year, in order to measure a country's economic performance. Deane and Cole had British GDP growing at about 2.5 per cent per year between 1780 and 1831; Crafts' figures suggested an annual growth rate of GDP of just over 1.7 per cent.[10] A detailed breakdown is provided in Figure 2.2. Again, the effect of this annual difference was large when compounded

Deane and Cole (1962)	GDP
1760–80	0.65
1780–1800	2.06
1801–31	3.06
Crafts (1985)	GDP
1760–80	0.7
1780–1800	1.32
1801–31	1.97
Crafts and Harley (1992)	GDP
1760–80	0.64
1780–1800	1.38
1801–31	1.9

Figure 2.2 *Estimates of growth of gross domestic product (GDP) in Britain (per cent per year), 1760–1831.*
Sources: Crafts, British Economic Growth, table 2.11, p. 45; Crafts and Harley, 'Output growth', table 2, p. 711; table 4, p. 715.

over 50 years. The earlier estimates had implied that GDP had increased by nearly three-and-a-half times in the half century between 1780 and 1831; in Crafts' estimates, the economy grew to less than two-and-a-half times its original size over the same period.[11] Given that the population had almost doubled in size during these years, the increase in GDP per capita was rather modest. Crafts' new figures indicated that gains within the British economy had been slow and uncertain prior to 1830. He could convincingly conclude 'the acceleration of growth was a more gradual process than metaphors such as "take off" imply.'[12] Though this, it should be recalled, was in fact just as Deane and Cole had also argued.

Crafts went a step further than measuring the size of the economy and its rate of growth throughout this period. He also sought to measure how *productive* the different sectors were and whether they were becoming more productive over time. This question is of particular interest, as it sheds light on the causes of rising prosperity. Imagine a successful factory increasing its output. It might be doing so simply by taking on more workers and by processing more goods. Each of those new workers is doing the same job as the old ones: with so many more workers on the shopfloor the factory's output inevitably increases, but the productivity of the factory has not changed. Our imagined factory might, however, increase its output not by taking on more workers, but by improving the efficiency of each worker – through the use of new machinery, new materials or new working methods. In this scenario, the same number of workers is producing more goods than once they did – their productivity has increased. It is clearly important to distinguish between these two different ways of raising output: the first might be achieved through simple population growth; the second implies that industrial processes are changing. This is why Crafts tried to measure changes in productivity as well as the overall rate of growth. He used a measure of productivity called 'total factor productivity' (TFP), which is defined as the part of output that cannot be explained by the amount of inputs. He was seeking to identify what was causing economic growth, in particular whether technological or organisational innovations, rather than a simple increase in the amount of inputs, were responsible.

Given that Crafts demonstrated industrial output growing slowly during the industrial revolution, it is unsurprising that he also found slow changes in improvements to industrial productivity. His figures suggested that TFP in manufacturing increased by 0.2 per cent per year between 1760 and 1801 and by 0.3 per cent per year from then until 1831 – a rate of growth that he described as 'slow'.[13] Furthermore, most of the gains were located in just two industries, textiles and iron, with practically no change in the rest of the manufacturing sector. The cotton industry alone, he argued, probably accounted for half of the improvement in productivity in manufacturing during this period, with transport, iron and other textiles making up most of the rest of the gains.[14] This account implied that while one industry was perhaps revolutionised, the rest developed in a wholly unrevolutionary way. Owing to the highly localised nature of productivity improvement, Crafts concluded that '[T]he term "Industrial Revolution" . . . should *not* be taken to imply a widespread, rapid growth of productivity in manufacturing.'[15] Though this too, despite Crafts' revisionist tone, was in fact largely as Deane and Cole had earlier argued.[16]

This downward revision of productivity in the industrial sector contributed to a downward revision of productivity improvements in the economy as a whole; Crafts put the figure for TFP at 0.1 per cent per year between 1760 and 1801, rising to 0.55 per cent per year between 1801 and 1831.[17] All the estimates for TFP, as well as the most recent revisions, are contained in Figure 2.3. He also shifted the location of improvements in productivity throughout the economy: one-third of the growth in productivity, his figures implied, was owing to improvements in one of its most traditional sectors – agriculture; manufacturing (textiles and iron) and transport (railways, canals and shipping) provided most of the remaining two-thirds. Less than 10 per cent of productivity growth occurred outside these 'modernised' sectors.[18] Furthermore, the lion's share of overall economic growth was not achieved through gains in productivity at all, but instead by extra factor inputs – more capital and more people.[19] This then completes the picture of the British industrial revolution that Crafts painted. Crafts did not simply recast industrialisation as slow; he also suggested that it was a highly localised affair. British economic growth had been achieved largely thanks to underlying demographic growth and to the accomplishments of agriculture and a handful of other modernised industries. Once more, though, it is important to stress that while Crafts' estimates differed quite

Crafts (1985)	TFP (Industry)
1760–1801	0.2
1801–31	0.3
Crafts (1985)	TFP (Economy)
1760–1801	0.1
1801–31	0.55
Crafts and Harley (1992)	TFP (Economy)
1760–1801	0.1
1801–31	0.35

Figure 2.3 *Estimates of total factor productivity (TFP) in industry and the economy (per cent per year), 1760–1831.*
Sources: Crafts, British Economic Growth, p. 84; table 4.2, p. 81; Crafts and Harley, 'Output growth', table 5, p. 718.

sizeably from those of Deane and Cole, his interpretation was considerably less novel. They too had stressed the atypicality of the modern industries and argued that much of Britain's economic growth had been caused by concurrent population growth.

Before proceeding to consider these estimates in more detail, it is helpful to make two further observations about Crafts' calculations. Firstly, it is worth emphasising the new chronology of change that Crafts offered. Crafts' estimates for industrial growth are often characterised as 'slow', but placing the emphasis on the speed of change is in fact less illuminative than focussing upon the timing. Although Crafts' estimates implied that growth had been quite muted during the years 1780–1830, by the end of this period the British economy had reached roughly the same size in both sets of estimates. In other words, his 'slow' growth did not result in a smaller, less industrialised economy at the end of our period; instead he argued that the British economy must have been considerably larger in 1780 than Deane and Cole had believed. Crafts dated growth from the early decades of the eighteenth century, so by 1780 significant economic expansion had already taken place. As Crafts and Harley clarified in their 'Restatement' of 1992, slow growth in the period 1780–1830 implied a 'wealthier and more industrial economy' at the start of that period, not a less fully developed one at its end.[20] One implication of these figures, therefore, was to recast the *whole* of the eighteenth century as a period of steady and sustained economic growth.

Secondly, it bears pointing out that Crafts' estimates for the nineteenth century were in fact anything but slow. One consequence of the highly revisionist tone that pervaded his work was to obscure how substantially the economy picked up after about 1800. Whether one looks at industrial output, GDP or TFP, a noticeable upturn in the rates of growth is evident as we move into the nineteenth century. This element of Crafts' analysis is confirmed by the independent estimates of Charles Feinstein and other researchers for various economic indicators in the nineteenth century. Between 1830 and 1870, the figures for industrial output, GDP and TFP all remain buoyant, and significantly higher than the levels that had been reached prior to 1800.[21] The figures are provided in Figures 2.4 and 2.5. Taken together, therefore, the most robust estimates available point towards two distinct phases of growth: a period of slow and sustained growth through the eighteenth century, followed by more accelerated growth in the nineteenth, which, while it never quite reached the heady heights implied by Deane and Cole's work, was nonetheless well in excess of anything that the British economy had previously achieved and marked a departure from existing trends.

	Industrial output	*GDP*	*TFP* (Economy)
1831–60	3.3	2.5	0.8
1856–73	2.6	2.2	0.6

Figure 2.4 *Estimates of growth in industrial output, GDP and TFP (per cent per year), 1830–73.*
Sources: Feinstein, 'Capital formation', table 25, pp. 139, 141; Crafts, *British Economic Growth*, pp. 32, 45, 81; Matthews et al., *British Economic Growth, 1856–1973*, pp. 22, 28, 133, 228–9, 501.

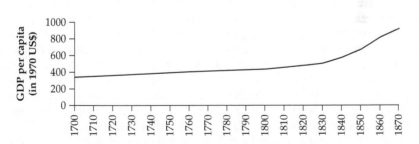

Figure 2.5 *Graph of growth of GDP per capita in Britain, 1700–1870.*
Sources: N. F. R. Crafts, 'Gross national product in Europe 1870–1910: Some new estimates', *Explorations in Economic History*, 20 (1983), table 1, p. 389.

Crafts' estimates for GDP per capita indicate a period of slow, steady growth throughout most of the eighteenth century, followed by a shorter period of more rapid growth in the nineteenth.

Despite providing a rather different outline of economic progress over the eighteenth and early nineteenth centuries, Crafts' estimates met with a very similar response to that of his predecessors, sparking interest and controversy among the academic community in almost equal measure.[22] These criticisms ran upon two different lines. In the first place, considerable effort was devoted to demonstrating that Crafts' figures, if not wholly inaccurate, were certainly less reliable than he appeared to suggest, and that many of his key assumptions, moreover, tended to understate the rate of growth rather than to exaggerate it. Secondly, critics argued that growth rates, even if they could be reliably measured, were simply not relevant to our understanding of an event so complex, so multifaceted and so diverse as the British industrial revolution. Let us consider both of these responses to the work of Crafts in turn.[23]

In order to address the first tranche of criticisms, concerning the reliability of Crafts' figures, it is helpful to begin by clarifying exactly what Crafts was trying to measure and how he sought to do it. Crafts set out to measure the size of the economy at different points in time in order to establish the rate of growth over the period. He further sought to identify which parts were growing, and whether or not this growth was achieved through improvements in productivity. Of course, measuring the size of a complex economy at two centuries' remove is no easy task, and Crafts began by disaggregating the economy into a number of different sectors, and measuring what was happening in each one. Crafts broke the economy into five sectors – agriculture; industry; commerce; rent and services; and government – and estimated growth rates in each. With so much of the controversy turning upon his calculations for industry, let us concentrate our analysis on that one sector.

The starting point for determining the size of the industrial sector was the measurement of the output of certain industries. Crafts did not measure the output of every industry, but of a sample, presumed to be representative of the whole: 13 in all – cotton, linen, silk, beer, leather, soap, candles, paper, wool, building, iron, copper and coal. His first task was to establish the output of each of these in cash terms. Next he sought to measure the 'value added' of each of the industries. Value added is defined as the additional value of a finished product over the cost of the materials used to produce it. It may be understood as the contribution that a manufacturer makes in terms of labour, capital and tools to raise the value of the unprocessed goods it began with, and it is used in national accounting to measure national income and to compare the size of one industry relative to another. Crafts' analysis of the industrial sector of the economy was completed by determining the relative importance – or the appropriate weight – of each of the 13 sample industries. With information on the rate of growth of the 13 industries and of the weight of each relative to the others, Crafts was able to compile an aggregate growth rate for the whole of his industrial sample.

Every element of this procedure is open to criticism. Consider, for example, the difficulties involved in measuring the basic building block: the output of industry. In the absence of systematic record-keeping by either government or companies, how can we quantify how much cotton, beer or soap was produced? Like his predecessors, Crafts turned to tax records: the excise duties that were levied on a number of industries such as beer, leather, soap and candles; and the custom duties that were applied to the import of raw cotton. His detractors were quick to point out that given the perennial problems that the government faced with tax evasion the tax data upon which his estimates of output were based were likely to underestimate industrial outputs. Others such as wool, linen and iron were not taxed at all and the output of these is yet more difficult to capture.[24]

Besides these difficulties in measuring the output of different industries are a host of problems concerning the measurement of value added. Value added is measured by comparing the costs to the manufacturer of purchasing materials to make his goods with the price he receives for them at the point of sale. While the idea is straightforward in theory, a look at the account books of some late-eighteenth-century cotton cloth manufacturers reveals the complexity of measuring value added in practice. Cardwell, Birley and Hornby was a firm of cotton manufacturers based in Blackburn in the late eighteenth century. They bought yarn and weaved it into various types of cloth. The most basic forms of cloth were sold for between two and three times the cost of the yarn; bleaching the cloth as well raised its value marginally higher and most of the company's cloth was sold in this form. If, however, the cloth was dyed before it was sold, its value was raised by a further quarter; and if it was printed, it was raised by up to a half.[25] Meanwhile, at the Peels' Brookside works, rolls of white calico (unprocessed cotton cloth) were bought at £1 6s each; Peels' printed them and then sold them for between £4 and £5 each.[26] Even within one factory the amount of value added varied significantly from one product to the next, and each factory's overall value added depended upon the relative proportion of the different products sold. Furthermore, the value added by each of these two cotton manufacturers was not identical – how is one to decide which is most representative of the industry as a whole?

Now imagine the challenge involved in constructing estimates for value added across the cotton sector as a whole, as well as across the other 12 sample industries, over the entire period in question. Accurate measurement of value added calls for extensive knowledge of the costs of inputs, the prices for which different outputs sold and the relative quantities of each output; and of course, such comprehensive information simply does not survive. With only the most fragmentary records for measuring the prices of goods, it is extremely difficult to establish with any degree of certainty how much value was added by manufacturers to the raw materials they processed.[27]

Once the value added of each of the 13 industries had been calculated, Crafts' analysis of the industrial sector was completed by establishing the relative size – or weight – of each over the period in question. The key problem here is that one sector – cotton – displayed a highly atypical growth curve. With cotton manufacture growing so much more quickly than most other industries, the weight it is given will powerfully influence the estimates for the sector as a whole – given too high a weight it will distort the sector's growth upwards; given too low a weight it will drive it downwards. Given the general paucity of data for the overall output, costs and prices of industry during the eighteenth and nineteenth centuries, it should come as no surprise that there is little hard information upon which to determine the size of the cotton industry relative to the rest of the manufacturing sector. Records of this nature were not kept prior to the middle of the nineteenth century, and in their absence it is extremely difficult to determine the relative share of cotton's manufacturing output. As Crafts and Harley themselves admit, the weight of cotton 'cannot be established with any precision'.[28]

Finally, it should be remembered that Crafts did not calculate the growth in output of every industry throughout this period, but rather that of a sample. How representative were the 13 industries that Crafts selected? Critics were quick to point out the many industries that were omitted: pottery, glass, lead, chemicals and metalworking, for example.[29] This list includes many of the most impressive industries in the period – the Staffordshire potteries, for example, or the metalworking trades in Birmingham and the Black Country. How far might the image of an atypically dynamic cotton industry within a generally stagnant manufacturing sector be modified by the inclusion of fast-growing industries such as these? Clearly, measurements of the industrial sector are bedevilled by a number of problems at every level. The heart of the problem is that the kind of data that is collected by modern economies in order to construct national accounts was not collected in the eighteenth and nineteenth centuries. Historians must work from scattered records compiled for other purposes and as a result, their estimates will always subject to sizeable margins of error.

Measuring the size and growth rate of the industrial sector of the economy is fraught with problems, but the difficulties in assembling indices of economic growth do not end there. Industry was just one of the five sectors that Crafts measured before constructing national indices of growth; so, having estimated the output of the industrial sector, Crafts proceeded to make similar calculations for the other four – agriculture, commerce, rent and services, and government. Evidently, the data needed to measure these sectors was no more widely available than it was for the industrial sector, and historians have developed a number of criticisms of Crafts' measurements of these four sectors similar to those that we have considered here.

Having broken the economy down into five distinct parts, Crafts' final task was to determine the relative sizes of the five different sectors in order to piece everything back together again. Just as each of the 13 industries had been weighted in order to give a picture of overall industrial growth, so these five sectors of the economy now needed to be weighted in order to measure growth across the national economy. The challenge here lay in establishing exactly what proportion of the total economy was devoted to agriculture, industry, commerce and so forth.

Deane and Cole had approached the problem by looking at the occupational structure of the economy, basing their estimates on the size of the agricultural sector (for example) on the proportion of the population working within it. While basing economic structure on occupational structure is uncontroversial in theory, in practice it is difficult to accomplish. The only figures that Deane and Cole had for occupational structure before the mid-nineteenth century were the rough-and-ready estimates that a few contemporary observers, most notably Gregory King, Joseph Massie and Patrick Colquhoun, had provided. Crafts' method was identical; he too sought to assign weights to each sector of the economy based on the number of people working in them, but he had at his disposal the superior social tables that Lindert and Williamson had recently constructed.[30]

Lindert and Williamson's occupational tables suggested that the contemporary estimates used by Deane and Cole had understated the size of the industrial sector in the eighteenth century, and this revision was in fact critical in reshaping Crafts' curves of industrial growth. By increasing the overall size of industry in the middle of the eighteenth century the growth that occurred between then and the 1820s was rendered less significant: what had looked like spectacular growth from an insignificant base now looked more like the continuation of long and steady growth.[31] But, of course, this conclusion was only as good as the social tables upon which they were based, and critics consequently subjected them to considerable scrutiny.

Lindert and Williamson used local censuses and burial records listing male occupation to provide estimates for the percentage of the workforce employed in agriculture, industry, service and so forth. At the time, their research gave a far more comprehensive breakdown of the structure of the economy than anything previously available, but historians have now raised some serious concerns about the reliability of their results.[32] They have questioned, for example, how appropriate it is to ascribe to each worker just one occupation when we know that many labouring men moved from one job to another over the course of their working lives in their endless struggle to make ends meet. Consider, for example, the career of John Tough, a labourer from Aberdeen, who, between the ages of 17 and 39, turned his hand to no fewer than 11 different jobs. He began his working life as a gardener; 3 years later he moved into land surveying; and next worked travelling for a hosiery manufacturer. He then had a succession of office-based jobs: first as an assistant clerk to a cotton mill, next as a bookkeeper for a brewery and then as the 'Collector of Freights' for the London Shipping Company – though this proving to be 'a very disagreeable situation' he soon left. Finding himself without work, he filled in a little time by hiring a vessel and travelling to Danzig to collect a cargo of wheat, before returning to Aberdeen and trying to eke out a living with a horse and cart and three cows. When this small enterprise failed, he travelled with his family down to the Central Belt of Scotland to work first in a mill and then at an iron works, before finally returning to the hosiery business in Aberdeen.[33]

Clearly, a complex working life such as this cannot be easily slotted into one sector of the economy or another. Indeed, attempting to do so betrays a grave misunderstanding of the nature of work in the eighteenth and nineteenth centuries.

Perhaps yet more problematic, though, is the fact that most official records did not list the occupations of women and children. Both are accordingly entirely omitted from Lindert and Williamson's tables. Yet we know that many of the factories springing up in south Lancashire and the West Riding of Yorkshire were filled with women and child workers; that new machines were sometimes designed and built to fit a child, not a man; and that employers often preferred to hire women and children in the belief they would be more tractable and submissive than a male workforce. In all sections of the textile industry – cotton, woollen textiles, silk, linen, lace-making and stocking-knitting – women and children were to be found in large numbers, and occupational tables that exclude women and children will inevitably fail to capture a large part of the economic activity they performed.[34] Maxine Berg has questioned the extent to which estimates of national output have been based upon 'the industrial distribution of the wrong workforce. It was the female not the male workforce which counted in the new high-productivity industries.'[35] Certainly, without information about the distribution of female and child labour it is not possible to discern what proportion of the total workforce was employed by each sector, and their omission will tend to underestimate the extent of a wide range of developing industries.

Estimates of the size of the various sectors of the industrialising economy form the cornerstone of national accounts, but it is worth emphasising that the national accounts method does not in itself measure the relative size of each sector. Instead, it borrows this information from elsewhere and uses it in order to construct the larger picture of economic growth and change with which it is centrally concerned.[36] Detail on the occupational breakdown of the economy is extremely valuable to our study of the industrialising economy. It is information that historians are continuing to seek, and we will consider more recent approaches to this problem in Chapter 5. For the present, however, we must note that critics have raised serious doubts about the occupational data that were available to Crafts when he constructed his national accounts. And so long as there is uncertainty about the size of the different sectors of the economy, there must be uncertainty over the overall extent and pace of its growth.

The objections that historians have raised with the macroeconomic approach to understanding British industrialisation are legion and, initially at least, some of these critics expressed their views in quite hostile terms. Yet despite the criticism that was originally levelled against Crafts' figures, it is noticeable that over the last two decades there has been a begrudging acceptance of Crafts' three central arguments: that the mid-eighteenth-century economy was considerably larger than previously thought; that subsequent economic growth was probably slower; and that growth was more confined to a limited sector of the economy. In the early 1990s, Cuenca Esteban revisited Crafts and Harley's figures for the cotton industry and produced some startling different results. Cuenca Esteban suggested that the cotton industry was far larger in the 1770s than Crafts and Harley had believed and that estimates for growth in industrial output over the next half century therefore needed to be revised upwards in line with Deane and Cole's earlier estimates.[37] This research prompted a quick rebuttal from Crafts and Harley but otherwise attracted little attention: there was not much enthusiasm within the historical profession for Cuenca Esteban's attempt to reinstate the Deane and Cole view. Nor, we might add, has there been much interest in revisiting or reworking the figures that Crafts, along with Harley, has produced. Harley's estimates for industrial production were first published over a quarter of a century ago in the early 1980s and they remain, with only relatively minor modifications, the estimates for industrial production that we still use today. Indeed, Crafts and Harley's estimates have lasted longer than Deane and Cole's did, despite the fact that the discipline of economic history has expanded very significantly since the 1960s. Interestingly, the recently published *Cambridge Economic History of Modern Britain* does not even contain a chapter on national accounting, perhaps because the available research in this area is now relatively old and has already been widely disseminated.[38] How, then, did the outright hostility that Crafts and Harley's reworking of national economic growth initially provoked evolve into such a comfortable accommodation among all?

Understanding how such contentious research has been incorporated so unproblematically into the mainstream historical narrative involves returning to that second line of criticism that historians initially developed: that whatever the accuracy or otherwise of these figures, they are simply not relevant to our understanding of the British industrial revolution. As Berg and Hudson argued, 'the national accounts approach to economic growth and productivity change is not a good starting point for the analysis of fundamental economic discontinuity.'[39] At the outset, historians recognised that slow economic growth and fundamental transition were not irreconcilable, and once the essential complementarity of these two versions of industrialisation is fully grasped, the necessity of demolishing Crafts' results largely disappears.

In pursuing this line of argument it is important to note that this is not so very far from what Crafts himself argued. Crafts never rejected the notion of an industrial revolution. Instead, his estimates led him to believe that the then dominant perspective of rapid economic growth driven largely by improvements in manufacturing productivity was untenable, and that a new definition needed to be found. The concept of an 'industrial revolution' still had value, he concluded, but in terms of a 'structural shift' in the economy, by which he meant a shift of human labour out of agriculture and into industry. In his own words: 'the main feature of British industrialisation involved getting a lot of workers into the industrial sector, not getting a high level of output per worker from them once they were there.'[40] Crafts never failed to stress 'the importance of the first industrial revolution'. He continued,

> Even if we now believe that it proceeded at a relatively modest pace, and that the really revolutionary changes were for long confined to a limited part of the whole economy, it remains true that Britain had brought about a remarkable transformation in the way a society provided itself with material goods. This will always be seen as an event of the greatest historical significance.[41]

Crafts and his critics agreed that slow national growth and radical transition were not incompatible.

Macroeconomics is just one way of seeking to study and understand economic change, and there can be little doubt that it has yielded some valuable insights into the nature of the British industrial revolution. For the present, at least, macroeconomics has decisively demolished the older interpretation of the industrial revolution which emphasised a short period of rapid economic growth fuelled by advances in manufacturing. But macroeconomics has been less successful in providing a new interpretation to take its place. Crafts placed the emphasis upon the shift that occurred in occupational structure, but this argument was ultimately derived from Lindert and Williamson's social tables rather than from his national accounts, and these tables raise a host of further questions and problems of their own. So, while we might agree with Crafts that Britain underwent an 'event of the greatest historical significance', we are still left with many questions about what exactly this event was – questions which the national accounting framework is unlikely to be able to answer. Let us then leave the 'facts and calculations', 'figures [and] simple arithmetic' and turn to explore some alternative ways of shedding light on this transformation. We shall start by looking at that most precious of all resources: population – those men, women and children whose labour made industrialisation possible.

Chapter 3 . . . .

A Growing Population

> Men multiply like mice in a barn if they have unlimited means of subsistence.
>
> (Cantillon, *Essai*, c.1732)[1]

When nineteenth-century commentators sought to summarise the many social and economic changes that appeared to be occurring around them, they pointed to cities, factories, new machines and increased wealth – all seemed to be integral to the transformation they were witnessing. Population, by contrast, was given rather less attention. Early censuses (the first was recorded in 1801) clearly indicated that population, just like the economy, was growing; nonetheless, it remained possible for one commentator to declare in 1822 that he was 'quite convinced that the population, upon the whole, has not increased in England one single soul since I was born [1763]'.[2] While entirely incorrect (population had probably grown by about 90 per cent over these 60 years), it is striking that the claim that recent economic advance had occurred *without* a corresponding growth in the population was at least plausible in the nineteenth century.[3] In the twentieth century, however, historians placed a very different emphasis on the relationship between demographic and economic change in eighteenth- and nineteenth-century Britain. Not only did they argue that population grew considerably during this period, they also maintained that this growth was a key element of Britain's transition from a pre-industrial to an industrialised society. In this chapter we shall explore the history of population more fully. We shall outline the magnitude and mechanisms of growth; we shall assess the methods historians have used to measure growth; and we shall evaluate the explanations they have provided for it. We shall also consider what possible relationships might exist between population growth on the one hand and the process of industrialisation on the other.

Despite a general conviction through most of the twentieth century that the British population had grown significantly during the eighteenth and early nineteenth centuries, historians remained largely unable to identify the precise dynamics of this change.[4] The difficulty was not, for once, a lack of available evidence. On the contrary, historians were aware of the existence of a vast amount of information about the population contained in the registers of baptisms, marriages and burials kept in every parish by the Anglican church. The problem was that they had yet to devise ways of extracting and manipulating that information in a way that shed meaningful light upon population trends. In the 1950s and 1960s, new techniques for analysing parish registers and the advent of computing together promised to solve some of these problems, and in 1964 a group of historians founded a research group – the Cambridge Group for the History of Population and Social Structure – with the goal of harnessing these new techniques and technologies to their research on population. The Group had varied interests in population and family history, but its most lasting contribution has arguably been its work extracting data from parish registers and turning it into information about the size of the population and the mechanisms and causes of growth.

By the early 1980s, the Cambridge Group's work had revealed that some extraordinary changes in the population were occurring in the eighteenth and nineteenth centuries. Most significant perhaps was the sheer increase in size: during the eighteenth century the population almost doubled; in the following 50 years, it almost doubled once more. In all, this amounted to a more than threefold increase in just 150 years – growth on this scale had never been seen previously in Britain. Furthermore, through the second half of the nineteenth century and into the twentieth century, the population continued on a gradual upward curve. It was not simply the rate of growth that was unprecedented, it was that the growth seemed able to continue, ever upwards; it was open-ended, and appeared to have no limits.[5]

Certainly there had been periods of accelerated growth in earlier times. Though our knowledge of medieval and early modern demography is sketchy, there appears to have been a steady rise in numbers between the twelfth and the thirteenth centuries and again in the sixteenth and the early seventeenth centuries.[6] But these periods of growth had always been halted by some kind of catastrophe that brought the population back down to more sustainable levels – those 'Malthusian checks', dearth or famines, plagues, fires or wars, that brutally wiped out a section of the population, thereby forcing numbers back in line with the available resources. The most notable example of this was the Black Death – the great plague that swept across Europe in the middle of the fourteenth century bringing a swift and devastating end to the steady population increases of the preceding centuries: in England, somewhere between a third and a half of the population are estimated to have died.[7] The forces reining in the surge of population in the sixteenth and seventeenth century were rather less dramatic: increased celibacy, transatlantic migration and the concentration of population in a notoriously unhealthy London all played their part in keeping the British population at a sustainable size. Nonetheless, it is clear that the open-ended growth of the eighteenth century marked a break with earlier patterns and is suggestive of a splitting of the age-old link between population and natural resources. Something fundamental in the economy had changed, enabling resources to be used in a way that permitted not only rapid demographic growth, but continuous growth, free of the Malthusian checks that had haunted population expansion in earlier times.

Let us begin by looking at the exact dimensions of growth in a little more detail. In 1701, the population of England and Wales stood at just over 5 million. Numbers started to rise in the 1690s but only slowly: by the 1730s population had reached 5.5 million. After the 1730s, however, growth continued far more rapidly. By 1800, the number of people in England and Wales had reached 8.6 million, and in the following 70 years climbed to over 20 million.[8] The Cambridge Group had at last put some definitive figures to the population growth that contemporaries had sensed, but been unable to measure. Figures 3.1 and 3.2 provide a visual representation of this growth.

Although the sheer increase in population was one of the most striking discoveries of the Cambridge Group, the evidence they produced concerning the mechanisms by which that increase occurred was also highly significant. There are three ways in which a population may grow: there may be more births (higher fertility); there may be fewer deaths (lower mortality); or the number of migrants entering the country might increase. We may largely discount immigration as a significant force at this time, so the population growth must have been caused by either falling mortality or rising fertility, or some combination of the two.[9] One of the Cambridge Group's key findings was that it was a rise in the birth rate, rather than a fall in the death rate, that underpinned population growth in the eighteenth and nineteenth centuries. Between the 1680s and the 1820s, average life expectancy from birth steadily rose from around 31 years to 38 or 39 years, and in the period of relatively slow population growth between the 1690s and 1740s, mortality in fact made a greater contribution to the rising population than did fertility.[10] After the 1740s, however, although life expectation

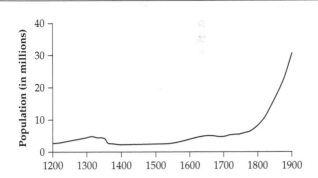

Figure 3.1 *Graph of population growth in England and Wales, 1200–1900.*
Source: Hinde, *England's Population*, p. 2.

This graph of population growth over the long term illustrates both the limited nature of population growth before the late eighteenth century and the much more rapid and sustained growth that was achieved thereafter.

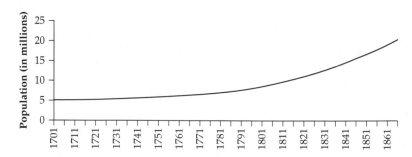

Figure 3.2 *Graph of population growth in England and Wales, 1701–1866.*
Source: Wrigley et al., *English Population History*, table A9.1, p. 614.

It is interesting to compare this graph of population growth between 1700 and 1866 with Figure 2.5, showing the rise of GDP over the same period. Notice how both follow a broadly similar trend, with steady growth over the eighteenth century followed by a sharp upturn in the nineteenth century.

continued to increase, its influence on growth rates, was (in Wrigley and Schofield's words), 'swamped by sweeping changes in fertility', and for the following century, an increase in the birth rate was the main driving force behind population growth.[11] Wrigley and Schofield concluded that the rising fertility rate had contributed two-and-a-half times more to the expansion of the population than had improvements in mortality, accounting for about 70 per cent of the total growth.[12] In a subsequent revision, the relative contribution of rising fertility to population growth was reduced to about 64 per cent.[13]

It is worth emphasising both the importance and the novelty of this finding. Earlier generations of demographic historians had certainly considered that rising fertility may have contributed to eighteenth-century population growth, but much of their attention remained focused upon the role of mortality. After all, it was on this front that the really significant changes seemed to be taking place: the spectre of famine largely disappeared during this period, and noticeable improvements were being made on the healthcare front, both through medical advances such as smallpox vaccination and through a simple rise in living standards. It seemed likely that some combination of these forces had led to improvements in mortality, which had, in turn, fuelled population growth.[14] Indeed, this line of argument was not entirely incorrect, as these developments had helped to create a reduction in the death rate. It was simply that this reduction made only a rather modest contribution to population growth as whole. Fertility, according to Wrigley and Schofield's new research, was the main driver of growth, and this necessitated a comprehensive rethinking of population change during the period of industrialisation.

Inevitably, as the Cambridge Group pioneered new ways of measuring past populations, it also attracted a considerable degree of controversy, and before accepting their re-writing of English demographic history, it is necessary to pause and address their critics in some detail. After all, we can only accept their conclusions if their research is reliable. So let us consider how Wrigley and Schofield measured demographic change and explore the possible flaws and biases their methods contain.

Wrigley and Schofield's estimates of population totals, mortality and fertility derive from a technique known as 'back-projection'. The method has since been refined and goes by the name of 'generalised inverse projection', or GIP, but we shall employ the original term here. Parish registers cannot shed light on the total size of the population in any given place: they simply contain information about movements in (baptisms) and out (burials) of it. However, combined with knowledge of the size of the population at a fixed point in time, this information about movements in and out can be used to provide a headcount at various intervals previously. Wrigley and Schofield used the census of 1871 as their starting point, as this not only measured the size of the population but also recorded the age of every man, woman and child. The principle is relatively straightforward. All those that had been buried in the previous 5 years were added to the total, while all those who had been baptised were taken away. In this way, Wrigley and Schofield were able to construct a new total for the size of the population (and its age structure), 5 years earlier. By continuing the procedure at 5-year intervals back to the middle of the sixteenth century they were able to reconstruct the size of the population over three centuries. In addition back projection yielded fertility and mortality rates, and information about the relative importance of each to population growth throughout the period.[15]

If the principle of back-projection is relatively straightforward, in practice, every stage of the method is fraught with difficulty. In the first place, it is not in fact possible to measure total movements in and out of the population. This would require information on every baptism and burial in all 10,000 English parishes, and such information was, unsurprisingly, unavailable to Wrigley and Schofield. They used instead a sample of 404 parishes and attempted to convert the baptisms and burials for these 404 parishes into monthly and annual birth and death rates for the whole country. In contrast to earlier attempts at demographic history, the number of parishes (about 5 per cent of the total) was impressive, but critics queried the extent to which this sample provided an accurate cross-section of English parishes. The difficulty was that Wrigley and Schofield had not selected their 404 parishes with a view to constructing a representative sample. Instead, they chose parishes where registers of good quality had survived and where transcriptions of the registers had been completed by volunteer historians; and these two conditions did not result in a perfectly balanced sample of parishes. The final sample ended up heavily weighted towards larger than average rural parishes, with small rural parishes and urban parishes under-represented. London was not included at all.[16] There were other imbalances; southern parishes dominated the sample, there were none from Cornwall and 12.5 per cent of the total came from just one county – Bedfordshire.[17] Yet these criticisms are less compelling than might at first appear, as Wrigley and Schofield were fully aware of all these omissions and imbalances and attempted to correct their results for them. For London, for example, they substituted the Bills of Mortality as well as some evidence from parish registers, and the whole sample was re-weighted before being converted into national totals, to allow for the imbalances in their sample of 404 parishes.

Perhaps more serious is the problem that these registers do not record the births and deaths with which we are really concerned. In place of births and deaths, parish registers list the baptisms and burials that took place within the established church. Poor-quality record-keeping by absent, barely literate or idle clergy might result in the omission of some of the vital events we are seeking to count. Likewise, the decision of those who chose to worship outside the Anglican church to baptise their children, marry or bury their dead in their own churches would result in these vital events not appearing in the parish registers at all. For these, and other reasons, there existed a gap between the ecclesiastical record-keeping and the actual occurrence of birth, marriage and death.[18] Throughout much of the period, levels of religious conformity were high and one can fairly assume that most births, marriages and deaths took place within the parish church and were duly recorded. From the late eighteenth century, however, nonconformity grew, and with it the problem of under-registration becomes more acute. Once again, however, Wrigley and Schofield were aware of this problem and sought to adjust their figures for it accordingly. Indeed, part of their motivation for starting back-projection in 1871 was the existence of nineteenth-century national censuses dating back to 1801 which could provide a check against which to measure the new procedure. There is a high degree of agreement between the two sets of figures. Estimates from the census and from back-projection are within 2 per cent of each other, indicating that the adjustments Wrigley and Schofield had made for under-registration accurately captured the births and deaths missing from the parish registers.[19]

Back-projection was a pioneering and novel procedure in the 1970s, and historians were inevitably keen to scrutinise and evaluate every element of it. There are clearly problems in converting the details recorded in parish registers into aggregate statistics, and experts will no doubt continue to debate the finer points of these complex issues. At the same time, however, there is a broad consensus among demographic historians that these figures are vastly superior to any alternative estimates and can be taken as a fair guide to English population history. It follows, therefore, that it is reasonable to accept the conclusion that rising fertility was the key driving force behind population growth in the eighteenth and nineteenth centuries.

It is clear that any explanation of population growth over the long eighteenth century will need to focus on the long-term rise in fertility, but it is in fact possible to pinpoint the exact motor of growth yet more precisely. Fertility can rise in a number of different ways. In a society in which most births took place within the context of marriage, it is helpful to structure our discussion around births occurring inside and outside marriage. One way then in which the birth rate might rise is by an increase in the number of births taking place outside marriage – an increase in the rate of illegitimacy. Throughout this period illegitimacy did rise significantly. At the start of the eighteenth century, just 2 per cent of all births took place outside marriage; this rose to 6 per cent by the end of the century.[20] But while this was a considerable increase, hinting at some interesting changes in sexual and marital practice, the overall contribution that it made to population growth was quite limited, for illegitimate births only accounted for a small fraction of the total.[21] Wrigley suggested that just under 15 per cent of the rise in fertility could be attributed to rising levels of illegitimacy through the period.[22] Furthermore, rising illegitimacy in fact had rather mixed results for the fertility rate and for population growth. In the first instance, women who had illegitimate children tended to marry later than their peers, which in the long term served to depress their fertility and reduce the rate of population growth. Secondly, as infant mortality among illegitimate births was much higher than average, perhaps even twice as high, the overall contribution made by rising illegitimacy to population growth was smaller than the figures for illegitimate births would imply.[23] In order to understand the rise in the birth rate, therefore, it is clearly necessary to look at births occurring within the context of marriage.

There are two distinct mechanisms by which couples produced more births within marriage. Each marriage might have produced more offspring – in the language of demographers, 'marital fertility' increased; or there might have been more women of child-bearing age within marriage – a rise of 'nuptiality', as it is termed by demographers. Let us consider both of these possibilities in turn.

Marital fertility is not constant across space and time. Even in the absence of modern contraceptive techniques, couples may use various methods to limit their family by increasing the spacing between births or by stopping before the end of the wife's child-bearing years; conversely, marital fertility may be increased by reducing the space between each birth, or by continuing to bear children for as long as is possible. The Cambridge Group's 1981 publication found 'no evidence of significant fluctuation' in marital fertility throughout the long eighteenth century, and this was accordingly discounted as a significant contributor to the overall rise in fertility.[24] However, in a second volume, *English Population History from Family Reconstitution*, published in 1997, this position was revised. Fresh research indicated that

marital fertility had undergone a substantial rise between the late seventeenth and the early nineteenth centuries, largely owing to a reduction in
the space between each birth of about 3 months, particularly in women aged
35 and over.[25] This rise, they argued, had been caused by a decline in the
rate of stillbirth and had contributed an estimated 15 per cent to the overall rise in the birth rate.[26] Together, the rises in illegitimacy and in marital
fertility accounted for about 30 per cent of the overall rise in the birth rate.
This leaves the bulk of the rise in fertility unexplained by increases in either
illegitimacy or marital fertility, and it is accordingly to the third variable –
nuptiality – that we must turn.

An increase in nuptiality, that is, an increase in the number of married
women of child-bearing age, may be achieved in two ways: by a higher proportion of women marrying, or by a drop in the age at which they marry.
Both will lead to a rise in the birth rate. Given that most procreation takes
place within the context of marriage, if a higher proportion of the population get married, then one should obviously expect a rise in the birth rate
to follow. Alternatively, if women abstain from sexual activity until they
marry, but begin marrying at a younger age, their child-bearing period is
effectively lengthened; once again, this should cause a rise in the birth rate.
Wrigley and Schofield's 1981 figures highlighted the importance of both
of these factors: they indicated that the proportion of women never marrying fell from 15 per cent to 7.5 per cent, while the mean age at which
women married for the first time dropped by about 3 years, from 26 to 23
years of age.[27] They concluded there had been 'substantial secular changes
in nuptiality sustained over long periods of time in England . . . of a magnitude to cause wide swings in overall fertility and in the rate of population
growth'.[28]

Following the publication of the *Population History* these figures were
refined in two significant ways. Firstly, David Weir demonstrated that prior
to 1700 it was the rising proportion of the population marrying that contributed most to the rise in fertility, whereas after 1700 it was the fall
in the age of marriage. Given that, as we have already noted, the greatest rise in the growth rate occurred after 1750; it, therefore, follows that
falling marriage ages were a more significant factor in population growth
than changes in the marriage rate.[29] Next, a re-examination of the figures
by J. A. Goldstone revealed that the drop in the age of marriage should not
be interpreted as the result of women throughout the population opting for
marriage 3 years earlier. Instead, this drop was caused by the emergence
of a small subset of the population marrying at much younger ages – a
set of men marrying aged 19–23 and of women marrying under the age
of 22. As Goldstone wrote, 'It is as if a fraction of the marrying population, about twenty per cent of men and about fifteen per cent of women,
withdrew from the population of "traditional" marriers, whose marriages
spread into the late twenties and thirties and beyond, and entered a separate category of "young marriers" who uniformly married during their late
teens or very early twenties.'[30] Both these contributions helped to specify

the exact mechanism by which population was rising in the eighteenth and nineteenth centuries and, therefore, to clarify exactly what change needs to be explained. The majority of the rising birth rate was caused by a drop in marriage age, the result of one section of the population marrying several years younger, rather than a uniform shift of 3 years across the population. The second volume on English population history published by the Group in 1997 largely reinforced these findings. The proportion of the population never marrying fell from 20 per cent to less than 10 per cent and this declining celibacy rate was pushed back to the seventeenth century. The fall in mean marriage ages remained 3 years and was relocated to the second and third decades of the eighteenth century.[31] This essentially amounted to a refinement, rather than a revision, of their original views. Of the two forces – age at marriage and rate of marriage – the former was considerably more important in fuelling population growth: Wrigley's figures suggested that about 60 per cent of the increase in the birth rate was caused by the drop in the age of marriage, and about 10 per cent by changes in the rate (Figure 3.3).[32]

Once again, it is worth pausing to consider the novelty of these results. Contemporary observers had fully appreciated that the marriage rate did not remain constant, but varied from one year to the next. For example, John Rickman, the nineteenth-century pioneer of the national census, noted that 'a great variation in the annual amounts of marriages is caused by the circumstances of the times, and especially by the price of provisions.'[33] Yet, in twentieth-century demographic history, the idea that changing marriage patterns were a significant factor in changing population trends had largely

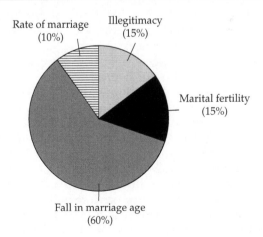

Figure 3.3 *Factors contributing to the increase of the birth rate in the long eighteenth century.*
Source: *Wrigley, 'British population', pp. 71, 75–6.*

receded from view. Prior to the publications of the Cambridge Group, historians looking at fertility had tended to look at the spacing between births within marriage, that is, at marital fertility, rather than nuptiality. Indeed, this was precisely the line of argument that Wrigley himself had pursued in an earlier work. His study of the parish of Colyton in Devon linked a decrease in the fertility rate with the adoption of some form of birth control and its later rise with the abandonment of these techniques.[34] Although the Group's latest work has re-emphasised the role of marital fertility, it still remains the case that primacy remains with nuptiality, and in particular the age of first marriage. The inconstancy of marriage formation across time, and the significance of this inconstancy in driving population trends, stands out as a novel and unexpected finding.

And equally, it is once again worth pausing to consider how Wrigley and Schofield were able to locate the relative importance of illegitimacy, marital fertility and nuptiality in driving the growth in the birth rate so precisely – for if their methods are not robust, these claims about the mechanism of population growth do not stand either. It is not possible to measure the variables considered here – marital fertility, the rate of marriage and the age at first marriage – using back-projection alone. Marital fertility and age at first marriage are measured using a second technique known as family reconstitution; and the rate of marriage is measured using the two methods in conjunction.[35] In contrast to back-projection, a technique that was pioneered by the Cambridge Group, family reconstitution is a well-established demographic tool, having been developed by a French demographer, Louis Henry, in the 1950s. A small part of the Group's first volume drew upon family reconstitution and the second volume was devoted to this technique. It is perhaps important to emphasise at the outset that the Group's work on family reconstitutions yielded broadly similar results to those obtained through back projection – a method so intrinsically different in nature that similar results lend significant credence to both.

Family reconstitution starts once again with the parish registers. Each baptism, marriage and burial is considered a unique event and recorded on a separate card. Imagine the marriage of an 'Eliza Wright'. The family reconstitution seeks to retrieve all those cards containing the name Eliza Wright. Perhaps she had been baptised 20 years earlier: we know her age at marriage. Maybe a daughter is born 5 months after the marriage: we know she was 4 months pregnant at the time of her marriage as well as her age at the time of her first birth. As each of her subsequent children are baptised, we learn the spacing between her births as well as her completed family size (marital fertility). Of course, this procedure will not simply yield information about the age of first marriage and marital fertility. It can also be used to shed light on mortality. In time the name 'Eliza Wright' will crop up in the burial records, and we learn her age at death (life expectancy). Child and infant mortality can also be measured using this technique: the space between the baptism and burial of any of Eliza's children will indicate their age at death. And so on. This procedure is repeated for the thousands of different names that appear in the registers. In this way we are able to reconstruct a remarkably detailed history of the life and family formation patterns of the thousands of families residing within the parish.[36]

Family reconstitutions can provide an exceptional level of detail about family history, but this detail is inevitably bought at a price. A reconstitution is a time-consuming and laborious procedure, likely to produce several thousand life histories, and cannot be conducted on a large canvas. The *English Population History* is in fact based upon the family reconstitutions of just 26 parishes. Owing to deficiencies in the parish registers at certain points in time, not all of these covered the entire period: only eight, for example, covered the period 1789–1837. The 26 parishes amount to a quarter of 1 per cent, a considerably smaller total than was used for back-projection. It is arguably a very slender base on which to make generalisations about national trends in population.[37]

Perhaps more significant than the total number of reconstitutions on which the study is based is the issue of whether this sample is representative of English society. With the sample comprising such a very small minority of the national total, some measure of representativeness is clearly essential. But these 26 parishes were selected from the original 404, and many of the observations concerning the types of parish that dominated the original sample may be repeated here. For example, the final sample of parishes misses out both ends of the demographic experience: the most rural parishes at the one end and the towns and cities at the other. The parish registers of small, sparsely populated rural parishes rarely meet the criteria of completeness required for family reconstitution, and these accordingly are under-represented in the sample.[38] All manner of urban parishes are likewise absent: none of the parishes were located in provincial towns, nor were any of the country's great cities – Manchester, Birmingham, Bradford, Leeds and so on – included. London, housing at least 10 per cent of the population throughout this period, is also absent from the sample. Yet the late eighteenth and early nineteenth centuries coincide with the onset of rapid urbanisation in England: by 1831 over one-quarter of the population was living in towns over 20,000 people; just a decade later more than a third did.[39] It is regrettable that none of this historical experience is represented in the final sample. Instead we are left with a sample of medium- to large-sized rural parishes and small urban centres. The 26 parishes were on average two-and-a-half times the size of the typical English parish; they had higher levels of population density and higher-than-average levels of the population engaged in manufacturing.[40]

Not only are certain types of settlement incompletely represented by the sample, but so too are certain regions. Once again the omissions mirror those already noted of the 404 parishes used for back-projection. Most notably, the North, rural as well as urban, is heavily under-represented: the sample contains just two parishes from south Yorkshire, one from the far north, and none from the North West. In the period after 1789, the exclusion of the North is particularly pronounced.[41] As in their earlier volume, the authors applied weighting procedures in order to bring the sample more into line with the national average – they used the occupational census of 1831 as a benchmark for comparison. But those familiar with the census have raised questions about how accurate this census really is.[42] Clearly, in the absence of robust information about the precise make-up of the English economy at any point during this period, it is extremely difficult to weight the sample, known to be unrepresentative in a number of ways, appropriately.

There is a further problem with the technique of family reconstitution, and this concerns the method itself, rather than the sample of parishes that the Group has used. There are two problems of particular significance. In the first place, the whole method relies upon linking names across the registers. This is a straightforward matter when dealing with unusual names, but more problematic when dealing with common ones – linking the marriage of, say, Zelah Wholey with her own baptism is far easier than doing likewise for Mary Smith. Secondly, family reconstitutions only ever capture the full life histories of men and women who were baptised, married and buried in the same parish. An individual might travel no more than a few miles to a neighbouring parish, but is lost to the family reconstitution once he or she has done so. Wherever an individual moves, it becomes impossible to trace their life history from baptism to burial – though of course a partial history tracing a chunk of their lives may still be reconstituted. The high rate of migration means that most family reconstitutions exclude many more people within the parish than they include: typically they are able to detect a baptism for only around 40 per cent of marriage partners. In effect, those who were baptised, married and buried in the one parish formed the minority, not the majority, in any parish and one needs to question whether those that lived out their lives in the place of their birth are fully representative of the rest who did not.[43]

As ever, as soon as one starts to interrogate the statistical record, a number of potential sources of error quickly appear, and scholars have not been slow to explore the significance of these problems for the overall results. Yet for all the many criticisms that scholars have levelled at the work of the Cambridge Group over the last four decades, it is undeniable that they have provided widely accepted parameters to early modern population growth. Their family reconstitutions have very usefully shed light on hitherto neglected aspects of population growth and they provide largely separate confirmation of the Group's original findings, namely, that sustained population increase was driven by rising fertility, which in turn was driven by earlier and more universal marriage.

What is perhaps less well established is how far the national picture they paint for the whole country captures the diversity of local experience. The authors of *English Population History* stress the comparative homogeneity of nuptiality and fertility across the country. While they accept the existence of local and regional variations, they nonetheless emphasise that such variations are of relatively minor importance and insist that their 26 parishes stand as fair representatives of England as a whole.[44] Yet while family reconstitution undeniably adds unparalleled depth to our understanding of demographic processes in certain parishes, it does not capture a broad spectrum of experience across different parishes, and it is this, the difficulty of generalising from the local to the national, that forms the most problematic aspect of their recent work. A new trend in demographic history attempts to disaggregate the data, to look parish by parish and consider the (possibly) unique motor of change in each, rather than clump it altogether and try to tell stories about the 'English' experience.

Hudson and King's recent family reconstitutions of two Yorkshire townships – Calverley and Sowerby – have yielded some unexpected results and point the way towards an alternative way of conceptualising population change during this period.[45] Though Calverley and Sowerby closely resemble the villages in the 'proto-industrial group' studied by the Cambridge Group, neither conformed neatly to the demographic patterns sketched for such places with Calverley, in particular, failing to do so quite spectacularly. Beyond the fact that both parishes underwent natural population increase driven by rising fertility rather than falling mortality, a number of local peculiarities abound. Consider, for example, the highly distinctive fertility trends in Calverley. In contrast to the steadily rising illegitimacy rate in the national sample, illegitimacy actually fell in Calverley over the eighteenth and nineteenth centuries, never rising above 2 per cent of all births after 1700. Likewise, changes in both the age and the rate of marriage failed to mirror national trends. Mean female marriage ages were already low at the start of the eighteenth century, on average about 23 years for women, and they dropped by only a few months in the following 100 years (compared to the drop of 3 years that occurred nationally). The proportion of women remaining unmarried was also low at the start of the eighteenth century, about 7 per cent, and it actually rose rather than fell over the next 100 years. Clearly, neither changes in illegitimacy rates nor marriage patterns could have fuelled the steadily rising birth rate in this industrial village, and rising marital fertility must instead have provided the stimulus for natural population increase. Furthermore, in a pattern that should by now be familiar, this rise in marital fertility was not the result of a steady reduction in birth-spacing across all women, but stemmed instead from the emergence of a small subset of women (about 15 per cent) with consistently short birth intervals.[46]

In the parish of Sowerby changes in fertility resembled the national pattern more closely. Illegitimacy rose significantly through the period 1680–1820, from about 2.5 per cent of all births to over 8 per cent, thereby exceeding the national average. Nuptiality also rose. The mean age at first marriage dropped by about 18 months, roughly half the national average, and female celibacy also declined, dropping by more than half, from about 12 per cent of the population at the start of our period to just over 5 per cent at its end. At the same time, marital fertility increased steadily over the period, resembling the national trends more closely than the more marked increase in Calverley.[47] Such findings should warn against making national generalisations on the basis of a handful of local examples. Two parishes, just 15 miles apart and both with local economies dominated by farming and textiles, nonetheless experienced unique patterns of population growth, and much of this diversity will be lost by combining the parishes' results rather than looking at them separately.[48] And if such apparently similar villages could nonetheless experience such different patterns of demographic change, what might be lost in considering parishes with very different social and economic characteristics together rather than apart?

One further point these two reconstitutions reinforce is the fact that demographic trends in England were driven not by small changes across the whole population but by very marked changes in small subsets of the population. In Calverley, for example, there were no 'early marriers' – as we have seen, marriage ages did not move much through the eighteenth century in this parish. There was, however, the emergence of a small subset of women exhibiting a marked increase in their marital fertility. In Sowerby, the very significant rise in illegitimacy was not spread evenly across the women in parish but was concentrated in a small subset of women (about 8 per cent) who repeatedly gave birth to illegitimate infants. When one looks closely at the results of parish reconstitutions, therefore, it becomes clear that change and continuity co-existed at the local level, with certain small sections of the community undergoing rapid transformation in their patterns of family formation, while the rest continued to copy the behaviour of their parents, grandparents and even great-grandparents and beyond.

It is unfortunately not possible to sketch the history of population growth in Scotland or Wales to such a fine degree of detail. In Wales, the parish church recorded baptisms, marriages and burials in the same way as in England, and there may well be registers of sufficient quality to undertake some analysis of Welsh population history. At present, however, no one has yet sought to locate and work with them, and there is insufficient recent research on Welsh demography upon which to base an informed discussion of that country's population history. Meanwhile, Scotland did not share the English system of parochial registration at all and such registers as were kept north of the border do not contain the requisite information for modern demographic techniques. Scattered sources such as the early nineteenth-century censuses, patchy parish registers, local tax records and private statistical surveys are all that exist for the historian of Scottish demography. Consequently, while the demographic history of Scotland is rather more advanced than that of Wales, it is important to emphasise that the picture here is, necessarily, incomplete in contrast to the thoroughly documented population history of England.[49]

Nonetheless, it is possible to outline the main trends in Scottish population growth with a reasonable degree of confidence. For most of the eighteenth century, population growth north of the border was rather muted compared to that experienced in England, and began to catch up only after 1750. In the first half of the eighteenth century, the Scottish population grew slowly from 1 million to about 1.2 million. In the following

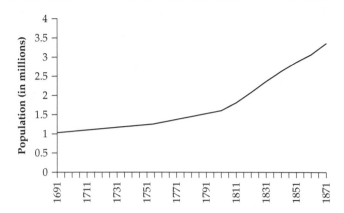

Figure 3.4 *Graph of population growth in Scotland, 1691–1871.*
Source: Flinn, *Scottish Population History*, table 3.8.6, pp. 198–9; table 5.1.1, p. 302; Tyson, 'Demographic change', p. 195.

While population totals and the rate of growth in Scotland are lower than in England, the general trend is not dissimilar, with a more rapid rate of population growth in the nineteenth century than in the eighteenth.

50 years, the annual rate of growth increased taking the total to 1.6 million in 1801.[50] Between 1800 and 1871, population growth increased more rapidly again, now running at an annual rate of 1.1 per cent, just slightly lower than that of England. As a result, the Scottish population had swelled to over 3 million by 1871.[51] In the absence of high-quality parish registers, the task of establishing the relative importance of fertility and mortality is considerably more difficult, though a number of tentative conclusions about the mechanisms of change may be offered.

In contrast to England, where as we have seen fertility was driving population growth, the birth rate in Scotland failed to increase significantly during the period.[52] As the birth rate remained largely stable, fertility could clearly not have been a significant force behind Scottish population growth. It is nonetheless instructive to consider the component parts of fertility – illegitimacy, marital fertility and nuptiality – in order to shed light upon how these variables were changing. In Scotland, as in England, illegitimacy rose steadily (from about 4 per cent at the beginning of the eighteenth century to 9 per cent of all births in 1861).[53] By contrast, nuptiality and marital fertility appear to have followed quite different paths in the two countries. While nuptiality steadily rose in England, both marriage ages and the celibacy rate remained stable and high in Scotland throughout the eighteenth century. The mean age for first marriage hovered around 26 or 27 until the 1820s, dropping then by about a year. The celibacy rate remained largely stable: at about 20 per cent, it was almost double that of England.[54] The figures for marital fertility in Scotland cannot be directly measured. However, given that there was a modest rise in illegitimacy and that nuptiality remained stable, it is reasonable to infer that marital fertility decreased slightly over this period. We will clearly need to look at mortality in order to understand what fuelled population growth in Scotland, and we shall do this below where we study mortality in greater detail. For the present, however, it is interesting to note that the nuptiality tap that was switched on in England in the middle of the eighteenth century appears to have remained firmly closed in Scotland. There is no convincing evidence of a dramatic change in any aspect of family formation in eighteenth-century Scotland.

We will return to consider the role of mortality, both sides of the border, more fully in due course. For the present, however, let us pursue the findings of the Cambridge Group one step further. The significance of rising fertility in driving population growth is well-demonstrated, as is the primacy of rising nuptiality in many, if not all, parishes. This, then, leads to one final question: why were more women choosing to get married and others opting to marry so much younger? Or, to put the question another way, why had women traditionally had to wait so long before tying the knot? And why had such a sizeable minority failed to do so altogether?

The key to this question lies in understanding the impediments to marriage that existed in early modern England. These included, of course, the timeless difficulty of finding an attractive and suitable partner, but they also included a number of more historically specific obstacles. Marriage in Britain was traditionally a rather expensive business. There was the cost of the wedding itself (a day off work, fees for the vicar and a little money for a drink with friends and family). More significantly, however, there was the cost of setting up home together after the wedding had taken place. A newly married man was not expected to lodge with his parents or in-laws, but to take a dwelling for himself and his wife and become an independent householder. So marriage also required money for rent, and to buy the few sticks of furniture that would make a home habitable. The obstacles to marriage were summarised by the political economist Richard Cantillon in the early eighteenth century.[55] Cantillon considered it evident that 'most men desire nothing better than to marry.' At the same time, though, he thought no man would marry unless 'in a position to maintain his family in the same way that he wishes to live himself'.[56] Marriage, he explained, required some sort of economic opportunity, and unless a man could see 'the necessary means of raising children, [he] will not marry or will only marry late, after having put something aside for the support of the household'.[57] The result was that across much of Europe, the young either delayed marriage until they had the economic security to set up an independent household or failed to marry at all. According to this logic, if couples were marrying younger, it suggests they were finding it easier to scrape together the resources required to set up a household of their own. And this, in turn, suggests that something was changing at the heart of the British economy.

Quite how it was that couples were finding these resources remains something of a mystery. Wrigley and Schofield originally linked earlier marriage to a rise in real wages. Superimposing the graph for fertility trends over that for real wages, Wrigley and Schofield observed a striking pattern of similarity and concluded that 'wide, slow oscillations in fertility ... broadly mirrored the real-wage fluctuations.'[58] But historians were quick to identify a number of problems with this explanation. Firstly, the shifts in fertility that Wrigley and Schofield had uncovered only followed shifts in the real wage 40 years after they had happened. Many critics simply found this implausible, for why should improvements in real wages only lead to changes in marriage patterns 40 years – nearly half a century! – later?[59] Next the real wage data that Wrigley and Schofield had borrowed in order to illustrate the correlation between marriage rates and the state of the economy were replaced by fresh research in this area. Lindert and Williamson's new estimates for real wages over the period did not follow the same curve, and when they were superimposed upon the nuptiality trends the neat correlation that Wrigley and Schofield had found simply disappeared.[60] With it, the foundations for the original argument were removed at a stroke.

Yet if changes in fertility could not be straightforwardly mapped on to changes in real wages, many historians nonetheless agreed that changing marriage patterns could be explained with reference to England's developing economy. A number of different possibilities were suggested. David Levine, for example, linked younger marriage ages with the growth of 'proto-industry', that is, small-scale cottage industry in rural areas.[61] This, he suggested, gave the young a source of income earlier in life and enabled them to marry without awaiting the inheritance of land. But critics were quick to point out that the drop in marriage ages was not confined to proto-industrial villages: it was also 'happening elsewhere in wholly different economic circumstances', including places with little or no rural industry.[62] J. A. Goldstone linked the drop in marriage ages to the emergence of 'proletarianisation', that is, the switch from self-employment and farm service to wage labour.[63] This enabled young workers to dispense with the need to save before marriage and allowed them to marry with nothing more than the *prospect* of regular wages in the future. But this argument assumes a fairly radical switch to wage labour in the century after 1750, when studies of work have revealed that daily wage labour was already widespread long before this period.[64] The Poor Law, the decline in farm service and changes in women's working patterns have also been implicated in changing marriage patterns during the eighteenth and early nineteenth centuries.[65] In reality, historians have found it extremely difficult to pin down the precise changes in the English economy that caused changes in nuptiality, and there is little consensus over why the young were finding it easier to set up their households during this period.

Nonetheless, despite the disagreement between historians concerning the exact reasons for younger and more universal marriage, the ground between Wrigley and Schofield and their critics is far smaller than might at first appear. Their original formulation, linking nuptiality to real wages, was no doubt an oversimplification, but just as there was a general acceptance of the broad thrust of their figures, so too were historians largely agreed that Wrigley and Schofield were looking in the right place. Historians have largely accepted that something was changing at the heart of the English economy which enabled more men and women to marry, and enabled some to do so at a very much younger age than before, though they remain uncertain as to what exactly this 'something' was.

Yet before accepting that growth in the economy were responsible for changing marriage patterns, there is one final point to consider. This argument rests upon the claim that marriage throughout this period was delayed until couples had the wherewithal to set up their own household. A close look at the historical record, however, suggests that the reality of courtship and marriage frequently deviated from the model of independent nuclear households.[66] Of course, generalising about the motivations behind an act so individual and private as marriage is notoriously difficult. Nevertheless, investigating the cultural context of marriage is an important issue, for if marriage was not linked to economic circumstances in the way that a generation of historians has assumed, then our attempt to link changing marriage patterns, and therefore population growth, to the fortunes of the economy quickly appears misplaced.

It is possible to shed some light upon this problem by looking at autobiographical evidence. Marriage was an important step in anyone's life, and those who wrote their life history usually had something to say about the circumstances surrounding their wedding. These sources provide an extremely varied array of reasons for marrying. Consider, for example, the case of William Swan, a London bricklayer, who explained he wished to marry as the fighting between 'my Landlord and his Lady' left him feeling 'somewhat uncomfortable in my lodgings'.[67] Or John Bates, for whom the costs of a long-distance relationship proved too much: 'postage was very expensive then, each letter costing 10 d, and rail was almost as dear, so I made short work of it and gained her consent. We were married the day after Christmas day.'[68] Meanwhile, Joseph Arch, who in time became the first president of the National Agricultural Labourers Union, decided to marry because he needed a housekeeper to keep his house in order. Living at home with his father he found life so uncomfortable following the death of his mother; he concluded, 'there was nothing for it then but to marry and settle down.'[69] Clearly, motives for marriage could be complex and often defy simple classification.

Nonetheless, it is not difficult to find writers who made firm links between marriage and economic independence. John Green, for example, explained his decision to marry at the end of a varied career as a soldier overseas in terms of having the financial means to do so: 'having employment, and a little property at my disposal', he wrote, 'I began to think of changing my way of life; and on the 1st of June 1815 I entered on the marriage state.'[70] Arnold Goodliffe, a grocer's assistant from Nottingham, did not even consider marriage until he had set up his own small grocer's shop. Even then, he resolved to do 'the best I could and try for about a year before I set up housekeeping and married'.[71] A Scottish flax-dresser described falling 'deeply, thoroughly and unmistakably in love', but he nonetheless continued to work and save for two full years before getting married.[72]

Counterpoised to these careful, saving workers with their prudent marriages, however, were those who walked down the aisle with little economic planning and no savings, and these too abound in the autobiographical literature. Consider, for example, James Nye, an agricultural labourer in Sussex, who agreed to marry with 'only one sovereign in my pocket to do everything with, and no constant work and winter coming on … after I bought a wedding ring and a wedding dinner and paid the parson my money was gone and no house furnished'.[73] Or James Bowd, who got married with a bed and a 'very good Family Bible', but very little money – 'only three shillings not much to start in Life', he confessed.[74]

Meanwhile, Benjamin Shaw married his heavily pregnant Betty at the age of 19, while still an apprentice and having, by his own admission, 'no Prospect before us but extream Poverty'.[75] Without a penny to set about housekeeping – 'we had neither furniture, or monney, nor friends' – Betty at first continued living with her father and then moved into Benjamin's lodgings, where they 'found their own vituals, & were poor enough'.[76] The poverty that Benjamin had feared did indeed lurk at the door throughout their union. Time proved his forebodings about their fitness to marry correct, yet his understanding of the financial burdens imposed by marriage had not been sufficient to prevent his improvident marriage taking place. Autobiographers like Nye, Bowd and Shaw clearly recognised the desirability of married independence, but it was something that they had failed to achieve on a personal level. Such examples should caution us that the creation of an independent household was more precarious and more haphazard than some demographers have assumed.

As so few autobiographies were written before 1750, such evidence will never reveal precisely how the process of family formation changed during this period, but it is nonetheless instructive that a core of mid-nineteenth-century writers forged ahead with marriage despite lacking the means to set up an independent household of their own. Writing at the end of the demographic revolution, Nye, Bowd and Shaw married without the means to set up their own household, and this suggests a possible reason for changes in nuptiality that historians have thus far neglected to consider: that the social and cultural norms that had for centuries served to restrict access to marriage were starting to weaken. If this is so, it implies a shift of emphasis in our explanations for eighteenth-century population growth. Since Wrigley and Schofield, the taproots of demographic growth have been located in an expanding economy: the culture of marriage, it has been assumed, remained the same, but the economic context in which marriages took place became more propitious. Autobiographical evidence, however, suggests that it might be helpful to explore the culture of marriage more fully before dismissing the role of social change in driving the age of marriage downwards. In other words, the precise balance between social and economic causation remains unclear. Wrigley and Schofield have convincingly demonstrated that a fall in the age of marriage played a pivotal role in driving demographic growth. But exactly why marriage ages were changing, and in particular whether it was a consequence of economic expansion or of cultural change, has not yet been established with any certainty.

It seems clear that rising fertility was a key component of demographic growth in the century-and-a-half after 1700. Nonetheless, it should not be forgotten that a decrease in mortality also helped to fuel Britain's spectacular growth, and in the final part of this chapter let us turn our attention to the ways in which changes in mortality contributed to this process. In England, the decline in the death rate in the first half of the eighteenth century was in fact the primary driver of population movement, although the upward trend was relatively slow before 1750 compared to what then followed. A second phase of improvements to mortality occurred at the end of the eighteenth century; while no longer the most significant variable, it certainly helped to add to the overall increase. Taking the period as a whole, life expectancy at birth rose from a low point of 35 years in the 1720s to 40 years in 1801, and then hovered stubbornly between 40 and 41 years for the next 70 years.[77] Improvements in mortality were uneven and often faltered, but the general trend is unmistakable and long-term improvements over the period 1700–1870 were a significant force helping to buttress English population growth. In Scotland, as we have seen, the role of mortality is of considerably greater importance. Here a very marked increase in life expectancy occurred in the second half of the eighteenth century, rising from about 31 years in 1750 to about 39 years half a century later. This was a substantial improvement and was largely responsible for Scotland's rapid population growth during this period.[78] It is time to consider what might have caused these falling death rates and how improvements in mortality might be related to the concurrent process of industrialisation.

Just as breaking fertility into its component parts – illegitimacy, marital fertility and nuptiality – enables us to pinpoint the precise dynamics of change more clearly, so does disaggregating the death rate. Although there are a number of different ways of doing this, as a disproportionate number of deaths during this period occurred in babies and small children it is helpful to disaggregate the experiences of infants, children and adults. Separating the various components of mortality in this way indicates that England's steady fall in the death rate was caused by an uneven process of change across the different age groups. In the early eighteenth century, for example, while adult life expectancy rose, infant and child mortality actually deteriorated.[79] After 1750, adult mortality continued its steady improvement and infant and child mortality began improving too, though each at different rates. Infant mortality improved most significantly; whereas almost one in five babies born had died before their first birthday before that date, by the early nineteenth century the figure was closer to one in seven. A sharp reduction in the number of infants dying in the first month of life was largely responsible for this drop.[80] Child mortality also improved after 1750, though the improvements for children were less dramatic than those for infants.[81] In the first half of the nineteenth century, mortality hardly moved for infants under 1 year of age and deteriorated for older adults – those aged 40 years and more; there were, however, quite significant improvements for those aged between 1 and 40, in particular for those aged between 5 and 19.[82] The complex nature of decreasing mortality in Britain in the century-and-a-half after 1700 with infants, children and adults all experiencing improvements at different times suggests there is unlikely to be one single factor driving the fall in the death rate over this period.

In addition to the diverse mortality experiences of different age groups, the picture of mortality improvement is further complicated by the existence of very marked regional variations. Urban mortality was generally higher than rural mortality, and, with the exception of London, the larger the town, the greater the mortality.[83] In fact, this helps to explain why increases in life expectancy halted in the first half of the nineteenth century. This period corresponds with the large-scale movement of population from the relatively healthy rural environment (expectation of life at birth over 40 years) to the far less healthy industrial towns and cities (expectation of life at birth closer to 32 years). This migration is considered more fully in Chapter 4; for the present it is merely necessary to observe that urbanisation, all things being equal, should have caused a further deterioration in the death rate. Instead, it remained largely stable. Robert Woods has demonstrated that underlying England's unmoving life expectancy between 1800 and 1871 were improvements in most rural and urban areas counteracted by the movement of population from country to town.[84] Furthermore, high mortality rates were not just the preserve of large cities: semi-industrial rural parishes also tended to experience death rates higher than the national average. Death rates actually rose in most of the proto-industrial parishes in the Cambridge Group's sample over the eighteenth and early nineteenth centuries in contrast to the steadily falling death rates elsewhere, a fact which can be obscured when looking at national aggregates.[85] Nowhere are the pitfalls of making national generalisations about England's demographic experiences more evident than in the history of mortality, and without clear national trends the task of explaining changes in mortality becomes extremely difficult. Indeed, so complex is the pattern of mortality decline over the period 1700–1870 that Wrigley and his team have steered clear of attempting to explain it.[86]

In the absence of the detailed parish reconstitutions that have enabled the Cambridge group to outline the various components of mortality in England so well, our knowledge of the precise mechanism of change in Scotland is necessarily less complete. Heavy emphasis has traditionally been laid on the role played by the decline of subsistence crises in the eighteenth century in increasing life expectancy after 1750.[87] More recent analyses have questioned the extent to which this one development can be held responsible for Scottish mortality decline, but have had difficulty clarifying what other factors should be emphasised instead.[88] The problem stems from the fact that Scottish demographers are not really sure about what needs to be explained. Did life expectations increase for all age groups, or was the increase located in particular age groups – infants, children or young adults, for example? There is evidence to suggest that infant mortality steadily improved between the 1790s and 1850, falling from one in six to one in nine, but how did other age groups fare?[89] A study of Scottish lawyers has suggested that this group of adults witnessed no increase in life expectancy in the second half of the eighteenth century, though it would be foolhardy to believe that this relatively affluent section of Edinburgh society can be taken to represent adult mortality as a whole.[90] How did mortality differ between rural and urban areas? And what combined effect did these differentials between rural and urban mortality have on overall mortality trends? Without answers to questions such as these it is difficult to clarify exactly what needs to be explained. Little wonder, therefore, that one recent study has concluded that the improvement in life expectancy that occurred in Scotland in the eighteenth century was 'a conundrum that as yet has no satisfactory explanation'.[91]

Movements in the death rate are difficult to measure and yet more difficult to explain, and our understanding of mortality is far from complete both sides of the border. Yet it is interesting to note that wherever we have detailed information, we find mortality rates moving in a similar fashion to fertility rates. We have already noted that rises in the birth rate were driven by the emergence of a small subset of 'early-marriers' in the population rather than a more general drift towards lower marriage ages. In the same way, changes in mortality did not affect the entire population, but tended to be localised within small pockets of the local population. In proto-industrial parishes, for example, with their generally worsening infant mortality, a handful of families experienced very high levels of infant death, while the rest experienced an infant death rarely or never. When the death rate rose and fell, it did so because the number of families experiencing numerous infant deaths rose and fell, not because there was a general shift in infant death spread across the population.[92] This local perspective helps to illustrate the nature of change during the industrial revolution. This period undoubtedly witnessed spectacular population growth, and it is tempting to look for some large-scale general causes to explain it. But we should almost certainly be mistaken to do so. Rather than broad general shifts across the nation, we find pockets of highly concentrated change.

This characteristic – change that is rapid and dramatic, but confined to small areas or social groups – is key to understanding the industrial revolution, and a theme to which we shall frequently return.

Finally, it is important to note that mortality, like fertility, bore a complex relationship to contemporaneous economic developments, a relationship that is as yet imperfectly understood. Rising fertility, we have already seen, occurred at the same time as substantial economic growth, but it has not been demonstrated beyond doubt that it was caused by that economic growth; changing social mores surrounding marriage may also have helped to lower the age of marriage. It is equally difficult to establish a clear connection between improving mortality and the broader economic context. An influential thesis advanced by Thomas McKeown in the 1970s argued that rising living standards leading to improved nutrition must have been largely responsible for falling mortality in eighteenth-century Britain as the alternative possibilities (medical advances, developments in public health, improved personal hygiene and changes in either the virulence of disease or the disease resistance of the population) could together account for only small improvements in the death rate.[93] The detail of this argument predates most of the research published by the Cambridge Group, and the goalposts have clearly shifted considerably in the interim. McKeown may be correct that the wealth generated by improved agriculture and industrialisation helped to ameliorate mortality by raising nutritional standards. At the same time, however, one cannot escape the fact that British industrialisation was also associated with urbanisation, a process that has been clearly demonstrated to have had pernicious consequences for life expectations. As Wrigley has concluded, 'increasing wealth bore an ambiguous relationship to improved mortality.'[94]

Let us end this chapter where we began, with Richard Cantillon, and his observation that 'men multiply like mice in a barn if they have unlimited means of subsistence.' Writing in the early eighteenth century, Cantillon could not have known that England was on the cusp of the most rapid and sustained era of population growth in its history. Yet he nevertheless displayed a remarkable understanding of some of the forces that were involved in driving numbers upwards: the lion's share of population growth was caused by a rising birth rate, which in turn rose owing to younger and more frequent marriage. Marriage, furthermore, bore some relationship to the means of subsistence. Yet for all that Cantillon grasped the building blocks of English population growth, he made a fatal miscalculation in the outcome of these forces. Observing that the English enjoyed a higher level of subsistence than most of Europe, he concluded they must be achieving this by limiting their numbers. For Cantillon, the fruits of the soil were fixed; so if the English peasantry wanted to enjoy luxuries like leather shoes, beer, meat and butter, they had to make sure there were not too many of them. 'Englishmen, in general', he concluded, 'consume more of the produce of the Land than their Fathers did,' so there *had* to be 'fewer Inhabitants than in the past'.[95] This line of reasoning led him to scoff at the notion that the population of England could possibly be growing. And it also, of course, led him into serious error.

During the period 1700–1870, not just England, but Scotland too witnessed significant population growth without a catastrophic drop in living standards and Cantillon's belief that population growth was limited to what the land could provide had simply ceased to be true. The means of subsistence, which had for so long placed a ceiling over population growth, seemed to be expanding, permitting numbers to grow not just in short-term cycles, but over the longer term as well: from 5 million in 1700 to around 60 million today – three centuries of growth without any significant interruption.[96] As a consequence, this period marks a new phase in British history. This does not explain exactly what the industrial revolution was, but it is evidence of a fundamental shift within the British economy, and in subsequent chapters we shall seek to identify what happened during these years that enabled the economy not simply to provide for so many more people but also to provide them with ever-greater levels of comfort.

Chapter 4 ....

A Mobile Population

Day after day, such travellers crept past, but always ... in one direction – always towards the town. Swallowed up in one phase or
other of its immensity, towards which they seemed impelled by a
desperate fascination, they never returned.

(Dickens, *Dombey and Son*, 1848)[1]

We noted in Chapter 3 that population was increasing rapidly, particularly
after 1750, largely as a consequence of falling marriage ages. But we also
noted that while falling marriage ages were linked in some way to the process of industrialisation, historians as yet remain largely unable to agree
on what these links may have been. The riddles of population, however,
do not stop here. With a fourfold increase in population between 1700 and
1870, we might reasonably expect most villages, towns and cities to swell to
something like four times their original size. This though is far from what
happened. Growth across the country was extremely uneven, with the population of the largest cities increasing an incredible thirtyfold while that of
some provincial towns and villages either stagnated or actually declined. In
other words, people were not simply increasing in number, but they were
also moving from some parts of the country to others – a clear sign that
new patterns of economic opportunity were being established throughout
the land. In this chapter we shall complete our analysis of population trends
in the period 1700–1870 by looking at population movement and assessing
what light the evidence from internal migration might shed upon the British
industrial revolution.

Let us begin by reconsidering the figures for population presented in
Chapter 3 in greater detail. Building upon his totals for national growth,
Tony Wrigley has recently provided new estimates for demographic change
in each of England's 41 historic counties, estimates which unambiguously
reveal a pattern of uneven increase across the land. Between the years 1761
and 1801, the national population grew by 37.4 per cent. In fact, just two
counties grew by this amount. Two-thirds increased by 37.4 per cent or
less, and the other one-third increased by more than the national average.
Although the precise factors that determined the extent of growth were
unique in each case, there is a strong correlation between regional growth
rates and the composition of the local economy.[2]

We can see this correlation by looking more closely at those counties that grew at a slower-than-average rate and at those that exceeded the national average. Considering the slow-growers first, these counties were largely rural and agricultural with little in the way of manufacturing, industry or mining. Heavily agricultural counties such as Wiltshire, Hertfordshire, Berkshire, Herefordshire and Buckinghamshire, for example, languish at the bottom of Wrigley's population tables.[3] By contrast, those counties exceeding the national rate of growth, 12 in all, included all of those with marked concentrations of industrial employment: Cheshire, Derbyshire, Staffordshire, Warwickshire, Nottinghamshire, West Riding of Yorkshire and Lancashire. Nowhere underwent such rapid and extensive industrialisation as Lancashire, and it is surely significant that this county also experienced the highest rate of population growth by a considerable margin. The population here more than doubled in this 40-year period, with the result that the county's share of England's total population rose from less than 5 per cent to over 8 per cent.[4] Five counties with smaller, though nonetheless sizeable, pockets of growth in either mining or manufacturing – Shropshire, Durham, Leicestershire, Cumberland and Cornwall – experienced growth close to, or just slightly below, the national average (Figure 4.1).[5]

It is clear that these wide regional variations were created largely by migration rather than by local variations in fertility and mortality. We noted in Chapter 3 that changes in the rate and age of first marriage were largely responsible for driving population growth in the century following 1750, and while these differed from one parish to the next, the differences were relatively modest and cannot explain the very large divergence in the overall rates of growth between counties. Mortality varied more widely between settlements, but as the highest rates of mortality were generally to be found in densely populated industrial areas, this clearly cannot account for the higher rates of population growth that such places experienced.[6] The counties that were undergoing high rates of growth, therefore, must have been achieving this largely through the effect of migration.

Although our knowledge of population trends in Scotland and Wales is generally less complete than that for England, it is nonetheless clear that broadly similar processes were at work in these two nations as well. In Wales, for example, industrialisation was largely located in the two south-eastern counties of Monmouthshire and Glamorgan, and, as we should expect, these two counties also saw the greatest levels of population growth. Both grew to five times their original size between 1800 and 1871 as migrants left the English rural counties of Gloucestershire, Somerset and Herefordshire to work in the region's mines, quarries and iron and steel industries.[7] At the time of the 1851 census, only half of those living in Monmouthshire had actually been born

County	Rate of growth	County	Rate of growth
Wiltshire	5.9	Bedfordshire	24.9
Hertfordshire	6.4	Somerset	26.0
Rutland	8.3	Shropshire	26.3
Northamptonshire	9.9	Leicestershire	27.1
Huntingdonshire	11.1	Hampshire	30.3
Norfolk	11.5	Durham	33.6
Berkshire	13.3	Kent	36.7
Herefordshire	13.9	Cumberland	37.2
Buckinghamshire	15.9	Cheshire	42.4
Essex	17.9	East Riding of Yorkshire	44.5
Westmorland	18.5	Cornwall	47.0
Cambridgeshire	18.8	Derbyshire	48.0
Oxfordshire	19.4	Middlesex	48.9
Worcestershire	19.4	Staffordshire	56.7
North Riding of Yorkshire	19.6	Warwickshire	57.0
Lincolnshire	20.0	Nottinghamshire	60.9
Devon	20.0	Sussex	61.2
Northumberland	20.5	West Riding of Yorkshire	65.3
Dorset	21.3	Surrey	68.1
Gloucestershire	22.2	Lancashire	133.3
Suffolk	24.8		

Figure 4.1 *Estimates of rate of population growth in the English counties, 1761–1801.*
Source: Wrigley, 'English county populations', table 5, pp. 54–5.

in the county.[8] In Scotland, the general movement of population was towards the heavy industry of Lanarkshire, the textile towns of the Border and parts of the Central Belt – the two great cities of Edinburgh and Glasgow absorbed much of the overall increase.[9] Whereas about 36 per cent of Scotland's population had resided in the Central Belt in 1750, by 1801 about 42 per cent did; and by 1850 this had risen to 52 per cent.[10]

Furthermore, just as population grew unevenly from one county or region to the next, so within each county wide variations in the rate of growth existed. In the county of Northumberland, for example, the county-wide growth masked some sharp local variations. Between 1800 and 1870, the population more than doubled from 170,000 in 1801 to nearly 400,000 in 1870 – an increase that closely corresponds with the increase in the whole of England over the same period.[11] But not all parts of the county increased by this amount. The lion's share of the growth was located in just two small, but densely populated, districts: Newcastle, with its heavy engineering industry and its iron and steel manufacture; and Tynemouth, with its rapidly expanding coalmining industry.[12] Conversely, rural and unindustrialised parts of Northumberland grew at a slower-than-average rate. The county's average rate of growth, therefore, conceals at least two different patterns: rapid expansion centred upon the county's commercial and industrial centres and more muted change in much of the rest of this overwhelmingly rural county.

A similar pattern can be seen in south Wales. Monmouthshire's five-fold increase in population between 1800 and 1871 was considerably in excess of the national average. Furthermore, this buoyant county average masks a more complex local picture, with pockets in the county growing far more rapidly and much of the rest growing slowly or barely at all. Growth was most pronounced in the western part of Monmouthshire, in the major town of Newport with its thriving ship-building industry and in the town of Tredegar experiencing mushroom growth largely on the back of its successful ironworks. Newport grew to 14 times its original size in just 50 years, while Tredegar grew tenfold.[13] More generally, the demographic experiences of Northumberland and Monmouth encapsulated a recurring characteristic of social, demographic and economic change during the industrial revolution. Repeatedly we find that developments are not spread evenly through society. It is not difficult to identify revolutionary change throughout this period, but we find it limited to one social group, one area or one industry, sitting in a sea of relative continuity.

It should also be clear that the national totals for population growth presented in Chapter 3 obscure a pattern that was in fact far more complex and uneven than the national averages suggest. Changes in fertility and mortality were causing population growth throughout Britain, but the traditional rural economy could not accommodate all the extra men, women and children created by natural population increase. In earlier centuries, a mismatch between population and natural resources had been resolved by some kind of Malthusian check – plague, famine or dearth – that cruelly brought population and resources back once more into line with each other. There was no resort to this response now. In the eighteenth and nineteenth centuries, the British economy was able to support its rising numbers, but only through a significant redistribution of the population.

An alternative way of illustrating the changing economic make-up of Britain can be obtained by looking at the proportion of the population living in cities and towns. Urbanisation is an excellent way of assessing a nation's historical development, as it is suggestive of numerous changes taking place at the heart of the economy: improvements in agriculture; a decline in the proportion of the workforce employed on the land and corresponding rise in those working in industry or service; a rise in incomes; a growth in specialist employment – any or all of these may accompany the movement of people from the country to the city. Taking settlements with a population of 5000 souls or more as a somewhat artificial definition for a town, the extent of urbanisation in England is easily illustrated. In 1700, 17 per cent of the population lived in towns with a population of 5000 or more. By 1800, this had risen to 27 per cent.[14] As ever, however, these plain statistical totals conceal a more complex picture. The overall drift to towns was more marked than this suggests, because at the earlier date most of the urban population (nearly 70 per cent) had lived in just one city, London, with the remaining 30 per cent living in all the other towns of 5000 or more combined. Over the eighteenth century, London's growth just kept pace with national growth and its share of the urban population held steady at about 11 per cent; so the rise in the proportion of the population living in towns stemmed from the growth of provincial towns and cities – their share of the total urban population doubled, from 30 to 60 per cent.[15]

The urbanisation of England continued in the following 70 years, picking up speed after the turn of the century. The proportion of the population living in towns doubled between 1801 and 1871, thanks both to the growth of pre-existing towns and to the emergence of new towns altogether. Over a hundred new towns emerged in Britain in the half century following 1800, most of them located in just one of four industrial regions: the West Midlands, the North West, Yorkshire and the Scottish Lowlands.[16] One set of estimates suggests that by 1851 over 50 per cent of the population of England and Wales lived in urban areas, and by 1871 over 65 per cent did.[17] Figure 4.2 provides an illustration of the steady advance of urbanisation between 1700 and 1871.

The most striking examples of these demographic changes are to be found in the emergence of a handful of northern towns, some of which exhibited unprecedented rates of growth. Manchester, Liverpool, Birmingham, Leeds and Sheffield, for example, had all had populations of fewer than 10,000 at the start of the eighteenth century; by the end of the century, they had populations ranging between 89,000 (Manchester) and 46,000 (Sheffield).[18] In the case of Manchester, the town had grown to ten times its original size. Many more new inhabitants continued to flock to these towns in the following 50 years, swelling their numbers yet further. Through the first half of the nineteenth century the population of Manchester, for

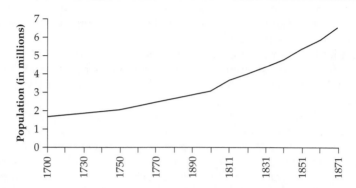

Figure 4.2 *Graph of urban population growth in England, 1700–1871.*
Sources: Wrigley, 'Urban Growth', table 1, p. 686; Law, 'Growth of urban population', table 5, p. 130.
Note: Wrigley and Law used slightly different definitions of a town in their calculations. Defining a town as a settlement with a population of 5000 or more Wrigley concluded 27.5 per cent of the population was urban in 1801. Law set the size of a town at 2500 but also used measures of population density and nucleation in defining urban settlements and on these criteria established that 33.8 per cent of the population was urban in 1801. The mean of these two estimates has been used in Figure 4.2.

example, doubled between 1801 and the 1820s and then doubled again by 1851.[19]

While urbanisation initially proceeded more slowly in Scotland, after 1750 population moved to the towns at a prodigious rate, rapidly transforming the previously agrarian country. In 1775, about 12 per cent of the population lived in towns of 5000 souls or more; in the next 15 years, this increased to 19 per cent – just slightly above the 17 per cent of English inhabitants who had lived in towns in 1700. By the end of the following decade, however, the proportion of Scots living in towns had risen to nearly 27 per cent – thereby achieving a level of urbanisation in one decade that had taken a century to accomplish in England.[20] Whereas in 1750 Scotland was ranked as the seventh most urbanised nation, it had risen to second place by 1850, just one place behind England and Wales.[21] Much of the increase in the urban population can be accounted for by the growth of just four cities: Glasgow, Edinburgh, Dundee and Aberdeen. Glasgow was growing at a rate of over 3 per cent per year in the 1830s.[22] Like Manchester, the city's population doubled twice in the first half of the nineteenth century; the total number of inhabitants was approaching half a million by the 1870s.[23]

By the 1870s, Britain was unmistakeably a more urbanised country than it had been 170 years earlier. In 1700 only London had had a population in excess of 100,000 and the next largest town, Norwich, had a mere 30,000.[24]

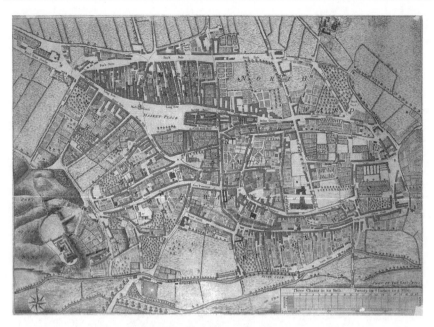

Illustration 4.1 Badder and Peat, *Plan of Nottingham*, 1744.

By the 1820s there were now five British cities besides London with a population of more than 100,000 (Birmingham, Edinburgh, Glasgow, Liverpool, and Manchester) and a further ten with more than 40,000 (Aberdeen, Bath, Bristol, Leeds, Newcastle, Norwich, Nottingham, Plymouth, Portsmouth and Sheffield).[25] Fifty years later, there were many more towns in both of these categories: 17 with more than 100,000 and 31 with more than 40,000.[26]

While the headlong growth achieved in some northern and Scottish cities was one of the more dramatic manifestations of demographic change in the century after 1750, growth is not the full story. Hardly less important than the overall expansion of the urban sector was the radical reorganisation of the urban hierarchy that occurred simultaneously. Although in Scotland, urban growth was largely concentrated in the country's historic regional centres – Edinburgh, Glasgow, Dundee and Aberdeen – in England this was far from the case.[27] As a number of northern English towns rose to prominence they eclipsed the older regional centres that had long dominated the urban hierarchy. Of the major urban centres in late-seventeenth-century England, only London, Bristol, Newcastle and Norwich still remained among the country's 10 largest towns in 1800 – and Norwich was just clinging on in tenth place.[28] The six newcomers were, in order, Manchester,

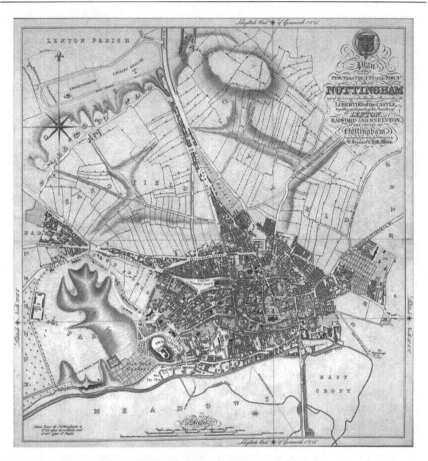

Illustration 4.2 Staveley and Wood, *Plan of Nottingham*, 1831.

Liverpool, Birmingham, Leeds, Sheffield and Plymouth. Bristol continued to expand owing to its vibrant Atlantic trade and Newcastle benefitted from the steady expansion of London, with its demand for Northumbrian coal; but Norwich only remained in the top ten because it had been so large in 1700 rather than because of significant growth thereafter. Norwich, along with Exeter, York and Colchester, failed even to keep pace with national population growth over the period, let alone to match the rapid urban growth occurring elsewhere.[29] In other words, this is not simply a tale of urbanisation, with all towns steadily adding to their populations. Instead, we witness a more fundamental transformation in the fortunes of different towns, with populations rising and falling in response to the opening of new economic opportunities in some, and the closing of established

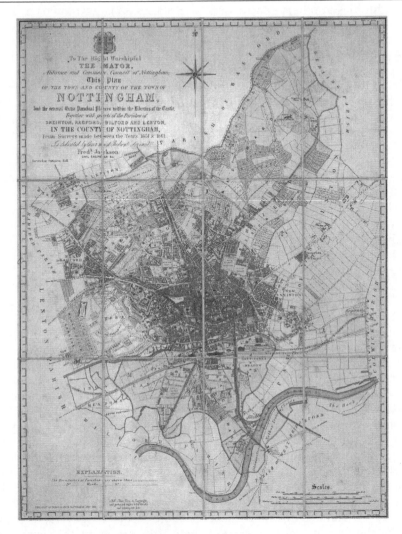

Illustration 4.3 Jackson, *Plan of Nottingham,* 1861.

These three maps of Nottingham, drawn between 1744 and 1861 clearly illustrate the town's rapid growth. In 1744, the town remains firmly within its roughly circular boundaries and much of this area comprises fields and orchards. By 1831, virtually all of the green space within these boundaries has been filled in and the town has begun to spread up the Derby Road to the west and the Mansfield Road to the north. By 1861 much of the land between these two roads has been developed and the town has begun to creep beyond its original southern-most boundary into the agricultural land called the Meadows. The town's large and distinctively shaped market place in the north-west corner of the town provides a useful reference point for assessing the town's growth.

opportunities in others. Map 4.1 shows Britain's 30 largest towns in 1871. Although a number of historic towns are included, the rise of the industrial north and midlands up the urban hierarchy can be clearly seen.

Although the emergence of towns with populations in excess of 50,000 was particularly pronounced, there was considerable growth in many smaller towns as well. The Black Country, for example, was transformed by the appearance of towns with a population between 10,000 and 50,000. Tipton, West Bromwich and Dudley all matched the rapid rate of growth seen in some of the country's great cities, increasing fourfold or more in the first half of the nineteenth century and ending up with populations ranging between 25,000 and 50,000.[30] A second tier of smaller towns underwent growth that was almost as rapid. Bilston, Rowley Regis, Sedgeley, Walsall and Wednesbury increased to around three times their original size in the half century following 1801, housing populations between 10,000 and 25,000 by the end of the period.[31]

The growth of medium-sized towns was also of particular significance in the industrialising districts of South Wales. We have already noted the very fast growth seen in some of south Monmouthshire's towns, but this did not translate into the emergence of great cities as found in Scotland and northern England. Instead, urbanisation in Wales consisted in the proliferation of towns with between 10,000 and 40,000 inhabitants. Even Cardiff, the nation's capital, located in the neighbouring county of Glamorgan, numbered less than 40,000 souls by 1871.[32] Yet the steady growth of these smaller towns was highly significant in the overall urbanisation of the country and all helped to make England, Wales and Scotland the most urbanised nations of Europe by the third quarter of the nineteenth century.

Once again, one must look to migration rather than natural population increase, in order to explain the urbanisation of Britain. It is worth repeating that rapidly urbanising districts often had the highest rate of mortality owing to their unhealthy living conditions, and their rising populations must therefore have been the product of either higher fertility or in-migration, or a combination of the two. As towns tended to house a younger-than-average (and therefore more fertile-than-average) population, they tended also to have a high birth rate, and this helped to counter-balance the impact of a high death rate. But the higher urban birth rate was not sufficient to fuel growth of the magnitude seen in many nineteenth-century towns and cities. The sustained year-on-year increases in population recorded in scores of British towns are testimony to the high levels of migration. Jeffrey Williamson has suggested that prior to 1811 in-migration accounted for about 60 per cent of city growth, and after that it accounted for about 40 per cent.[33] In Scotland, where the seven largest towns more than doubled in size in the half century after 1750, it has been calculated that between 4500 and 6500 new migrants must have entered them each year in order to achieve this growth.[34] Many of the migrants were from rural counties, though the population of some cities, most notably,

Map 4.1 Map of Britain's thirty largest towns in 1871. Adapted from B. R. Mitchell and Phyllis Deane, *Abstract of British Historical Statistics* (Cambridge, 1962), pp. 24–7.

Glasgow, Liverpool and Manchester, was also boosted by a steady flow of migrants from Ireland.

The movement of population from countryside to town provides strong evidence that new employment opportunities were opening in the manufacturing and service sectors of the economy. No less importantly, however, migration from the countryside suggests that changes in the rural economy were also occurring. In pre-industrial societies, most labour – typically over 50 per cent – is directed towards procuring the means of subsistence. Evidently, the steady flow of people towards towns also resulted in the flow of labour out of agriculture, which suggests that each worker remaining on the land was producing more food than his or her predecessors; in other words, that agricultural productivity was increasing.

Measuring changes in the performance of agriculture during this period is, as might be imagined, fraught with difficulty, but most recent studies suggest that agricultural output increased steadily, albeit not dramatically, during the long eighteenth century. Recent estimates suggest that agricultural output was increasing at a rate of somewhere between 0.2 per cent and 0.5 per cent per year throughout the eighteenth century, and at a markedly faster rate of 1 per cent per year in the first half of the nineteenth century.[35] This was a respectable performance, but hardly enough to sustain the idea of an 'agricultural revolution', as an earlier generation of historians sometimes claimed.[36] Furthermore, these increases built upon the accomplishments of the sixteenth and seventeenth centuries and are therefore best regarded as the continuation of a long-established pattern of growth, rather than as a phenomenon unique to this period. Nonetheless, it is interesting to consider the progress of agriculture and its possible contribution to the process of industrialisation.

In reality, the causes of the slow and steady rise in agricultural output that occurred over the long eighteenth century were complex and numerous. There are many different ways in which agriculture could raise its output, but most historians find it helpful to analyse growth in terms of an extension of the amount of land or labour devoted to agriculture, or of an improvement in the productivity of land or labour. These forces are not mutually exclusive, and all worked together to produce the increases outlined here. The most straightforward way of increasing agricultural output is to put more land to agricultural use, and this simple strategy was an important component of growth throughout this period. It has been estimated that the extent of arable, pasture and meadow rose from 21 million acres in 1700 to 30.6 million acres in 1850, an increase of nearly 50 per cent.[37] Most of this increase was achieved through the reclamation of woodlands and wastes – land that had previously been of rather little agricultural value. In addition to increasing the acreage of farmland, however, the output per acre was also raised by making improvements to the land.

Improvements to the land were made in several ways.[38] The enclosure movement, which involved replacing the collective management of open

villages with a system of enclosed, private farms, was one of many strategies. While a number of historians have convincingly demonstrated that
the extravagant claims sometimes made for the advantages of enclosure
have often been exaggerated, it is nonetheless clear that enclosure was one
of many factors that helped to drive up yields, as the owners of enclosed
farms tended to adopt new farming methods more readily than those
who farmed in open systems.[39] Also significant was the introduction of
the Norfolk four-course rotation, which replaced the fallow cycle of crop
planting with clover and other legumes to feed nitrogen back into the soil.
This both improved soil quality and permitted the growing of crops during years where the land had previously been left fallow.[40] Output was
further increased by the development of better strains of seeds, which
helped to raise grain yields in many southern counties in the late seventeenth and eighteenth centuries.[41] In the pastoral sector, improved breeds
of animal led to similar gains in productivity.[42] By a variety of strategies,
therefore, farmers in different parts of Britain, working with very different soils, climates and landscapes, coaxed ever-greater yields from their
lands.

In addition to extending and improving the land under cultivation, agricultural output was increased by changes in the supply and quality of
labour used to work the land. Just as extending the land under cultivation
will help to raise agricultural output, so putting more workers on the land
is a simple way of achieving the same effect. Extra hands can be put to
use preparing the land for cultivation: careful digging, weeding, application of manure and so forth will all help to improve crop yields. Despite
significant population growth throughout the eighteenth and nineteenth
centuries, however, the agricultural workforce remained roughly constant
between 1700 and 1850, at about 1.5 million workers.[43] Rather than adding
extra farm workers, therefore, output was raised by improving the productivity of the workforce. In part this was achieved through changing its
composition. The eighteenth and nineteenth centuries witnessed a decline
in the employment of women and boys and a rise in the employment of
adult men; although the total numbers employed remained roughly stable,
there was effectively some modest improvement in quality.[44] In addition,
the productivity of farm labour was pushed up through the use of extra
draught animals and new farming tools and machines. The substitution
of animals for human muscle power was a particularly important way of
improving labour productivity. The number of draught animals at work on
British farms rose steadily from the middle ages to the nineteenth century,
horses replaced oxen and the size (and therefore the strength) of horses
rose considerably: all three factors helped to improve the productivity of
each worker by a considerable margin.[45] The purchase of new implements
had a similar effect. One recent study of ploughs, for example, has demonstrated how improvements in plough design enabled farmers to economise
on expensive inputs such as men and horses – though as ever in the world
of agriculture, there was considerable regional variation in the take-up of

the new technology.[46] Just as the productivity of the land was improved in many different ways according to local conditions, therefore, so too was the productivity of labour pushed up by numerous different strategies.

Although the combined effect of piecemeal improvements to land and labour over the period 1700 to 1870 was to increase both the output and the productivity of agriculture, most historians today are sceptical of arguments that accord agriculture a pivotal enabling role in British industrialisation.[47] Agricultural improvement created a steady rise in output throughout the period, but these increases were not sufficient to feed the rapidly growing population, and part of the rising demand was met through imports rather than domestic agriculture. Prices also rose, leading to downward pressure on the living standards of the bulk of the population.[48] Nonetheless, the steadily rising productivity of agriculture went far in enabling the country to feed itself on a workforce that, in relative terms, was becoming ever smaller. In 1700, over 50 per cent of the population were working in agriculture; by 1801 that had fallen to 36 per cent; and by 1851 it had dwindled yet further, to around 20 per cent.[49] The great achievement of agriculture, therefore, was to release labour from the ancient, back-breaking toil of working the soil. Steady, and long term improvements to agriculture underpinned the twin processes of migration and urbanisation and led to the creation of a non-agricultural workforce that in historical and global terms was unusually large.

It is clear that the direction of much population movement was from villages to towns and the growth of medium and large towns certainly provides one of the starkest illustrations of high levels of migration throughout Britain. Nonetheless, rapid population growth and movement were not, in fact, a purely urban phenomenon. Some fairly surprising redistribution of population in rural areas was also occurring, and we should be mistaken to assume that the flow of migrants was always from country to town. Across south Lancashire and south Yorkshire, and through parts of Staffordshire and Nottinghamshire, sharp increases in the rural population were taking place as newcomers flocked to take advantage of the opportunities presented by new rural industries. The process was described many years ago by one scholar of industrialisation as a 'thickening of the population over the countryside' – a memorable phrase that helps to remind us that industrial growth was not only to be found in the large factories of the new northern towns.[50]

The scale of migration to rural areas is seen clearly in the county of Lancashire. Migrants moved into the region's many large- and medium-sized towns – most obviously to Manchester, but also to Preston, Bury, Bolton, Oldham, Rochdale and Wigan – but there was sizeable migration into rural Lancashire as well. A detailed study of the Shaw family, employed mostly in agriculture and the woollen industry in various parts of Lancashire in the century after 1750, illustrates the wide range of migratory experience within just one family and also powerfully underscores how much economic opportunity was to be found in industrial villages as opposed to towns.[51] Within this century, various members of three generations of the Shaw family moved a total of 167 times. Over time, there was a gradual shift from countryside to town, though the shift was far from linear and proceeded in a piecemeal fashion via circulation between agricultural areas, industrial villages and larger towns. For the Shaw family, rural to rural moves were as common as rural to urban moves: both constituted about 30 per cent of total moves. Twenty per cent of the family's moves were from towns to rural areas, while just over 10 per cent were from one town to another.[52] It is clearly an oversimplification, then, to suggest population movement in industrialising Britain was invariably from country to town. Rural counties certainly did send their surplus populations to the great cities, but this was only one element of a more complex matrix of migration processes. Many opted to move to industrial villages and hamlets rather than to larger towns and cities. Furthermore, movement into the industrialising regions did not mark the endpoint of migration: once there, workers continued to move about between villages, townships and cities, searching for fresh work opportunities in expanding but often fragile new industries.

A similar pattern of both urban and rural growth is also evident in south Yorkshire. The region's major towns – Leeds, Sheffield, Bradford and Halifax – all experienced rapid population growth in the nineteenth century, but migration into industrial villages and hamlets was hardly less significant. Steven King's micro-study of Calverley illustrates the process of migration in one West Riding parish. The population of Calverley was divided between four distinct townships – Calverley-cum-Farsley, Pudsey, Idle and Stanningley – and grew rapidly over the eighteenth and early nineteenth centuries, rising from about 3200 in the late seventeenth century to over 14,000 in 1821.[53] As with most places, natural population increase helped to swell its numbers: but even had Calverley retained all its natural increase in-migration of about 3000 new people must have occurred in order to achieve this growth. Yet even with the combined forces of natural population growth and in-migration, none of the townships met the criteria of a 'town' in 1821, as it is usually defined for the nineteenth century, that is home to 10,000 inhabitants or more. The largest of the townships was Pudsey with a population of just over 6000. Idle had 4600, Calverley-cum-Farsley 2600 and Stanningley less than 1000.[54] This is the 'thickening of the countryside' to which scholars have referred – the expansion of once small villages into industrial townships with large numbers employed in cottage industry or small mills. Across south Yorkshire, a growing rural textile industry acted as a powerful magnet for migrants, and, for many, settlement here formed an attractive alternative to life in the neighbouring large towns.

The reasons for the high levels of mobility in industrial Britain are inevitably complex and it is important to emphasise that migration was not a new phenomenon in this period. Studies of sixteenth- and seventeenth-century England have revealed surprisingly high levels of mobility and much of the migratory activity in the following 200 years can be seen as a continuation of this older pattern of population movement.[55] Two motivations stand out as being of long-standing importance. Marriage and family provided one major spur to migration. One study of several thousand life histories has revealed that among women, the single most common cause of migration was marriage, and a number of local studies have confirmed that up to one half of all female moves were for marriage purposes.[56] In addition, family members often moved close to one another during times of particular emotional or financial crisis – the death of a spouse, sickness in the family, the loss of employment or the birth of an illegitimate child, for example. Family matters continued to provide much of the motivation for population movement and can appropriately be regarded as a continuation of much older patterns of migration.

The second motivation that stands out as being of particular significance is economic need, and once again much of this movement can be interpreted in the context of a long-established pattern of mobility. Migration from the Scottish Highlands perhaps provides the clearest illustration of migration undertaken from economic necessity. Harvest failures and famines in the 1780s and in the 1830s and 1840s and the deliberate clearance of Highland farms caused spikes of migration out of the region, and the combination of high rents and a chronic lack of any alternative to agricultural employment helped to contribute to a high underlying rate of migration.[57] Economic pressures of this magnitude were unusual, but movement in search of work was not, and in most parts of Britain migration was more likely to involve a careful balancing of the different work opportunities available between different areas. Women tended to migrate more often than men and they were more likely to move to towns, reflecting their predominance in one of the most traditional sectors of the economy: domestic service.[58] Studies of nineteenth-century migration to the Scottish Lowlands reveal large numbers taking up employment in such established trades as agriculture, the herring fisheries, the building industry and domestic service.[59] Furthermore, migration in search of farm work was not simply a rural phenomenon. King's study of the proto-industrial parish of Calverley in west Yorkshire suggests that the availability of land provided a stimulus to in-migration here in parts of the eighteenth century.[60] In sum, much of the population movement that we have described in this chapter was motivated by the search for work in traditional areas of the economy and, along with movement for family reasons, can be understood as part of a larger and much longer history of population movement within the British Isles.

There remains, however, some element of eighteenth- and nineteenth-century migration that cannot be explained simply by reference to existing patterns of labour mobility. The thousands that took up residence in Black Country townships such as Bilston, Wednesbury and Smethwick after 1800 were not moving in order to marry, to work as domestic servants or to farm the land. They were drawn in by the astonishingly wide array of

employment opportunities provided by the region's expanding metalworking industries. The population of south Lancashire doubled in just 40
years between 1761 and 1800 and the county's urban population increased
tenfold in the eighteenth century and thirtyfold between 1801 and 1841
largely in response to the astonishing development of the cotton industry.
Although population growth was occurring nationally between 1750 and
1870, wherever we find the most rapid rates of growth, we can also observe
a significant expansion in manufacturing or mining. An idea of the labour
needs of these industries is given by a South Wales newspaper which ran the
following advertisement in 1840: 'WANTED, ONE THOUSAND MEN at
the MONMOUTHSHIRE SALE COAL COLLIERIES, where good men can
earn from Four to Five Shillings per day. Applications for employment to
... the NEWPORT COAL COMPANY'.[61] Employment opportunities on this
scale mark a decisive break with anything the region could have offered half
a century earlier. Undoubtedly, migration was deeply engrained in British
culture, and has a history stretching back well before the industrial revolution. At the same time, however, this period witnessed the emergence of a
new tier of industrial employment that triggered population movement on
a greater scale than ever previously seen before.

Furthermore, in the 170 years following 1700 migration had some far-
reaching consequences. Down the preceding centuries, British population
had drifted from rural areas to towns, and to London in particular, but this
drift had not radically altered the nation's composition: however many people moved, the majority of the population continued to live in villages; and
most of those living in towns were still to be found in London. Eighteenth-
and nineteenth-century migration permanently changed this centuries-old
pattern of population distribution. By 1870, the majority now lived in towns,
and while London remained far and away Britain's largest city, the country
now had a far more complex urban structure, with dozens of large towns
and cities outside the metropolis and an extensive network of small- and
medium-sized towns as well.

Coupled with the movement of people from rural to urban areas was
a shift of population between different regions. Prior to about 1750, the
south of England had been the most populous and prosperous part of the
country. Daniel Defoe, writing in the early eighteenth century, had considered that the counties south of the Trent were 'infinitely fuller of great
towns, of people and of trade'. In the mid-1750s, 70 per cent of all fairs
took place south of a line drawn between the mouth of the Severn and
the Wash, and one historian has concluded that 'the greater weight of economic activity still lay to the south.'[62] But the movement of large numbers
in the eighteenth and nineteenth centuries out of agricultural counties and
into industrial ones reversed the economic significance of north and south.
Gerard Turnbull has observed that population was moving towards the
coalfields: 'migrants flocked to jobs of all kinds, in traditional as well as
new industries, on the coalfields. Population gathered there in concentrations far in excess of previous levels.'[63] (A comparison of Map 4.1 detailing

Britain's largest towns in 1871, with Map 7.1, showing the distribution of coalfields, clearly illustrates the movement of population towards the coal-producing regions.) Migration to cities in the north and the midlands, as well as to the rural-industrial hinterland around many large towns, created a strip of relatively thickly populated areas running from south Lancashire, across to west and south Yorkshire and down through Nottingham and Leicester to the west Midlands. In Scotland, population congregated in the Central Belt, running from Greenock and Glasgow in the west across to Edinburgh in the east. During this period, therefore, migration effected a fundamental shift of population away from southern agricultural areas to northern urban and industrial areas, and in the process significantly altered the human geography of Britain.

The full extent of the economic restructuring that underpinned eighteenth- and nineteenth-century migration can be grasped by looking at those parts of the country which failed to match the national rates of population growth. As should by now be clear, this was largely a consequence of their inability to retain all their natural population increase, that is, of out-migration, rather than the existence of an entirely different demographic regime. An examination of regions with local economies dominated by agriculture clearly illustrates what was 'missing' in the slow-growing counties.

Consider the counties comprising East Anglia: Norfolk, Suffolk and Essex. At the start of the eighteenth century, all three had strong economies combining both agriculture and industry. The region was widely regarded as the centre of one of the most successful and progressive systems of agriculture in eighteenth-century England, with the cultivation of grains, peas and beans, turnips and potatoes, and the breeding of sheep and cattle in Norfolk; grains, butter and hard cheese in Suffolk; and wheat and cereals in Essex.[64] At the same time, the region was home to a flourishing industrial sector. East Anglia's regional capital, Norwich, was the centre of a great worsted industry, and in 1700 was England's second city – second in size only to London.[65] In Suffolk and northern Essex, there was a thriving woollen industry, as well as a small but expanding silk industry centred upon Colchester and extending to a number of smaller surrounding towns and villages. The region boasted a number of thriving ports, particularly those at King's Lynn and Yarmouth, trading in grain, cloth, timber and fish. It all combined to make East Anglia a prosperous region with excellent prospects for further growth in the eighteenth century.[66]

By the middle of the eighteenth century, however, it was clear that population growth in East Anglia was not even keeping pace with national growth – still less with the fastest rates recorded in the industrialising counties. Between 1761 and 1801, population in Suffolk grew by 24 per cent, in Essex by 18 per cent and in Norfolk by a mere 13 per cent.[67] The relative population decline of the three counties continued in the nineteenth century. These poor growth rates are in part explained by the predominance of agriculture within the region's economy: as we have already suggested, agriculture was generally unable to accommodate the growing numbers, and out-migration tended to be found in regions dominated by farming. But in East Anglia, out-migration was also connected with changes in the three counties' industrial composition. East Anglia's textile industry, once a major source of employment, went into decline in the eighteenth century: the silk industry survived until the 1820s, but then entered a period of rapid contraction.[68] Not all of the region's natural population increase could be accommodated by local agriculture and a declining industrial sector, and at least some of those born here were faced with a stark choice: to accept a sharp reduction in their living standards or to move away.

A similar combination of forces may be found at work in most of the counties that failed to keep pace with the national average for population growth. In Wiltshire, for example, numbers grew more slowly than in any other English county in the second half of the eighteenth century, expanding by a negligible 1.5 per cent each decade. Once again, the local economy combined agriculture and a declining woollen industry and was unable to support a rising population. The once-thriving textile industry centred upon Bradford-upon-Avon could not withstand the competition from the rapidly expanding woollen industry in the West Riding of Yorkshire and entered a period of prolonged stagnation and decline at the turn of the century.[69]

The difficulty of earning a living in such an environment is vividly portrayed in autobiographical testimony. Take, for example, John Bennett, one of nine children born to a poor carpenter living in South Wraxall, Wiltshire, a small village not far from Bradford-upon-Avon. At the age of eight his meagre education was ended and he began working in the carpentry trade with his father. As he reached adulthood, though, it became clear that South Wraxall could not provide a living for all the Bennett's nine children. Noting he had an uncle, a father and a younger brother 'getting up', John concluded 'there would not be work enough for all of us.'[70] He headed off to Bristol one Sunday morning through snow and rain, reaching the city before dark and starting his search for work the following day.[71] There he enjoyed higher wages and more regular work than South Wraxall could ever offer – and he also, by his own admission, enjoyed spending most of his money 'in visiting and walking about Sundays with the young ladies, and sometimes the old ones' as well.[72] Over in Rutlandshire, Arnold Goodliffe, the second son of a small farming family, left the tiny village of Belton for Nottingham when he realised he was one of 'two brothers at home where one would have been better'.[73] It did not take much for workers like Bennett and Goodliffe to realise there was insufficient work in their sleepy villages to maintain a decent standard of living for all in their family. Both men clearly perceived moving to a nearby large town as a necessary and normal part of the transition to adulthood.

It is evident that alongside the rapid population growth described in Chapter 3, a fairly dramatic redistribution of people was also occurring. It was not simply the new industrial towns of the north to which migrant workers flocked; many small towns and even many villages in south

Lancashire, south Yorkshire, the west Midlands and the Scottish Lowlands also attracted large numbers of migrants. The evidence from migration, as the evidence from population growth more generally, is not itself proof of an industrial revolution, nor does it help to explain exactly what that revolution was. It does, however, hint at some momentous changes occurring at the heart of the British economy. And as the search for work prompted much of the migration that we have been considering here, it is fitting to turn our attention in Chapter 5 to the changing nature of work.

Chapter 5 . . . .

Worlds of Work

Labour divides itself into ten thousand forms.
(London Saturday Journal, 1841)[1]

In Chapters 3 and 4 we looked at the history of population. First we noted the sustained increase in overall numbers and identified changes in the practice of marriage – most notably more universal and younger marriage – as the key mechanism by which this growth was achieved. In Chapter 4, though, we noted that many parts of Britain were not, in fact, able to maintain their expanding population and also noted that sustained demographic growth was accompanied by high levels of movement from some parts of the country to others. This chapter will look at the population once again, but consider the evidence from a new angle. We suggested in Chapter 4 that population drift was caused by different employment opportunities and, in particular, by the expansion of opportunities in some of the newly industrialising, coalfield districts. If this was indeed so, we should expect the employment profile of the country to gradually shift, reflecting the movement of labour out of farming and into urban, industrial employment instead. It is possible to consider this proposition more fully by looking in detail at patterns of employment, and the ways in which they changed throughout this period.

It has long been believed that knowledge about the structure of the workforce provides us with some kind of outline of the broader economy. In pre-industrial societies, the majority of the population were invariably involved in agriculture, whereas in modern societies, the proportion of the workforce employed by agriculture is negligible. Might not the movement of labour out of agriculture be pivotal to the process of industrialisation? And if so, would pinpointing the period when agriculture ceased to be the largest employer not also indicate when the industrial revolution occurred? As we saw in Chapter 2, this was effectively what lay at the heart of Nick Crafts' definition of the industrial revolution – though, as we noted there, he did not provide independent evidence for the proportion of the workforce employed by any particular segment. It is now time to confront this problem more squarely, to assess our current state of knowledge about the occupational structure of Britain in the period 1700–1870, and to explore what this tells us about the pace and path of British industrialisation.

As might be expected, there is little direct evidence for the employment of labour during the period of industrialisation. Although the first census was taken in 1801, the first to provide some systematic occupational information was not taken until 1831, and it was only in 1841 that individual occupations for the whole population were recorded. Thus, while the nineteenth-century censuses are invaluable for the study of occupations for the second half of the century, their use in evaluating changes in occupational structure before then is limited. In this chapter, we shall consider the various (and sometimes ingenious) ways in which historians have sought to uncover the distribution of the workforce in the pre-census period.

Our starting point must be the 'social tables' assembled by Gregory King, Joseph Massie and Patrick Colquhoun. Gregory King's 'Scheme of the Income and Expense of the Several Families of England' was drawn up in 1696 but referred to the year 1688.[2] Using a range of different tax records, King's intention was to calculate the number of families in England and their incomes in order to advise the government about possible future tax revenues. In the process, however, he divided the population into 26 different social groups, ranging from the lords, knights and baronets, through the merchants, clergymen and farmers, down to the 'Labouring People and Outservants', 'Cottagers and Paupers' and 'Vagrants, as Gipsies, Thieves, Beggars etc.'.[3] King estimated the total number of people in each of his groups, thereby providing a crude cross-section of the social structure of England and Wales. In the late 1750s, a rather more elaborate set of tables containing detail about the social and economic ranks of society was prepared by Joseph Massie.[4] Fresh tables of England's social structure were produced once again in the early nineteenth century by Patrick Colquhoun, for the years 1801–03 and 1812. Given the value of information about the employment structure of eighteenth-century Britain, historians have inevitably taken great interest in these tables and devoted considerable attention to evaluating how accurate they might be.

Their conclusion regarding this final point, however, has been far from encouraging. When King's tables were published in 1699, his editor declared that they were 'so accurately done, that we may venture to say they are not to be controverted in any point'.[5] The historical profession has generally been less convinced. King's primary motivation in preparing his 'Scheme' was to demonstrate that the onset of war with France in 1688 had depleted the nation's wealth and to argue, in effect, for its discontinuation: his template of the nation's social structure was therefore produced not for its own sake, but simply to underscore this argument. Furthermore, although King certainly did consult some tax records in order to construct his totals, doubt has been cast over how much data he really had access to. In any case, these records, both those he consulted and those he did not, did not contain the information necessary to construct an accurate and comprehensive social table. In the absence of such data, his tables, according to one critic, were 'far more the product of strained deduction, of mathematical juggling, or even plain guesswork, than of firmly grounded information'.[6]

Finally King's social tables present a suspiciously simple society running from the peer to the peasant, through 26 discrete social groups, each sharing common status, occupation and income. However, there is abundant qualitative evidence to suggest that England had become a highly complex society by the end of the seventeenth century, and that income could vary widely within any given occupational group, while individuals with different occupations could share similar incomes. King was undoubtedly a pioneer both in recognising the value of information about social structure and in attempting to measure it, but it is highly doubtful that he had the necessary resources to measure such a complex problem. One recent discussion of King's table has even concluded that it is 'semi-fictional' in nature.[7]

The social tables drawn up by Massie and Colquhoun, both inspired to some degree by King's earlier work, have been subjected to similar criticisms. Massie, like King, was politically motivated. As the title of his table indicates – 'A Computation ... Shewing How Much Money a Family of each Rank, Degree or Class Hath Lost by that Rapacious [sugar] Monopoly' – his interests did not really lie in providing a social table at all but lay, instead, in demonstrating the iniquities of the sugar lobby.[8] In accordance with these interests, Massie grouped society into four rather unusual categories: 'Labouring Families', 'Families which Drink Tea or Coffee Occasionally', 'Families which Drink Tea or Coffee in the Morning' and 'Families which Drink Tea, Coffee, or Chocolate, Morning and Afternoon'.[9] While these groups are further divided into more recognisable occupational groups – farmers, labourers, merchants and so forth – his table still contains some rather serious omissions. There was no one working in mining or the building trades, for example, and there were no paupers. These omissions stem in part from the fact that Massie was seeking to estimate the cost to English families of the sugar monopoly, not to produce an outline of social structure; but as the government was still not collecting the kind of information needed to construct an occupational breakdown, it is difficult to see how Massie could ever have accurately measured social structure, even had this been his primary aim.

By the time that Colquhoun turned his attention to the occupational make-up of Britain in the early nineteenth century, a wider range of sources was available than ever before. The censuses provided reasonably reliable population totals; more comprehensive tax records and the government's survey of expenditure on poor relief in 1803–04 provided some detail about the distribution of wealth among the population. In addition, Colquhoun had the benefit of intellectual advances in the study of political arithmetic since the time of Gregory King. From these building blocks, he fashioned a yet more detailed table of English structure, ranging from 'The King' at the top through nearly 50 distinct categories (encompassing, for example, 'Gentlemen and ladies living on income', 'Persons in the education of youth of both sexes', 'lesser clergymen' and 'Hawkers, Peddlars, Duffers etc'.) right down to the 'Chelsea, Greenwich, Chatham Pensioners' at the bottom.[10] Yet even with these advantages, Colquhoun's labours are of only limited use to the historian of industrialisation. Most problematic is the fact that he was so vague about the occupational differences that are most germane to economic history. Thus it remains largely unclear exactly which sector of the economy employed two of Colquhoun's three largest groups. His 'labouring people in husbandry' clearly refers to agricultural labourers, but his 'artisans, handicrafts, mechanics, and labourers employed in manufactures, buildings and works of every kind' seems to cover labouring of every description, lumping traditional employment in trades, such as carpentry and baking together with the employment offered by the emerging new industries – most notably, cotton and iron. It is similarly unclear what section of the economy employed the 'Paupers producing from their own labours in miscellaneous employments'.[11] In all, these three groups of manual labourers made up about half of the entire population of England and Wales; so the lack of a more detailed breakdown of the three labouring groups in Colquhoun's table poses a serious problem for those interested in the occupational structure of the economy. Indeed, taking the social tables produced by contemporaries one can hardly do more than agree with Peter Mathias, who half a century ago concluded that informed contemporary opinion provided 'historical enlightenment without quantitative accuracy'.[12]

It was precisely in order to provide some much-needed 'quantitative accuracy' to the discussion of English social structure that Lindert and Williamson set out in the late 1970s to move beyond the estimates that King, Massie and Colquhoun had provided and to search the archives for fresh evidence of occupational structure.[13] Their investigations revealed the existence of a hitherto largely unused source: parish burial registers. While these did not routinely provide information, Lindert's trawl through the archives indicated that a sizeable minority did, and he embarked on a project of research to extract occupational information from the registers and convert it into a series of national social tables. Inevitably, a project of this kind was not based on an analysis of all the available burial registers; rather Lindert looked at a sample between the years 1655 and 1814. This sample, together with the occasional local census taken by vicars or estate overseers (he surveyed 26 such local censuses in all), formed the basis of a new analysis of the occupational structure of England over the long eighteenth century.

Lindert and Williamson's analysis of the burial data strongly confirmed what historians had long suspected, namely, that Gregory King had seriously underestimated the size and strength of England's industrial and commercial sectors. Whereas King had estimated that about 50,000 men worked in commerce at the end of the seventeenth century, Lindert and Williamson increased this to over 128,000. They increased the size of the manufacturing workforce yet more significantly: from 60,000 to over 250,000. The number employed by agriculture they calculated to be one-third lower than King had suggested.[14] By contrast, Lindert and Williamson's results for the mid-eighteenth and early nineteenth centuries departed from the estimates of Massie and Colquhoun far less. For the first half of the eighteenth century, their estimates indicated that occupational structure remained largely stable. For the second half of the century, their figures implied a shift of labour away from agriculture and into building and manufacturing. The revisions together made England less agricultural, more industrial, and significantly richer at the start of our period and indicated a steady drift of population away from agriculture and into industry and manufacturing in the following century and a quarter.

While Lindert and Williamson's account of English occupations was clearly superior to earlier studies based upon the estimates of the contemporary observers, it also quickly attracted criticism of its own – owing in part, no doubt, to the central role it played in Nick Crafts' controversial income accounts.[15] As we noted when discussing Crafts' work in Chapter 2, scholars mounted criticism about the social tables he had used along two lines. In the first instance, they questioned whether Lindert and Williamson had, in fact, misunderstood the nature of the pre-industrial economy by ascribing to each worker just one occupation. Not only, was it suggested, did workers often combine more than one occupation, they also were likely to change occupation several times over the course of their working lives. Secondly, they challenged the exclusion of women from the occupational tables. As Lindert and Williamson recognised, women were recorded in the parish registers according to their marital, rather than employment, status: they were simply 'wives', 'widows' or 'spinsters'. There was no way of describing female employment patterns from labels such as these, and Lindert and Williamson's tables offered little more insight into women's working lives than a few figures estimating the number of servants. To this we might also add that the size of Lindert and Williamson's sample was in fact quite small. Lindert's sample captured about one-fifteenth of annual burials in selected years, which only amounted to about two out of every thousand living.[16] The results from the sample were inflated to national totals using statistical techniques, but the smaller the sample, the shakier such procedures become. Lindert admitted that the problem was most acute for the smallest occupational groups: his estimates for the total numbers of carpenters, shoemakers, bakers and miners, he conceded, were 'little more than guesses'.[17] The small sample size was also responsible for throwing up some rather surprising results, such as the nation becoming more agricultural in the early eighteenth century, the number of butchers more than halving in the second half of the century or the numbers employed in the textile industries declining in the early nineteenth century.[18] Yet despite the critical comment that Lindert and Williamson's revised social tables attracted, their central findings gained more general assent: that the English economy had been far more diverse at the start of the eighteenth century than King's alternative social table had implied and that the eighteenth century had witnessed an unmistakeable shift in occupational profile, away from agriculture and into industry. Moreover, Lindert and Williamson had identified the existence of a sizeable body of untapped material suitable for the study of social structure and illustrated how this scattered information might be used to provide an outline of the economy during the industrial revolution.

An alternative approach to the same problem was taken by Ann Kussmaul. Unconvinced that parish registers contained sufficient evidence about male occupations to make useful generalisations about the changing structure of the economy, Kussmaul turned instead to an indirect measure of occupational structure: the timing of weddings. Starting from the belief that couples were unlikely to take time off work in order to marry during the busiest times of their working year, Kussmaul argued that marriage registers should record a drop in marriages during the year's busiest months, followed by a rise soon after when all those who had delayed their wedding finally tied the knot. In grain-growing regions, the harvest of late summer and early autumn was the busiest time of year; in stock-rearing areas, the lambing and calving of spring was the busiest time. One would therefore expect to find couples delaying their wedding during these busy periods and to observe a cluster of weddings thereafter. As the pace of work was less influenced by the seasons in manufacturing areas, in these areas weddings should be spread throughout the year, without the seasonal clusters noted in agricultural economies.

In order to explore this idea, Kussmaul returned to the parish registers transcribed by local historians for the Cambridge Group's work on population history. Adding further material of her own from the registers, Kussmaul produced a sample of 542 English parishes between the middle of the sixteenth and nineteenth centuries, providing in all the timing of nearly one hundred thousand marriages. As ever, these registers did not produce a representative cross-section of the entire country, and Kussmaul, as the Cambridge Group had done before, used weighting procedures to compensate for regional bias. With such a wide spread of information about the timing of marriage both geographically and chronologically, Kussmaul argued that it was possible to pinpoint both moments and locations of change in the pre-industrial economy.[19]

Despite the large amount of data that Kussmaul collected, there were inevitably some things that could not be measured. Most notably, Kussmaul's method, like Lindert and Williamson's, revealed far more about men's work than women's work. Although both sexes worked prior to marriage throughout this period, decisions over when to marry were largely dominated by the groom's, rather than the bride's, occupation. Thus districts combining male labour in arable farming with female employment in straw plaiting and lace-making looked 'resolutely autumnal in their marriage seasonality, and are indistinguishable from areas without that women's industrial work'. Kussmaul's 'General View', therefore, described changes in male occupational structure, but had little to say about how female working patterns changed over the period.

Nonetheless, one remarkable feature stood out from Kussmal's study: the late seventeenth century emerged as a key period of transition. From this point, a number of regions recorded a constant increase in the proportion of non-seasonal marriages, indicating a male workforce moving out of agriculture and into industrial occupations. This steady industrial growth continued in rural areas through the entire eighteenth century with a corresponding decline in the proportion of the workforce engaged in agriculture. But these changes were not located in the classic period of the industrial revolution between the late eighteenth and the early nineteenth century. The evidence from the seasonality of marriage suggested that changes in the English economy had become established well before 1700 and that the eighteenth century was a period of consolidation, not change.

Measuring the seasonality of marriage patterns paints a sketch of English occupational structure with rather crude strokes, and though it appears to have captured the moment when local economies switched from agriculture to industry quite well, the information it provides for occupational trends thereafter is more limited. We are still left, then, with something of a gap between Kussmaul's evidence for the emergence of non-seasonal marriage patterns, crudely indicating the emergence of industrial employment, in the early eighteenth century, and the detailed information about occupational structure contained in the censuses from 1851 onwards. It is clearly desirable to have more detail about the distribution of the workforce in the intervening period.

More recently, historians have returned to the archives and suggested that the evidence they contain for occupations prior to the 1851 census may not be quite so spare as Kussmaul had believed. A large research project led by Leigh Shaw-Taylor and Tony Wrigley, designed to locate and extract evidence from the available scattered archives and to distil this information into an intelligible account of the evolution of English occupational structure in the century following 1750, is currently in progress. While its findings remain provisional, it seems clear that this project will enhance our knowledge of occupational structure in a number of fundamental ways. And while the results will be further refined as the project progresses, it is already possible to provide an outline of some of its central findings.[20]

In methodology, Shaw-Taylor and Wrigley's research draws on the tradition of Lindert and Williamson. At the heart of the project lies an extensive trawl of local archives, in search of any and every record that provides information about the work that people did. Shaw-Taylor and Wrigley have identified a variety of records that contain information about male occupations, many of them previously unused for this purpose. From these, they and their researchers have assembled a very large dataset, of the kind that Lindert and Williamson realised they needed, and recognised they did not have. By using modern computing power and mapping techniques, Shaw-Taylor and Wrigley are able to manipulate this very large body of data to provide an extremely detailed template of occupational structure in the century following 1750.

For the second half of the eighteenth century, their data have been collected from two types of records: the militia lists and parish baptism records. The militia lists were lists drawn up at parish level as part of the process

of selecting men to serve in the militia. Constables were required to provide the names and occupations of all the adult males in their parish, which
then formed the basis for a ballot to select men to serve in the militia. These
lists were not entirely comprehensive and they have not always survived
in sufficient numbers to be of much use to this project. Most notably, few
have survived in Lancashire and Yorkshire – two counties of particular
interest to historians of the industrial revolution. For the eighteenth century, therefore, the militia lists are supplemented with the baptism registers.
While there was no legal obligation in the eighteenth century to record a
father's occupation at the baptism of his child, many parish clerks opted
to do so, and wherever the practice was common, occupational detail has
been transcribed from the baptism registers. It is fortunate that the practice
was common in Lancashire and Yorkshire, as well as in a number of other
northern counties, which helps to fill the gap left by the absence of militia
lists.[21]

For the nineteenth century, the records containing occupational detail are
slightly more abundant. Shaw-Taylor and Wrigley look at two in particular: baptism registers and the 1851 census. In 1812, Rose's Act decreed
that parish clerks should record fathers' occupations whenever a child was
baptised: what had been fairly common practice thereby became universal, significantly expanding the amount of available information. Shaw-
Taylor and Wrigley have looked at a sample of parish registers for the 8
years between 1813 and 1820 – these, together with the eighteenth-century
baptisms registers, have yielded occupational data for over one million
baptisms in all. Finally, the project makes extensive use of the 1851 census.
This recorded (in theory) the occupation of every male head of household
and of all working members in the household; it is unquestionably the most
comprehensive and most robust of all the sources used.

Each of the different records lists the job title – or occupational descriptor – for an individual in a given place and at a given time. The project
has uncovered several thousand different descriptors, 20,000 in all, ranging
from the well-known (weaver, farmer, spinner, shoemaker, labourer, baker
and so forth) to the less common (such as 'razor grinder', 'enameller' or
'rag merchant') and the thoroughly obscure (the 'reclifier', for example, or
the 'reeler'). In order to make sense of this enormous number of different
occupations, Shaw-Taylor and Wrigley needed to enter each occupational
descriptor into a system of classification. They used a scheme devised by
Wrigley which divided all jobs between three different sectors: the primary, secondary and tertiary. The primary sector employed those engaged
in farming, fishing and mining. Those employed in the secondary sector
were involved in construction and the manufacture of goods such as food,
drink, textiles, clothing, pottery and glass. The tertiary sector employed all
those involved in the buying and selling of goods, banking, transport and
domestic service. Each of these three sectors contains many further subdivi-
sions, making it possible to track the growth or decline of particular trades
or industries: for example, the building of the railways, the stagnation of

the shoe industry or the expansion of the teaching profession can be traced by searching the databases for the appropriate occupational descriptors. For present purposes, however, our discussion will remain confined to the larger picture and consider the broad shifts of population between these three occupational sectors.

Shaw-Taylor and Wrigley's research to date has detected two distinct periods of growth: the first between 1750 and 1815; the second between 1815 and 1870. The first of these periods is characterised above all by stability in the occupational profile within counties, combined with very marked diversity between counties. It is possible to illustrate this combination of stability and diversity in greater detail by looking at Shaw-Taylor and Wrigley's results for the counties of Hertfordshire, Lancashire and Yorkshire. The three counties had strikingly different occupational structures, yet in each, the relative size of the primary, secondary and tertiary sector remained largely unchanged between 1750 and 1815. In the largely agricultural county of Hertfordshire, for example, levels of employment in agriculture were quite high in 1750, about 60 per cent of adult males, while rates of employment in the secondary sector were low, about 30 per cent.[22] They remained at roughly the same levels for the following 60 years. In Lancashire, by contrast, employment in agriculture was already low in 1750, about 25 per cent, while a very large secondary sector already existed, employing 66 per cent of adult males. Once again, these shares of the male occupational workforce barely moved between 1750 and 1815. The pattern in the West Riding of Yorkshire was similar to that of Lancashire. Here the secondary sector was large, about 67 per cent of male employment, and agriculture was small, about 20 per cent.[23] Once more, these proportions remained largely stable across the period 1750–1815.[24]

While the existence of occupational stability within these counties is clear, Shaw-Taylor and Wrigley also emphasise that this account needs to be modified in one major way. As we saw in Chapter 4, the counties of England were not growing at an even rate: in general, those with significant manufacturing sectors were growing much more rapidly than the agrarian counties, owing to their ability to attract migrants from the less dynamic rural areas. This differential growth of population therefore served to redistribute labour from primary sector employment in rural areas to secondary sector employment in industrialising districts. Yet the results were not dramatic. Whereas an estimated 40 per cent of the adult male population worked in the secondary sector in 1750, this had only risen to about 47 per cent by 1815 – a fairly modest rise given that over 60 years had elapsed. This has led Shaw-Taylor and Wrigley to conclude that the most remarkable discovery from the occupational data is not the extent of change that occurred during these years, but rather how much had already been achieved by 1750. It is perhaps worth emphasising how neatly this conclusion fits with Kussmaul's work, which also pointed to the late seventeenth century, rather than the eighteenth, as the moment of significant change in occupational structure.

In the half century following 1815, the occupational profile of England entered a new phase of more dramatic change, characterised above all by a decline in the percentage of the workforce employed on the land. This period also differed from the eighteenth century in that a new motor of change emerged: changes in male occupational structure prior to 1815 had been largely accomplished by migration; after 1815 they were achieved by structural changes at the regional level. Thus in Hertfordshire, for example, primary employment went into decline after about 1815, while secondary and tertiary employment began to rise steadily. Likewise in Lancashire and the West Riding, primary employment contracted from 1815 and tertiary employment began to expand: in both counties secondary employment also entered a period of slow decline after 1815. These trends were further reinforced by the ongoing migration of adult males from counties with high levels of primary employment to those with lower levels. The combination of structural changes at county level and high rates of migration managed to exert a greater influence on national trends than had previously been achieved by migration alone. This quickening in the pace of change has led Shaw-Taylor and Wrigley to refer to a 'second phase' of industrialisation, occurring between 1815 and 1870. British industrialisation, it seems, was not only protracted; it was also (possibly) a two-step process, composed of two distinct periods and patterns of growth.

It is important to emphasise that the research outlined here is yet in the course of completion. In time, Shaw-Taylor and Wrigley will provide further detailed county studies, which will enable them to ground their conclusions concerning the evolution of occupational structure more firmly. As their research is completed and more fully disseminated, it will no doubt also attract analysis and criticism from other historians, which in turn will help to clarify further its strengths and weaknesses. For the present, however, there is one cautionary point to consider and that concerns the gender composition of their sample. This study of occupational structure, like its predecessors, focuses on adult male, rather than female or juvenile, employment. This, of course, is hardly a point that has escaped the attention of those involved. Indeed, one element of Shaw-Taylor and Wrigley's recent project is devoted to identifying and analysing sources that might shed light on the evolution of female working patterns in the pre-census period. It is already widely recognised, however, that such sources do not exist in large number and that it will never be possible to assemble an account of female occupational structure as detailed as the one that is being constructed for male occupations. Nor, we might add, do we know much about the employment of children, beyond the miserable fact that children laboured long hours, in menial and sometimes back-breaking work, in all weathers, and from ages as young as four. Nonetheless, it is beyond dispute that the British economy was not powered by the work of men alone, and it is therefore worth summarising what we do know about female and child employment between 1750 and 1870.

Contemporary comment, gender history and numerous local studies all point to the importance of female labour throughout the period under review, particularly in those hotspots of the industrial revolution: Lancashire, Yorkshire, Nottinghamshire and Leicestershire, as well as Scotland's Central Belt.[25] Shaw-Taylor's recent analysis of the 1851 census provides strong quantitative support for the claim that female rates of employment differed very markedly from one county to the next and were generally highest in manufacturing areas. Female participation rates tended to be high wherever there was cotton or woollen textile manufacture (over 50 per cent in parts of Lancashire and west Yorkshire), lower in agricultural areas (between 30 per cent and 50 per cent in most rural areas) and lowest in the mining districts (17 per cent in Easington, north-east Durham).[26] The literature on child labour is considerably less extensive than that on women's work; nonetheless, it suggests the employment of children was also high wherever mills and factories were to be found.[27] It is not as yet possible to quantify the contribution of female and child labour to the economies of north-west and central England and of southern Scotland or the extent to which it changed over these one hundred years. It may never be possible. Yet even without precise quantification, Maxine Berg's response to Crafts' national income accounts perhaps bears repeating once again: 'it was the female not the male workforce which counted in the new high-productivity industries.'[28] All that is known for certain is that the contribution of female and child labour to the economy was high, but unknown. Given this, it is simply not possible to chart the evolution of occupational structure in Lancashire and Yorkshire, to identify periods of stability or turning points on the basis of evidence that looks at the contribution of men alone. Nor, by extension, is it possible to use this evidence to form generalisations about the nature of the industrial revolution.

Once again, autobiographical evidence helps to illustrate some of the developments that economic historians strive to measure. They demonstrate, repeatedly, that part of the attraction of the emerging factory districts for migrant families was that they provided employment not simply for adult men, but for their entire family. Consider, for example, the childhood experiences of one autobiographer in Scotland in the 1810s. When his father first moved away he failed to send any money home for a year, and his mother was obliged to break up the family: an older sister was sent into service, one brother was sent to live with an uncle and another was put to work herding cows.[29] By contrast, when his father migrated to the east central lowlands a couple of years later and got work at a flax-spinning mill, he also found jobs for all five of his children in the same factory: 'Our joint earnings', he recalled, 'amounted to a handsome sum weekly, which kept us all very comfortable.'[30] Autobiographical evidence is of course fragmentary and incomplete when contrasted with more quantitative approaches, yet certain themes do emerge. Unlike rural areas, factory districts offered secure work for husbands *and their wives and children*. Male occupational

Illustration 5.1 The Manufacture of Steel Pens in Birmingham. *Illustrated London News*.

Our knowledge of occupational structure is confined almost exclusively to men. How might the inclusion of women modify this knowledge? It is widely recognised that factory employers usually preferred to employ women and children, who they regarded as more flexible and manageable workers – hence the exclusively female workforce employed by this pen manufacturer. As men were employed in factories to a lesser extent, it is possible that studies of male occupational structure are failing to pick up the rise of factory employment that occurred between 1750 and 1820.

evidence suggests that men migrated to Lancashire and Yorkshire to work in both agriculture and industry. Autobiographies suggest, however, that when men with families moved into the factory districts, they were far more likely to find regular employment for the whole family. And if this trend was more general, it implies male occupational figures will understate the relative importance of employment in industry and manufacture.

Without comprehensive information regarding the employment pattern of women and children, our knowledge of occupational structure will always remain incomplete, yet even in the absence of this information, some conclusion can be drawn: Shaw-Taylor and Wrigley have demonstrated that changes in occupational structure, involving first movement into production, and then into the service sector, occurred over a very long timescale. Their evidence about male occupations indicates that by 1750 a handful of counties already had a highly distinctive economic structure with relatively small numbers involved in working the soil and well in excess of half the population engaged in the production of goods. With high levels of migration into these districts, occupational structure began to change at a national level, though the impression is very much of continued growth on previously laid foundations. It was only after about 1815 that these developments began to extend beyond Lancashire, the West Riding and the west Midlands and a more decisive change in occupational structure occurred.

Let us conclude by considering how this evidence about changing occupational structure fits into the history of the industrial revolution. The work by Lindert and Williamson, Kussmaul and Shaw-Taylor and Wrigley all points to the same conclusion: that occupational structure in England looked remarkably 'modern' at the start of this period, with large numbers, in at least some counties, already engaged in manufacturing rather than agriculture. Shaw-Taylor and Wrigley, moreover, point to the half century after 1815, rather than the eighteenth century, as the period of most dramatic change. In this respect, the information about occupations tells a similar story to that told by Crafts' national income accounts. His estimates implied that economy was already quite large and developed in 1700. It grew steadily, but rather slowly, through the eighteenth century and then underwent more dramatic growth in the early nineteenth century. Studies of both occupations and national income therefore delineate two stages of growth: slow growth in the eighteenth century, followed by a shorter period of more dramatic growth in the nineteenth.

Yet it would be premature to conclude that the industrial revolution was therefore a two-step process. The evidence from occupations and national income essentially describes certain aspects of the British economy in the period 1700–1870. It does not explain what caused the economy to follow the path that it did. It is time then to turn to consider what deeper forces may have shaped the patterns that we have been describing to this point. In Chapters 6 and 7 we will look at two possible causal forces that have attracted extensive critical attention from historians: technology and coal. We shall consider whether either one of these factors helps us to explain the evolution of the distinctive pattern of economic change sketched thus far. Clarity on this point will enable us not only to determine what the industrial revolution was but also to decide when it actually occurred.

The 'Mechanical Age': Technology, Innovation and Industrialisation

> Were we required to characterise this age of ours by any single epithet, we should be tempted to call it, not an Heroical, Devotional, Philosophical, or Moral Age, but, above all others, the Mechanical Age. It is the Age of Machinery.
>
> (Carlyle, 'Signs of the times', 1829)[1]

> It is upon the excellency of machinery that the superiority of British manufactures chiefly depends. In other countries labour may be cheaper, and in some the raw material may be more easily obtained, but as yet no country can equal Great Britain in the speed and perfection of machinery.
>
> (Lawson, *Geography of the British Empire*, 1861)[2]

For many Victorians, rapid advances in technology, in particular the use of machines to perform work that had previously been done by hand, were the most striking developments of the age. The mechanisation of the cotton industry, the invention of the steam engine and a myriad other contrivances and innovations in many branches of industry were taken as emblematic of nineteenth-century economic progress.

This emphasis on technology and machines has also continued throughout much of the twentieth century. In the late 1940s, for example, the economic historian T. S. Ashton spoke of a cadre of 'Inventors, contrivers, industrialists, and entrepreneurs . . . from every social class and from all parts of the country' busy at work fashioning the inventions that were to drive the industrial revolution. He continued, 'It was not only gadgets, however, but innovations of various kinds – in agriculture, transport, manufacture, trade, and finance – that surged up with a suddenness for which it is difficult to find a parallel at any other time or place.'[3] While not everybody shared Ashton's generally rather rosy interpretation of the industrial revolution, his emphasis on the transformative role of new technologies continued to resonate throughout the second half of the twentieth century. In the *Cambridge Economic History of Europe*, published in 1965, David

Landes offered a broad definition of the industrial revolution based upon a number of technical advances, encompassing the substitution of human strength with machines; new sources of power (fossil fuels and the steam engine); and new materials (iron and minerals).[4] More recently still, Joel Mokyr has argued that if 'European technology had stopped dead in its tracks – as Islam's had by about 1200, China's had by 1450, and Japan's had by 1600 – then Europe would not have continued down its path of industrialisation in the two centuries following 1750.' Britain's industries, he adds, 'displayed an unprecedented technological creativity that lay at the foundation of the British Industrial Revolution'.[5] For many, both contemporaries and historians, the rapid pace of technological change after 1750 is not simply a colourful historical curiosity; it is the key to understanding the world's first industrial revolution. This amounts to a large claim for the significance of technology, and in this chapter we shall consider whether inventions and technology do indeed deserve a place at the centre of our definitions of the industrial revolution.

It should immediately be clear that this account of pervasive and transformative technological change has been seriously challenged by the recent, and hugely influential, macroeconomic analyses of British industrialisation that we considered in Chapter 2. Crafts and Harley's estimates of national economic growth suggested that productivity growth was heavily localised in two 'modern' industries – cotton and, to a lesser extent, iron – with only meagre productivity gains elsewhere.[6] The poor productivity gains in industries outside the two modern sectors led them to infer that most 'other industries remained largely unchanged' and, therefore, to reject accounts stressing widespread technological change.[7]

We have already reviewed a number of criticisms of macroeconomic approaches to British industrialisation and cautioned that in the absence of reliable data to measure the various elements of economic growth the results must be viewed as subject to a sizeable margin of error. There are a number of further reasons why their description of a languishing manufacturing sector, if not incorrect, might be misleading. In the first instance, Crafts and Harley's estimates for industrial productivity were never based upon a complete analysis of the manufacturing sector. Their indices of industrial production were initially based upon a sample of around a dozen different industries, though the size of the sample was slightly extended in subsequent revisions.[8] Nonetheless, a recent study of industrial output for 26 industries for the period from 1815 to 1850 acknowledges that these industries amount to only about 60 per cent of total industrial production – still leaving fully 40 per cent entirely out of the account.[9] Most of those excluded were relatively small industries, and it has even been suggested that it was in precisely some of these small, dynamic industries that technological innovation was most pervasive – a claim that Crafts and Harley, unsurprisingly, dispute.[10] At any rate, our current macroeconomic estimates do not measure the productivity of these smaller industries, and the absence of such measurement should force us to pause before deciding whether change in manufacturing was localised in the 'modern' industries or was in fact more widely spread throughout the sector.

Peter Temin has turned to import and export data as an alternative way of gauging the extent and significance of technological change in some of the smaller industries not included in the Crafts-Harley analysis.[11] Between a quarter and a half of all manufacturing exports between the late eighteenth and mid-nineteenth centuries were of goods other than textiles and iron: they included items such as cutlery, pottery, clothing, glassware, books, umbrellas, hats and fishing tackles. If the manufacture of these items was undergoing improvements in productivity, one should expect their export to expand: without these improvements, exports should stagnate or be replaced by imports. Temin's analysis indicates that exports in such industries were keeping pace with exports in cotton, and he infers from this that technological progress must have occurred within them. This, it should be stressed, is not direct evidence for technological improvements in these smaller, older, industries, any more than Crafts or Harley ever provided direct evidence for its absence. Trade data reveal that Britain enjoyed a comparative advantage in these industries relative to her foreign neighbours, but does not indicate what underpinned this comparative advantage. Nonetheless, the existence of a buoyant export market in so many items outside the lead sectors of cotton and iron sits rather uneasily with the Crafts-Harley account of a stagnant traditional manufacturing sector.[12]

The evidence from patenting also paints a rather different picture of manufacturing progress to that depicted by Crafts and Harley. A patent is a grant by the state of exclusive rights for the use of a new invention for a defined period of time (during this period it was set at 14 years), and the granting of patents has been used by historians as a crude yardstick of inventive activity.[13] Care must be exercised in linking the patent series to technical and industrial change. A patent was expensive and difficult to obtain and some of the industrial revolution's most significant inventions – James Hargreaves' spinning jenny and Samuel Crompton's mule, for example – were never successfully patented, though the omission of major innovations from the patent series was in fact a rather unusual occurrence.[14] At the same time as some major inventions slipped through the patenting system, not every invention that was patented signified a fundamental technological breakthrough: while a handful were obtained for a radical new invention, many others were obtained for relatively minor improvements to existing techniques, or even simply in an attempt to evade the restrictions of existing patents.[15] Furthermore, the mere existence of a patent does not provide evidence that the patented device was ever produced and marketed successfully. More than one patented idea has failed to make the transition from inventor's workshop to commercially viable product. It is little wonder, therefore, that the historian of patents Christine MacLeod has cautioned that the patent series 'related to technological change in an erratic and tangential manner'.[16]

Despite these caveats, however, a number of clear and very interesting trends emerge from the patenting record. In the first instance, the scale and extent of patenting activity expanded considerably during this period, particularly in the years following 1750. The rate of change accelerated so sharply after 1762 that one historian has suggested that England 'entered her "Age of Invention"' at this time, defined as a period of self-sustaining growth in technology.[17] Given the great variety of inventions that underlie the patent series, it is helpful to break it down further, and consider which sectors of the economy were patenting new ideas, and what kinds of inventions they were seeking to protect. An analysis of the series by Richard Sullivan indicates the particular importance of machinery and motive power inventions (steam engines and other devices for transmitting power). Between 1750 and 1850, about a third of all patents concerned machinery and machine parts, while motive power accounted for about 7 per cent in the first 50 years rising to 14 per cent in the 50 years thereafter.[18] And while some of this machinery was for use in the textile industry, taken as a whole, the patent series is not dominated by the cotton industry in the way that productivity figures might suggest. Around 15 per cent of patents for capital goods between 1750 and 1800 were for textile machines (106 patents in all), and textile machines made up no more than 6 per cent of all patents issued.[19] This left over 1500 patents taken out on a very wide range of inventions and innovations spread across the economy – agriculture, ship-building, canals and chemical equipment, to name a few.

Once again, the evidence from patents does not fit with the claim that there was little technological change outside the cotton industry prior to 1850. The error lies in assuming that measures of productivity are a good indicator of the industrial processes at work in the economy. New technology is expensive to purchase, often prone to failure, and requires new workers to be trained to its use. All these factors mean that manufacturers are often slow to purchase new equipment and are likely to wait a considerable period before seeing much return on their outlay. To give one example, James Watt's separate condenser undeniably improved the fuel efficiency of existing steam engines, yet many manufacturers preferred to continue with their fuel-hungry Newcomen engines, as the cost of purchasing a Watt engine and paying his annual premiums outweighed any fuel savings that could be made, at least before his patent expired in 1800.[20]

Despite the fact that productivity gains were highly localised in two sectors of the manufacturing economy, the evidence from exports and patenting suggests that technological change was occurring on a much wider basis in the century following 1750. New inventions can be slow to diffuse and measurements of changes in the rate of productivity are unlikely to reflect the underlying changes in industrial techniques. It is one thing, however, to demonstrate that technological change was pervasive and quite another to evaluate its significance in powering the industrial revolution. As the history of earlier great civilisations demonstrates, it is possible to have extensive, and even revolutionary, technological change, without having an industrial revolution. In the case of Britain, industrialisation appeared to turn a switch, marking the end of a period of limited population growth and limited economic expansion and the beginning of an era in which both population and the economy appeared able to grow without limits. Our question concerns the role played by new technologies in turning that switch. Let us turn, then, from assessing the extent of inventive activity to evaluating its wider impact on the British economy.

Ever since Toynbee's popularisation of the term 'industrial revolution' in the late nineteenth century, the mechanisation of the cotton industry, and of cotton spinning in particular, has lain at the heart of historical accounts of British industrialisation. It is not difficult to understand why so much significance has been placed on this one industry. In the period 1772–74, England imported 4.2 million lb of raw cotton. By 1839–41, the annual average had risen by an astonishing one hundredfold to 452 million lb.[21] Over roughly the same period, the price of cotton cloth dropped by 85 per cent.[22] In fact, as this period also witnessed the rapid growth of muslins and fine cotton cloths, requiring less raw cotton to produce, it is likely that cotton output actually increased yet more rapidly than the figures for raw cotton imports suggest. Certainly, by any measure, the manufacture of cotton textiles underwent an extraordinary expansion in the century following 1750, experiencing an acceleration of growth that was unmatched in Britain's earlier industrial history. It is clear that something exceptional was happening in the cotton industry in the late eighteenth and early nineteenth centuries, and there can be no better starting point for considering the importance of technological change to Britain's industrial revolution.

While the myriad changes at work in the cotton industry escape simple classification, we must look to a series of major technological breakthroughs in the eighteenth century, causing the mechanisation of work that had previously been done by hand (and the subsequent movement of work out of the home into the factory), in order to understand the historical development of this one particular industry. Before cotton cloth can be woven, the yarn has to be spun into thread, and it was in this branch of the industry – the spinning industry – that some of the most significant advances were made. During most of the eighteenth century and earlier, cotton yarn had been spun by hand, between thumb and forefinger, at a small wheel turned by hand: it was women's work, and it was usually performed at home. It was a labour-intensive process, and so, despite the low wages generally paid to women, a relatively costly task. In the 1760s and 1770s, the process of spinning was revolutionised by a series of inventions: the spinning jenny, the water frame and the mule, which together replaced the work performed by women's hands with various mechanical devices.[23]

James Hargreaves' spinning jenny replaced the spinner's one spindle with several (initially 8 or 16), enabling the machine operator to spin the yarn onto several spindles at the one time, thereby considerably increasing the quantity of yarn that could be spun in a given period of time. Richard Arkwright's 'frame' (or 'throstle') produced a stronger thread by using three sets of paired rollers to produce yarn and a set of spindles to twist the fibres together; it was too large to be operated by hand, and after some experimentation was powered by a waterwheel instead, thereafter becoming known as the 'water frame'. Samuel Crompton's mule combined elements of both the jenny and the water frame to spin strong and good-quality cotton thread, which in turn facilitated the weaving of fine cotton cloth on a large scale. The mule required a skilled operator, but Richard Roberts' 'self-acting' mule, patented nearly 50 years later in 1825, made the operator unnecessary, and ushered in the first truly automatic machine. The mechanisation of elements of the process of cotton manufacture that had traditionally been performed by hand enabled industrialists to replace human skill and effort with machines and vastly increased the productivity of the industry within a matter of decades. Whereas a worker spinning cotton on a hand-operated wheel in the middle of the eighteenth century might take more than 50,000 hours to spin 100 lb of cotton, by the 1790s the same quantity of cotton might be spun in just 300 hours by mule, and the self-acting mule reduced the figure to 135 hours.[24] Illustrations 6.1–6.3 show the changing spinning technology and Figure 6.1 shows imports rising over the century 1750–1850 and clearly illustrates the great expansion of the industry that occurred during this period of rapid technological change.

Illustration 6.1 Woman Spinning on the One Thread Wheel. Baines, *Cotton Manufacture in Great Britain*.

A woman using a hand-operated spinning wheel could only spin one thread of yarn at a time. It was a labour intensive, and therefore relatively costly, procedure.

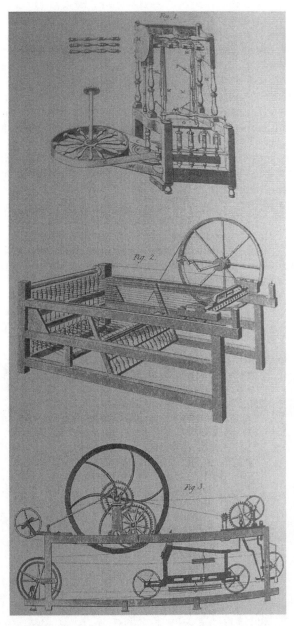

Illustration 6.2 Arkwright, Hargreaves and Crompton's Spinning Machines. James, *Worsted Manufacture in England*.

These three inventions – Arkwright's throstle or frame, Hargreaves' spinning jenny and Crompton's mule, which combined elements of the other two – enabled one operator to spin several threads at one time.

Illustration 6.3 Mule Spinning. Baines, *Cotton Manufacture in Great Britain*.

This image shows the interior of a large, steam-powered spinning factory, using the self-acting mule, first patented by Richard Roberts in 1825. Here a handful of employers oversee the spinning of hundreds of threads at once. The advantages over the simple spinning wheel are clear.

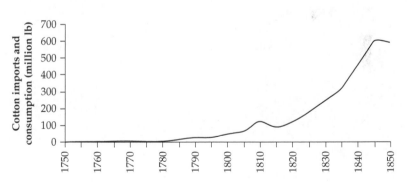

Figure 6.1 *Graph of retained imports of raw cotton, 1750–1810 and raw cotton consumption, 1810–50.*

Source: Daunton, *Progress and Poverty*, 'Statistical appendix', table 3.d.i.–ii, pp. 586–7.

While the spinning industry witnessed the most rapid increases in productivity in the late eighteenth and early nineteenth centuries, a host of new innovations in the bleaching, dyeing and printing sections of the cotton industry helped to transform these sectors too. In the bleaching industry, for example, the traditional method of open-air bleaching using buttermilk took up to eight months to complete. In the eighteenth century, this method was superseded by new techniques developed in the chemical industry, using at first dilute sulphuric acid, and then lime chloride to cut production times from months down to days.[25] New washing and drying machines introduced in the early nineteenth century speeded up the bleaching process yet further. In the printing branch, Joseph Bell's mechanised copper rollers replaced the older method of block printing by hand. One contemporary estimate suggested that a cylinder printing machine operated by a man and boy could do the same work as a hundred block printers, each with a boy to assist.[26] These innovations led to far-reaching changes in these industries, driving up both output and productivity, and changing the working patterns of the thousands of men, women and children employed in them.

Illustration 6.4 Calico Printing. Baines, *Cotton Manufacture in Great Britain.*

Cylinder printing using copper rollers. According to one contemporary: 'The saving of labour...is immense: one of the cylinder printing machines, attended by a man and a boy, is actually capable of producing as much work as could be turned out by one hundred block printers and as many tear-boys! In consequence of the wonderful facility given to the operation, three-fourths of all the prints executed in this country are printed by the cylinder machine' (Baines, *History of Cotton Manufacture*, p. 266.)

The cotton industry was in the van of technological progress, yet it is important to note even here the incomplete nature of change. Although productivity in the spinning and finishing branches of the cotton industry was quickly pushed up through the use of new powered machinery, change occurred much more slowly in the intermediate stage: weaving. With the advantages of powered machinery so evident in the spinning industry, cotton manufacturers held high hopes that machines might also replace human labour in the field of weaving and a series of power looms invented by Edmund Cartwright in the 1780s, William Horrocks (1803) and Sharp and Roberts (1822) appeared to herald the realisation of these hopes. In 1825, the Manchester Chamber of Commerce declared that the new power loom brought 'the whole process of manufacture, from the raw material to the cloth, into one connected series of operations, by means of which, a cheaper, more uniform and better fabric has been produced'.[27] But the reality was rather different from this hopeful vision. Cartright's and Horrocks' power looms did not work properly, and although Sharp and Roberts' version marked a noticeable improvement on its predecessors, even it could not weave fine or weak threads.[28] Furthermore, early power looms required very close attention from the operator as they needed to be stopped as soon as a thread broke or the shuttle became empty. Most weavers could only operate one, or at best two, power looms at a time, so gains in productivity were less significant than their purchasers might have wished.[29]

Given the difficulties that manufacturers faced in developing an effective automated weaving machine, inventive activity continued to be focussed upon creating a more efficient handloom. William Radcliffe's 'dandy loom', which enabled the woven cloth to be wound automatically onto a beam at the back of the loom, marked a significant improvement on the existing handloom: raising the hand weaver's productivity by as much as 50 per cent, it helped to sustain handloom weaving in the first half of the nineteenth century.[30] In the mid-1830s, there were about twice as many weavers operating a variety of different handlooms as there were power looms.[31] Determining the relative importance of the hand-powered branch of the industry on the one hand and of the water- or steam-powered branches on the other is difficult: the output of power looms was certainly greater than that of the handlooms, but the handloom weavers produced higher-quality cloths with greater profit margins. Wherever the balance lies, it is certainly the case that the weaving trade was only partially mechanised before about 1830, and that even so late as 1850, the handloom weavers made up a sizeable minority of the total weaving workforce.[32] Furthermore, despite the undoubted technological advances in some branches of the cotton industry, the endpoint of cloth manufacture – the turning of manufactured cloth into clothes, hats and accessories – was largely done by hand until the invention of the sewing machine in 1860.[33] Even in the cotton industry, then, where new technology undoubtedly ushered in some phenomenal advances, the technological revolution was not completed by the middle of the nineteenth century. Yet taken as a whole, the cotton industry, and the spinning industry in particular, demonstrate how powerful invention and innovation can be as a source of economic change and growth. Cotton manufacture combined a handful of path-breaking inventions with countless minor adjustments and modifications to existing processes to sharply cut the cost of producing cotton textiles. The mix of radically new inventions and small adaptations to existing machines underpinned explosive industrial growth of a kind that Britain had never seen before.

Outside the cotton industry, technical change proceeded far more slowly and with rather less spectacular results, but it is nonetheless possible to identify other industries that were revolutionised, at least to some degree, by the emergence of new technologies. The iron industry, for example, was the site of significant technological progress, and while this did not lead to growth rates as impressive as those of the cotton industry, it did help to revolutionise both this industry and other parts of the British economy.

The production of wrought iron depends on two processes. First the raw iron ore is smelted in a blast furnace to produce pig iron. Owing to its high carbon content, pig iron is hard and brittle; it can be cast into items such as pots, ovens and cannon, but its uses are rather limited. The soft, malleable wrought or bar iron, which can be fashioned into nails, locks, tools, cutlery, horse shoes, machine parts, railway tracks, and countless other items, has a far wider range of uses; so pig iron is therefore put through a second process, in order to refine it into wrought iron.[34] New technologies significantly improved both of these elements of iron manufacture – smelting and refining – during the eighteenth century. Smelting was transformed by the replacement of charcoal with coke and by the development of the 'hot blast' furnace, which used the furnace's own gases to heat the air inside. Refining was improved first by the Woods Brothers' 'potting and stamping' process, and soon after by Henry Cort's 'puddling and rolling' process, patented in 1783 and 1784. The work of refining pig iron had traditionally been performed by skilled ironworkers, who repeatedly heated and hammered the pig iron in small forges to beat out the impurities. Cort's procedure used iron rods to stir and beat impurities out of the molten pig iron, and then passed what was left between iron rollers to press the final impurities away. The technique heralded the end of small forges and helped to produce a more uniform and cheaper product. These various improvements to iron manufacture helped to raise the output of wrought iron by an average of 4.5 per cent per year in the first half of the nineteenth century and led to steep reductions in its cost.[35] Figure 6.2 provides an illustration of rising output over the century 1750–1850 and once again indicates that technological improvement during the period went hand in hand with a significant increase in output.

In many respects, the changes that occurred in the iron industry were less impressive than those that occurred in cotton. In iron refining, for example, Cort's puddling process was vital in increasing the production of wrought iron, but various rolling techniques had in fact existed for centuries; as the

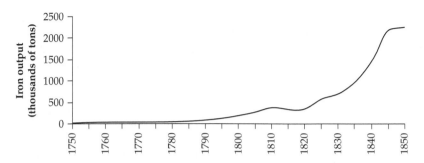

Figure 6.2 *Graph of pig-iron output, 1750–1850.*
Source: Daunton, *Progress and Poverty*, 'Statistical appendix', table 3.c, p. 585.

foremost historian of technology Joel Mokyr has noted, 'the conceptual novelty of the process was modest.'[36] Furthermore, improvements in smelting
and refining iron ore, though they certainly led to a significant expansion
of the industry, did not cause growth of the magnitude seen in the cotton industry. Whether measured in terms of its workforce, its output or its
growth rate, the achievements of the iron industry are overshadowed by
those of cotton.[37] Nonetheless, the technical achievements of the iron industry are perceived by many as the cornerstone of the industrial revolution,
as they made available a raw material – wrought iron – for which no substitute existed. Cotton textiles could be, and were, produced by hand. New
spinning, weaving, bleaching and printing technologies all replicated, with
greater or lesser success, processes that had previously been performed by
hand: by improving production processes they radically lowered the cost of
cotton cloth, but they changed the product in only minor ways. By contrast,
there was no alternative to cheap, wrought iron, and as its price dropped
it gradually began to replace the wood in bridges, ships, buildings and
machinery, and of course, it enabled the construction of new inventions,
such as the steam engine and the railways. Indeed, so numerous were the
uses of wrought iron that Cort's puddling process has been singled out by
one historian as 'a crucial invention which made the industrial revolution
possible'.[38]
    In their different ways, the cotton and iron industries both lend support to
the claim that technological change was the driving force behind the industrial revolution. Elsewhere, however, it is more difficult to demonstrate the
primacy of new technologies in powering British industrialisation. The difficulty lies not in identifying inventive activity, which was present, to some
degree, in almost every section of the manufacturing economy, but rather in
evaluating the overall significance of this inventive activity. Nowhere are
the difficulties of placing new technologies at the heart of the industrial
revolution more apparent than with the example of the steam engine.

Engines of various kinds had been available since the late seventeenth century, and their numbers had grown since the invention of Thomas Newcomen's self-acting atmospheric engine in the early eighteenth century – the first engine properly to use steam to operate machinery. But Newcomen's engine was large and noisy, operated in a jerky motion, and had a voracious appetite for fuel, all of which effectively limited its use to pumping water from mines, where the size and noise of the engine posed few difficulties and fuel was plentiful. As a result, most other industrial processes continued to be powered by other means: by wheels driven by water or by horses; or by small machines operated by hand or by foot. The value of steam power to manufacturing industry was greatly enhanced by James Watt's realisation that the two phases of the engine's cycle – the heating and cooling – could be separated. This enabled him to create an engine in the 1760s that was considerably more fuel efficient (four times so) and that ran with a smoother motion than its predecessors.[39] Both factors contributed to its early adoption in the mining industry and helped to facilitate its spread to the textile industry in the early nineteenth century.[40] By the 1830s steam had largely replaced the waterwheels that had powered the cotton industry through most of the eighteenth century; it was indeed an integral part of the technical revolution that occurred in that industry.

Outside the mining and cotton industries, however, steam power penetrated far more slowly, and its contribution to the industrial revolution is rather less clear. The mining and textile counties of Cornwall, Durham, Lancashire, Northumberland, Shropshire, Staffordshire and Yorkshire had between them well in excess of 1000 engines by the end of the eighteenth century, but several others – for example, Bedfordshire, Dorset, Hertfordshire, Suffolk, Sussex and Wiltshire – had not a single one.[41] The historian of the west Midlands a region, where steam certainly did penetrate in the early nineteenth century, has nonetheless concluded that 'many of the midland manufactures had no use for such a large measure of power which could not easily be turned on and off. For the majority of processes and in many works the traditional power of wind, water, man and animals continued to be used not only because they were cheaper but also because they were more appropriate and efficient in the particular context.'[42]

In the 1970s G. N. von Tunzelmann set out to put some figures to the importance of the steam engine by counterfactual analysis, or the 'social savings method', which seeks to measure the economic contribution of an innovation by calculating the saving in costs compared with the earlier alternative technology. His assessment of the number and use of steam engines based upon Watt's ideas in the early nineteenth century reveals that had they never existed, national income around 1800 might have been lower by about 0.11 per cent; without steam engines of any kind, it would have been 0.2 per cent lower – clearly negligible quantities.[43] These figures have received more recent confirmation from Nick Crafts. His calculations suggest that steam's contribution to improvements in labour productivity was never more than 0.02 per cent per year prior to 1830, rising to 0.2 per cent per year over the next two decades; the contribution of steam power to labour productivity growth, he concludes, was trivial before 1830.[44] Inevitably, measuring something so complex as the contribution of steam power to labour productivity in the early nineteenth century cannot be done with any great precision and the exact figures that von Tunzelmann and Crafts have provided should be taken with a pinch of salt. Nonetheless, the broad outline of their estimates fits neatly with a wide range of qualitative studies, and we might readily concur with Patrick O'Brien that the ' "age of steam" ... remained imminent rather than dominant during the first stages of the industrial revolution'.[45]

Clearly the history of the steam engine poses some difficulties for accounts that place technology at the base of the industrial revolution. The evidence concerning national economic growth rates and population growth and movement considered in the previous three chapters all points towards deep-seated change dating from as early as 1700; by 1800 Britain's economy and population appear to be following a trajectory different to both that of the rest of Europe and that of its own past. Yet steam power had no real impact until at least the 1830s, and prior to then Britain's economy was powered largely by its existing mix of waterwheels and hand power – indeed, the period 1760–1830 has been labelled the 'Age of Water Power' by one historian.[46] It is not simply, then, that the technology was slow to diffuse, as that so much was achieved without it. We will return to this problem in Chapter 7 where we consider coal – that vital fuel that made steam power possible. For the present, however, it must be emphasised that the steam engine, one of the most significant technological inventions of the entire period, does not fit within the timeframe of our traditional narratives of industrialisation.

Von Tunzelmann's demonstration that Britain's early industrialisation proceeded largely without the benefit of steam power has encouraged a generation of historians to turn attention away from the dramatic scientific breakthrough and to emphasise, instead the role played by small-scale invention and by successive improvements and modifications to existing techniques. These incremental innovations are sometimes termed 'micro-inventions' in contrast to 'macro-inventions' – the much rarer, ground-breaking discoveries that open the possibility of performing tasks in an entirely new way.[47] By expanding our framework for technological advance, it is possible to develop a much broader view of the ways in which new technology contributed to the industrial revolution.

In this vein, hand power is not viewed simply as the poor cousin of the steam engine, but as a viable alternative equally capable of fostering growth. Early steam engines were not well adapted to many manufacturing processes and machines or tools powered by human muscles offered a vital degree of precision or dexterity with which steam-powered machinery could not compete. We have already seen how this was the case with cotton weaving: the power looms could weave large quantities of coarse cloth but could not weave fine and fancy cloths as effectively as the handloom. Such examples can be multiplied endlessly. In ship-building, for example, timber needed to be sawed with an accuracy that machinery was as yet unable to impart, so hand-operated saws remained the mainstay of the industry. As one commentator explained, 'it might at first thought be imagined that machine-worked saws would be used; but the curvatures and angles of the timber are so extremely varied, not only in different timbers, but also in different parts of the same timber, that the precision and regularity of machinery would here be thrown away, and indeed unavailable.'[48] And of course, hand tools and innovation are not exclusive. On the contrary, hand tools could be, and were, improved, in ways that were more or less significant.[49] Once again, we have already described one such example from the cotton industry – the dandy loom – but countless other examples abound. Glassmaking, for example, was improved by the cylinder method adopted by the Chance Brothers at their Birmingham works in the 1830s. The cylinder method enabled the production of larger panes of glass than existing methods, yet it still remained a hand technique performed by a skilled workman rather than a machine.[50]

This more expansive approach to the role of technology has also encouraged historians to look beyond machines and industrial processes and to focus attention on the finished product instead. This reminds us that part of the inventive process lay in providing attractive and desirable goods to consumers: new fabrics, coloured and patterned cloths, shiny buttons, cheap buckles, affordable tableware – the list of new products designed to appeal to the changing tastes of consumers is endless. One study of the cotton industry has suggested that inventive energies were equally divided between devices aimed at reducing the costs of labour and raw materials on the one hand and product innovation – improvements to the nature and appearance of the finished cloth – on the other.[51] Similarly, Maxine Berg's study of patents for the manufacture of metalwares, glass, ceramics, furniture, clocks and watches demonstrates that one quarter of patents specified new products, improvements in ornamenting and finishing or imitations of existing goods.[52] These improvements involved inventions such as Keen and Schmidt's method of binding gold and silver to woollen cloth, John Peele's method of printing images onto linen handkerchiefs and Henry Clay's manufacture of black, lacquered buttons.[53]

It is doubtless important to emphasise that hand-powered technology was more than a simple precursor to steam and that it was often the site of significant innovation. It is also helpful to shift attention away from machines altogether and consider the range and extent of improvements to goods and products as well. Yet placing hand technology and product improvement at the heart of the industrial revolution would arguably be placing more weight on these small-scale developments than they can really bear. No matter how much hand technology was refined and improved, it still remained hand technology, an essentially older way of doing things. And whatever inventiveness was displayed in designing

more attractive consumer products, it is also possible to remain unconvinced about the wider significance of new techniques to decorate cloth
with gold, to print images on handkerchiefs and to manufacture lacquered
buttons. Enterprising producers had always sought to improve their existing methods of production and searched for new ways to make their goods
more attractive, and it is likely that during the eighteenth century they
became more inventive in their quest to do so. For our purposes, however, the critical question remains what role this played in promoting British
industrialisation. By any measure, the industrial revolution marked a great
discontinuity with the past, and however numerous and pervasive micro-
inventions and product improvements may have been, it is difficult to
see how they could have played more than a small role in forcing this
momentous transition.

If extensive, yet ultimately small-scale, invention seems insufficient to
account for the industrial revolution, it is also interesting to consider the
example of towns and regions that managed to industrialise without a
corresponding leap in inventive activity. While the fit between technology
and industrialisation is convincing in the case of Lancashire, the industrial
history of many other towns and regions demonstrates the complex relationship that existed between technical innovations on the one hand and the
process of industrialisation on the other. Consider, for example, the history
of Birmingham. As we saw in Chapter 4, Birmingham had grown to become
England's fourth city in 1800, largely as a consequence of in-migration. In
1700, its population of 6000 was roughly equivalent to that of Canterbury,
Cambridge, Salisbury and Hull; standing at about 74,000 a century later, it
had increased more than tenfold, vastly outstripping the growth of most
other towns of its original size.[54] Yet it is difficult to credit new technologies with a major role in this transformation from middle-ranking regional
centre to great city.

The economy of Birmingham had been dominated by metalwork since
the sixteenth century at least, owing in large part to its proximity to deposits
of iron ore and coal in Staffordshire and Worcestershire.[55] In the middle of the eighteenth century, three metal industries – gun-making, brass
and 'toys' (small articles of brass and iron, such as buttons, buckles, pins
and trinkets) – stood out in importance. All three branches developed and
expanded considerably in the century that followed, yet ground-breaking
macro-inventions are perhaps most conspicuous here by their absence. In
the gun-making trade, there were only two technological developments
of importance: the use of water- or steam-powered rollers to produce
gun-barrels and the invention of the percussion cap, which replaced the
flint-lock for firing the gun. Most other elements of gun-making remained
largely unchanged, and as the historian of Birmingham has observed, this
period witnessed 'no fundamental change in working techniques for the
majority of gun-trade workers'.[56] Illustrations 6.5 and 6.6 depict the traditional nature of gun-manufacture at mid-century. Likewise, although there
were a number of improvements to the making of buttons, there was no

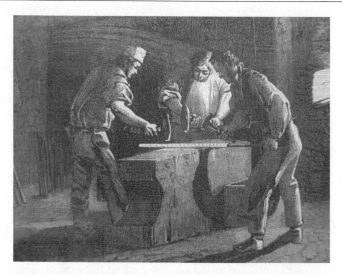

Illustration 6.5 Welding the Gun-Barrels, Birmingham. *Illustrated London News.*

Illustration 6.6 Grinding the Gun-Barrels, Birmingham. *Illustrated London News.*

These two engravings illustrate the traditional nature of gun-manufacture, Birmingham's foremost industry. Skilled welders heat the barrel in a furnace and use hammers to mould the heated iron into a perfect tube. The grinders' task is facilitated by the use of a large, steampowered grind-stone, yet even with the addition of steam-power, each man grinds just one barrel at a time and needs to exercise some skill to achieve a smoothly finished barrel.

clear technological break with the past in any branch of the toy industry.[57] Only the brass industry saw significant technical improvements: the crucible method for making brass and the production of seamless brass tubes, though these innovations came in the 1830s, rather late in the history of Birmingham's industrial and population growth.[58] None of this should be taken to suggest that innovation was unimportant to Birmingham's metalworking trades. Cumulatively, myriad minor improvements helped to increase output, reduce costs and raise profits. Nonetheless, Birmingham remained firmly in the world of skilled workmen operating their handheld tools in small workshops well into the nineteenth century. No matter how broadly we define the process of technical change, the overall impact of new technologies in Birmingham was relatively modest, and this town therefore offers us a path to industrialisation that did not involve major technical change.

Birmingham certainly stands out for the rapid growth it achieved on the basis of only minor (albeit numerous) innovations, but it was by no means unique in its marriage of industrial expansion and the continued use of older production techniques. The towns and industrial villages to the north and west of Birmingham that made up the Black Country were largely devoted to simpler forms of metalworking than were to be found in the regional capital, and they too developed largely through the use of existing techniques. The Staffordshire pottery industry provides another well-known example of an industry which expanded without the benefit of spectacular technological breakthroughs.[59]

A similar pattern of growth occurred in the hosiery (knitting) industry based in Nottinghamshire, Leicestershire and Derbyshire. The 'stocking frame' that formed the mainstay of the industry had been invented in the late sixteenth century. It roughly imitated the work of hand knitting and was used for the production of stockings and other knitted goods, such as waistcoats and gloves. In what must now be a familiar pattern, the process of framework knitting was improved throughout the eighteenth and early nineteenth centuries by a series of inventions. Attachments that could be added to a stocking frame, such as those patented by Jedediah Strutt in 1758 and John Morris in 1763, enabled its operator to knit a more elaborate and attractive stitch. Furthermore, the knitting industry responded to changes in fashions for its goods by countless innovations in the range of goods produced, offering new types of fabrics and knitted garments – velvets and brocades for waistcoats, ladies' silk mitts and woollen polka jackets, lambswool drawers and zigzag-patterned stockings, to name a few.[60] Despite these advances, however, down to 1850s, most of those employed by the knitting industry were working at frames that were fundamentally the same as those in operation two centuries earlier, and the industry's historian has concluded that hosiery provides 'an interesting case of an industry whose structure and organisation barely changed in the century 1750 to 1850'.[61]

No matter how widely we interpret technological change, it seems we are left with something less than an industrial revolution. This is not to deny the extent of inventive activity. The century following 1750 was undoubtedly a period of great innovation, involving both a small number of ground-breaking inventions and a far larger number of small improvements, adjustments and modifications to existing techniques; furthermore, this inventive process revolutionised some aspects of British manufacturing. In the cotton industry, a series of radical inventions vastly speeded up production processes, leading to an increase in output and reduction in price on an unprecedented scale. In metalworking, inventions helped to create a new product – wrought iron – at an affordable price, which in turn facilitated the creation and growth of many related industries and spawned a radically new form of transport – the railways.

Yet in other spheres of the economy, the overall contribution of technology is less evident. The steam engine, for example, was novel in conception, but it was not widely adopted until well into the nineteenth century, considerably after the date at which the industrial revolution is conventionally thought to have begun. And the countless micro-inventions of this period, though they reveal an inventive spirit at work at the heart of the economy and certainly helped contribute to economic growth, nevertheless remained small in scale and their significance should not be overstated. Finally, there are regions such as Birmingham and parts of Staffordshire, Nottinghamshire, Leicestershire and Derbyshire which underwent significant industrial growth yet without much in the way of a technical revolution at all. In fine, the emergence of new technology provides no more than a partial explanation for the industrial revolution. If we are to provide a full account of what caused this turning point in British history, it will be necessary to look beyond the machines and technology that so vividly captured the imagination of many Victorian commentators.

Coal: The Key to the British Industrial Revolution?

Far as the eye could reach . . . a wilderness of cottages or tenements that were hardly entitled to a higher name, were scattered for many miles over the land . . . interspersed with blazing furnaces, heaps of burning coal, and piles of smouldering iron-stone; while forges and engine chimneys roared and puffed in all directions and indicated the frequent presence of the mouth of the mine and the bank of the coal-pit.

(Disraeli, *Sybil*, 1845)[1]

Coal lay at the heart of Victorian accounts of their industrial revolution. Grimy northern cityscapes blighted by coal-dust and smog. The relentless motion of coal-driven machinery operated by soulless automatons. The railways puffing out their black smoke and travelling at speeds so fast they gave rise to fears about possible brain damage or even miscarriage in pregnancy. These and other images formed an intrinsic element of literary and artistic depictions of British industrialisation. At the same time, working with coal was regarded as a particularly dirty and unpleasant task. The employment of small boys as chimney sweeps and of women and children in deeply buried coal mines offended Victorian sensibilities and undermined contemporary ideas of Britain as a progressive and civilised nation. It is perhaps significant that these two trades lay at the heart of early and successful campaigns to place restrictions on the use of women and children in certain types of employment. Some modern historians have also suggested that coal was fundamental to the industrial revolution. Their research, however, has indicated that its significance in fact goes far deeper than the Victorian imagination allowed.

To understand the importance of coal it is necessary to return once again to population and our earlier observation that natural resources had always placed a cap on growth before the eighteenth century. Prior to 1700, there had certainly been periods of demographic growth, but these had been followed by stagnation and decline, as some kind of disaster brought numbers back into line with the capacity of the land to feed them. In fact, this account can be further complicated as the forces that kept the growth of population in check had also set limits upon the growth of industry. Prior to the industrial revolution, the expansion of both population and industry was restricted by finite natural resources, and by the competition that existed between the two. The population needed land to cultivate crops for food and trees for firewood, but industry also wanted the same land to grow timber to fuel the furnaces upon which production depended: agriculture and industry battled to take their share of the fixed resources the land could offer. As industry expanded, its claim upon woodland increased, forcing agriculture to feed a growing number of industrial workers on a dwindling proportion of the land, and while agriculture might initially respond to this challenge by improving productivity, these improvements always soon levelled off as there is a limit to the amount of energy that can be obtained from the soil. In other words, essentially the same forces that had placed a check on population growth through the centuries had also been limiting economic growth. As Tony Wrigley has explained, 'as long as the land remained the principal source not only of food but also of almost all the raw materials used in manufacture, it was inevitable that the productivity of the land should set limits to possible growth.'[2] This has been labelled an 'organic economy', that is, one in which all energy needs for both the people and manufacturing are derived from organic matter alone.

This is not to deny the possibilities of growth within an organic economy. It is well known that just as population had expanded before the eighteenth century, so too had the economy enjoyed periods of plenty. For example, historians of medieval Britain have sketched out a period of sustained economic growth beginning between the eleventh and twelfth centuries and drawing to a close with the onset of the Black Death in the mid thirteenth century.[3] Yet such periods of prosperity differ in a number of vital respects to the modern economy. In earlier times growth proceeded relatively slowly and ultimately flattened off and then stopped altogether: stagnation and decline followed. Gains since the industrial revolution have not taken this form. While the rate of growth has fluctuated, it has never entirely tailed off; the overall trend has followed an upward-bending curve. The organic economy had undoubtedly prospered at certain points in history, but so long as population and economy both depended upon organic matter, the growth that either one could achieve was limited.

This essentially was the world inhabited by the French thinker Richard Cantillon whose ideas about population we have already encountered in Chapter 3. To his understanding, a country might sustain large numbers living a very mean existence or a smaller number living well – 'a great multitude of Inhabitants, poor and badly provided [or] a smaller number, much more at their ease' – but nowhere in the world did you find large numbers living 'at ease'. The French and the English seemed to illustrate these two alternative ways of making use of an essentially finite set of resources. France, he believed (correctly), was a populous nation, so logically each family had to make do with a rather meagre share of the produce of the land: 'It will be seen that a Man who lives on bread, garlic and roots, wears only hempen garments, coarse linen, wooden clogs, and drinks only water, like many Peasants in the South of France, can live on the produce of an acre and a half of land of medium quality...' England, by contrast, was far less densely populated (once again he was correct on this point). So, he reasoned, each family could consume the produce of a significantly larger plot of land and, therefore, enjoy a rather more comfortable existence. He explained,

> On the other hand an adult Man who wears leather shoes, stockings, woollen cloth, who lives in a House and has a change of linen, a bed, chairs, table, and other necessaries, drinks a little Beer or Wine, eats every day meat, butter, cheese, bread, vegetables, etc. sufficiently and yet moderately needs for all that the produce of 4 to 5 acres of land of medium quality.[4]

As Cantillon makes clear, it was not simply crops and livestock that required a share of the land; manufactured goods also required land for their production. The Englishman ate meat, butter, cheese and so forth in place of the bread, garlic and onions consumed by the French peasant, but he also owned items such as woven cloth, knitted stockings and furniture – all required land for their production. Hence the significance for Cantillon of the opening statement of his treatise: 'The Land is the source or matter whence all Wealth is produced.'[5] Land produced all wealth, but the land-mass of each country was fixed. Inevitably, therefore, the wealth that any country could produce was also irrevocably fixed within certain limits.

Yet we know that the world Cantillon described is not the one in which we live today. Since the eighteenth century, population has grown steadily and living standards, far from declining in the face of population pressure, have also risen ever upwards. The size of the population is now at least ten times what it was when Cantillon wrote; yet living standards have risen so dramatically over the past three centuries that no meaningful comparison between those times and the present day can be made. Why does the economy that Cantillon described in the early eighteenth century look so utterly different from our own? One explanation for the difference between the early modern economy and the industrial economy focuses on their different use of natural resources, and of fossil fuels in particular. While this argument has been presented in various guises by a number of different historians in the past 30 years, Tony Wrigley has produced the most eloquent and forceful arguments underscoring the importance of coal. His work in the past two decades has helped to bring the significance of coal to the forefront of historical debate and to make expressions such as the 'organic' and 'inorganic' economy part of the working vocabulary of British economic historians.[6]

According to this line of argument, when industry began to burn coal rather than wood, the age-old constraints which had placed a ceiling to the growth of industry and population in previous centuries were at a stroke removed, and new and previously unimaginable rates of growth were now achievable for both. By digging under the soil, vast new expanses of economic possibility were opened; an apparently limitless source of fuel permitted long-term economic growth on a previously unimaginable scale. No longer were the needs of industry and human sustenance in competition for the same set of resources: the coal mines could provide fuel for industrial processes, cooking and heating, and the land could be used to cultivate crops to feed the rising population that an expanding industrial sector required. Though coal is, of course, itself a finite resource, in the context of the period, and in comparison with the fuel sources that had preceded it, the opportunities it presented for greater prosperity were seemingly endless.

Indeed, it is interesting to note that Cantillon himself recognised the significance of the contribution that coal could make. Commenting on Britain, he noted that 'The coal mines save them several millions of acres of land which would otherwise be required to grow timber.'[7] Yet Cantillon did not incorporate this insight into his larger scheme of the workings of the economy and remained wedded to the belief that the extent of available land placed a cap on the potential for rising incomes. More recently, however, historians have taken Cantillon's observation that 'coal mines save them several millions of acres of land' much further than he ever did, and even provided rough estimates of the amount of land that Britain's coal mines really did save. Thus Wrigley has suggested that the output of the British coal industry in 1800 (15 million tons) provided the equivalent energy supplied by about 15 million acres of land – it is as if, he suggests, 'the cultivable area of the kingdom [was] increased by 15 million acres towards the end of George III's reign, compared with its area when Elizabeth ascended the throne.'[8] By exploiting her coal reserves, Britain broke free from the constraints of the organic economy, and this, according to Wrigley, provides the key to understanding why Britain broke out of the older pattern of limited growth.

Defining the British industrial revolution as a shift from an organic to inorganic economy also provides a model for industrialisation that may be applied in other times and places. The precise path that each country takes to industrialisation will always be unique. Factories, small workshops and cottage looms; revolutionary inventions and small-scale technological improvements; cities, towns and villages – all will have their place in pathways to industrialisation. These particularities might be regarded as the foam on top of the waves for underneath the foam lurk much larger forces. Whatever the precise form that industrialisation takes, underpinning the process is the harnessing of new sources of energy. These might be new resources (coal and oil), new technologies (dams or nuclear power) or some combination of the two. In the process the age-old conflict between human needs and industrial production is finally broken, and the door is pushed open for society to move forward into a new era of sustained economic growth. Emphasising the pivotal role played by coal provides a remarkably coherent and compelling explanation for Britain's industrial revolution, and in this chapter we shall assess the evidence for this interpretation.[9]

Clearly, if the use of coal was integral to British industrialisation it is important to demonstrate that the use of coal increased during this period, and a quick survey of the available records for coal output indicates that such an expansion did indeed occur. Flinn's estimates for the eighteenth century suggest that coal output was increasing at around 1 per cent per year between 1700 and 1750. At that point, it appeared to enter a phase of more marked growth, with output growing at a little over 2 per cent per year for the next 80 years. In 1700, the annual output of coal was just under 3 million tons; this had risen to just over 5 million tons by 1750 and over 30 million tons by 1830 – in all a tenfold increase.[10] Growth in the nineteenth century was yet more impressive. Roy Church's estimates indicate that in the half century after 1830 the annual rate of growth was just over 3 per cent. By the 1870s annual output had risen fourfold and now reached 128 million tons, and Church concluded that 'It is difficult to exaggerate the importance of coal to the British economy between 1830 and 1913.'[11] Map 7.1 shows the location of the major coalfields in Britain.

Like much of the growth we have encountered in the pages of this book, however, the ever increasing output of the coal industry in the eighteenth and nineteenth centuries built upon previously established patterns. Paul Warde's survey of coal output suggests that the use of coal had been growing steadily from as early as the mid-sixteenth century and concludes 'there has been no significant trend break at any point in the history of British coal consumption between 1550 and the First World War.'[12] Nonetheless, 1750 stands out as the onset of a period of more accelerated growth, and 1830 as a period of yet more rapid growth again.

An alternative way of illustrating the rise in coal consumption can be provided by considering its contribution to the overall mix of energy in use. There were, of course, a number of alternatives to coal: energy could be supplied by the muscle power of humans or animals, by wind or by water; heat could be provided by burning wood. Warde has estimated that as early as 1620, coal was the largest single provider of energy in England and Wales, though only by a very small margin: at this point four major energy carriers – animals, humans, timber and coal – each provided around roughly a quarter of all energy consumed. From that point, coal steadily increased in importance and soon eclipsed the other major carriers: by the early eighteenth century coal was more important than the other three carriers combined. Nonetheless, the post-1750 period once again stands out as a period of more accelerated change. In 1750, coal was supplying about 60 per cent of England and Wales' energy needs; a century later that had jumped to 90 per cent.[13] At the same time, the overall energy consumption in Britain had also increased dramatically, doubling from approximately 30 GJ per capita in 1700 to 60 GJ per capita in 1820, and then doubling again to 120 GJ per capita in the next 50 years.[14] This evidence enables us to expand our understanding of the relationship between energy use and industrialisation. It indicates that the most notable feature of the period 1700 to 1870 was a

Map 7.1 Distribution of British coalfields. Adapted from John Langton and R. J. Morris, eds., *Atlas of Industrialising Britain* (London, 1986), p. 3.

sharp rise in the use of energy in all forms. Most of this extra energy was supplied by coal, but a slight increase in the energy squeezed from the land also occurred.

Demonstrating that energy consumption increased after 1700 is relatively straightforward; evaluating the connections (if any) between this increase and the industrialising process is considerably less so. Clearly, however, establishing the importance of coal in ushering in the world's first industrial revolution rests upon more than revealing that coalmining underwent an expansion at around the same time. Let us approach the problem by returning to some of the industries we considered in Chapter 6 and assessing what role coal played in their growth.

The pivotal place of coal in modern economic growth stands out with particular clarity with respect to the iron industry. Iron production depends on two processes: smelting the ore in the furnace to produce pig iron and then refining the pig iron in the forge. Both elements require very high temperatures, and therefore large quantities of fuel, and prior to the eighteenth century wood, in the form of charcoal, had been used. Wrigley has estimated that each ton of iron required approximately 10 acres of timber for its production.[15] So long as wood is the primary fuel for the iron industry, production must be accompanied with careful forest management involving techniques such as coppicing trees and letting them re-grow and rotating the area of woodland in use. Iron production was scattered in small-scale units, often situated in rural areas, and because it required large inputs of valuable and relatively scarce fuel, the finished product was expensive.[16] So well did this system work that when coke-smelting was developed in the early eighteenth century, most producers continued to work with charcoal instead: by 1750, 95 per cent of pig iron was still being produced using charcoal.[17] Nonetheless, the industry's dependence upon charcoal placed limits on growth. With a growing population, there could be little prospect of converting arable land to woodlands, and without more timber the industry's growth was hampered. Between the 1720s and the 1750s, the output of iron grew only modestly, from 25,000 tons to 28,000 tons. In fact, this modest expansion conceals the relative decline of the industry. Imports of iron from Russia and Sweden were expanding more rapidly than domestic production, so Britain's iron industry was in reality declining in importance.[18]

The switch from charcoal to coal in the 1760s brought a rapid and dramatic reversal in the fortunes of the iron industry. The introduction of coke-smelting and of the coal-fired blast furnace led to a sharp rise in the output of pig iron, and new refining techniques that used coal rather than charcoal increased the output of wrought iron. Thus the 28,000 tons of pig iron produced in the 1750s had increased six times by the end of the century, to 180,000 tons.[19] In the following 50 years, output increased a further 12 times: by 1850, well in excess of 2 million tons of pig iron were produced in Britain.[20] The switch from charcoal to coke also caused the centre of the iron industry to shift away from its traditional base in Shropshire to regions where there were both iron ore and plentiful supplies of coal, in effect to south Staffordshire and South Wales.[21] In the 1780s, Staffordshire and South Wales had together produced about one-third of Britain's pig iron; 50 years later this had risen to over two-thirds.[22] The growth of these two regions also coincided with some striking changes in the methods of iron production. Alongside the numerous but relatively small iron-producing manufacturers of the eighteenth century emerged a number of very large concerns combining coal mines, iron mines, furnaces and refineries – by 1830 there were about 50 such integrated works in the midlands alone.[23]

The switch from charcoal to coal was clearly integral to the expansion of the iron industry. According to Flinn's estimates, less than half of 1 per cent

Illustration 7.1 A Forge near Dolgellau, Gwynedd, Sandby, 1776.

Illustration 7.2 Cyfarthfa Rolling Mills at Night, Williams, 1825.

These two images of Welsh iron-making, separated by about half a century, reveal how significantly the scale of iron-making operations had changed during the period. The Dolgellau forge had been built around 1720: it used water power and charcoal for fuel and was housed in a wooden building; it was small and employed only a handful of workers. By the early nineteenth century, forges, furnaces, casting houses and rolling mills were usually constructed on the same site and all were several times larger than their eighteenth-century predecessors. Penry Williams' painting of the rolling mills at Cyfarthfa provides a dramatic illustration of some of the changes that had occurred in the industry by the 1820s.

of Britain's coal was being used by the iron industry in 1750; this rose to nearly 20 per cent by 1830.[24] Put another way, the iron-making industry was consuming a mere 21,000 tons of coal in 1750; by 1830 this had risen to over 5.5 million tons – the industry's coal consumption had increased over 250 times. If British charcoal was to have supplied the industry's fuel needs, it would have been necessary to convert 5.5 million acres to woodland – an area greater than the landmass of England's three largest counties (Yorkshire, Cumbria and Devon) combined. The growth of the iron industry undoubtedly depended upon the exploitation of an additional form of energy. Nowhere is the power of coal to untap new sources of economic growth so clearly demonstrated.

It is largely unsurprising that the steadily rising output of the iron industry was accompanied with an expansion in the metalworking industries as well. As we saw in Chapter 6, Birmingham and the Black Country underwent considerable growth in the eighteenth and early nineteenth centuries.[25] This region was the centre of the secondary metalworking industries, which transformed wrought iron into useful items such as nails, locks, hinges, tools and so forth. The industry continued largely along the traditional lines of production, with numerous, small-scale domestic workers employed either in their own home or in small family-owned forges, and while the metalworkers did not use much in the way of new technologies, they certainly did use large quantities of coal. The polluting black smoke produced by the iron industry and by the countless small forges dotted across south Staffordshire disfigured the environment to such an extent that the region acquired the unenviable epithet the 'Black Country'.[26]

The iron production and the metalworking industries provide a particularly vivid example of the power of fossil fuels to promote economic growth. What about that other industrial leviathan, the cotton industry? As we noted in Chapter 6, the cotton industry grew steadily throughout the eighteenth century: annual cotton imports doubled in the first half of the century; in the next 40 years they increased by more than 11 times, from 2.76 million tons in the 1750s to 30.74 millions tons in the 1790s.[27] Yet this very rapid expansion was achieved largely without the use of coal. The first cotton-spinning factory using power-driven machinery was constructed by Richard Arkright in Nottingham in the 1760s, but the power was provided by horses, wooden shafts and pulleys, not by coal and steam engines. More new spinning factories were constructed in the following decade in Derbyshire which used waterwheels driven by the River Derwent, and as the industry expanded in Lancashire in the late eighteenth century mills and factories were commonly situated in rural areas, so as to harness the power of fast-flowing upland streams.[28] The historian of technology Arnold Pacey has concluded that growth in the cotton textiles industry before the 1790s owed little to the use of new sources of energy. The machinery and factory buildings, he points out, were largely built of wood and waterwheels (or occasionally horses) provided the power: 'thus the new textile industry, however novel in mechanical detail and overall organisation was still using the old preindustrial resource base – timber, horses, water power – in complete isolation from the...new resource base – iron, steam power, coal.'[29]

Yet this situation altered significantly in the decades after 1800 as steam engines, in the view of one historian, 'spread rapidly and transformed an entire industry within a few decades'.[30] S.D.Chapman's estimates suggest that the industry moved quite slowly over to steam power down to 1820 and then switched from water power to coal more rapidly thereafter: by 1835 coal was providing power for three-quarters of the cotton industry in England and Scotland.[31] By this time, most of the cotton industry's machines were constructed from iron, housed in buildings reinforced with iron girders, and powered by coal-driven steam engines. The switch to the new resource base was complete.

The cotton industry was negligible in the middle of the eighteenth century, but with output increasing at an astonishing rate of 2200 per cent between 1770 and 1815, it rapidly grew to become one of Britain's largest sectors.[32] With much of this growth accomplished without the use of coal, the industry provides a powerful reminder of the extent of growth that was possible within an organic economy. Yet the cotton industry also brings into sharp relief the distinguishing features of both the organic and the inorganic economy and lends considerable support to arguments that stress the necessity of tapping new sources of fuel. A combination of revolutionary technical change and traditional power sources had permitted an extremely rapid rise in output during the eighteenth century, and no doubt some further rises along these lines might have been achieved in the nineteenth century. But so long as the cotton industry's machines were powered by waterwheels, there was a limit to how far it could expand, as the supply of sites close to fast-running rivers was limited. Steam engines provided a way out of this impasse, and their use thereby raised the ceiling for further increases in output. It is perhaps significant in this respect that the application of coal and steam did not revolutionise the industry's rate of growth: cotton inputs expanded approximately tenfold in the second half of the eighteenth century; they increased at roughly the same rate again in the first half of the nineteenth.[33] The significance of coal to the cotton industry, therefore, lies not in enabling a marked rise in the rate of growth but rather in enabling continuous growth.

Iron production, metalworking and textiles were all relatively fuelhungry industries and, therefore, provide strong support for arguments which stress the critical importance of cheap and plentiful coal. Inevitably, however, it is also possible to identify industries where the significance of coal is far less clear cut. In the paper industry, for example, output grew steadily between about 1750 and the early twentieth century, and while the use of coal-fired steam engines certainly underpinned the industry's gains in the middle decades of the nineteenth century, coal was far less critical to growth in the periods before and after. In the eighteenth and early nineteenth century, mechanisation, first of the pulping process and then of the paper-making process, was the key motor of growth, but the industry's new technology was water- rather than coal-powered at this stage. In this respect it mirrored the pattern of the textiles industry. After 1860, it was the scarcity of the industry's major raw input – linen rags – that constricted growth, and it was only with the switch from linen rags to wood pulp that the upward trend was able to continue.[34] Evidently, the switch to coal forms only one element in the long-term growth of the paper industry.

But while manufacturing growth without the use of new power sources was possible, it certainly was not the norm, and most British industrial expansion was accompanied by a significant increase in energy inputs. It is possible to demonstrate the importance of fuel-hungry industries by return-ing to Crafts and Harley's estimates for industrial production. Harley's estimates indicate that textiles (cotton, wool, linen and silk combined) and iron manufacture together made up 35 per cent of all industrial output in 1841.[35] Furthermore, improvements in industrial productivity were heav-ily concentrated in these two sectors. Harley's calculations indicate that 40 per cent of the improvement in productivity across the economy came from textiles and iron alone.[36] It is well known, of course, that these calcu-lations are subject to a sizable margin of error, yet it is unlikely that further revisions will do much to reduce the exceptional importance of textiles and iron. Without the switch to coal, the growth of these two industries would have been strongly curtailed; and without these two industries, the British industrial revolution (had it existed at all) would have looked very different indeed.

Inevitably, the suggestion that the switch from organic to inorganic fuels provides the key to explaining the world's first industrial revolution has not gained universal assent. One line of attack that may be fairly eas-ily dismissed is the recent attempt by Gregory Clark and David Jacks to demonstrate that organic fuel sources were sufficient to power Britain's industrial growth prior to the 1860s.[37] Clark and Jacks have downplayed the importance of coal by arguing that although Britain's forests could not have supplied its fuel needs for industrial production, the immense forests of northern Russia, Sweden, Norway and the Baltic states nonetheless could. Yet their evidence in fact does more to reinforce the importance of coal than otherwise. In the first instance, there were other markets for Baltic and Arctic timber, and it must be doubted whether Britain could ever have purchased the enormous quantities it would have required by the mid-dle of the nineteenth century in an open market. Furthermore, even if all the other purchasers of Russian timber had conveniently vanished in the nineteenth century, Clark and Jacks are forced to concede that Baltic wood would only have been able to sustain Britain's needs down to about 1860. At this point, Britain was consuming about 85 million tons of coal per year: it would have needed to purchase the timber from almost every last acre of sustainable woodland in the Baltic region to have replaced this with organic fuel sources. More significantly, had new forms of energy not become available after 1860, British economic growth would have faltered. As it was, with coal supplies nowhere near exhaustion in 1860, the British economy continued to expand through to the end not only of the nineteenth century but to the end of the twentieth as well.

Clark and Jacks' suggestion that British industrialisation may, hypothetically, have been possible without coal is not entirely without basis, but it also betrays a rather literal and narrow reading of Wrigley's argument and a refusal to recognise the fundamental difference that exists between the organic and the inorganic economies. Industrialisation, first in Britain and later elsewhere, was accompanied by a great surge in energy use, and as one small nation, industrialising Britain may have achieved what it did by exploiting the forests of a distant land. But had it done so, it would still ultimately have remained an organic economy, one in which growth was linked to the available natural resources. And as such, it would also sooner or later have reached the limits that natural resources imposed. The higher levels of energy use that accompanied industrialisation could only be sustained across space and across time by turning away from organic fuels to fossil fuels. That one small country in western Europe would have exhausted the immense natural resources of Russia and the Baltic as early as 1860 is testimony to the fundamental reorientation of the economy that was occurring.

Perhaps more compelling than this attempt to downplay the pivotal role played by coal reserves in fuelling British economic growth is Jack Goldstone's observation that coal was only put to work in the economy through the application of technology.[38] Goldstone has argued that the steady rise in coal consumption in eighteenth-century Britain cannot be separated from the emergence of new technologies, namely, engines, capable of converting heat energy into mechanical energy. Indeed, the links between coal and technology may go further than Goldstone implies, for engines were just one of many technologies that were required to put coal to work in the manufacturing economy. This is not to suggest that coal does not deserve its place at the centre of our definitions of the industrial revolution, but rather to argue that the transformative effects of coal cannot be separated from the emergence of new technologies that enabled coal to be used to maximum effect.

Possibly the most significant demonstration of the symbiotic relationship between fuel and technology is provided by the coalmining industry itself, which was only able to supply the ever-greater quantities of coal required by industry because of the development of new technologies which enabled the extraction of the coal in the first place.[39] By the early eighteenth century, the British had been mining coal for more than a millennium. Inevitably the most accessible deposits had long since been worked out, and the mining industry therefore needed to dig ever deeper in order to find good-quality reserves. Yet although the British Isles possess abundant deep coal reserves and there was therefore scope for further growth in the coal industry, deep mining had to overcome technical difficulties before that growth potential could be realised. Deep mines are filled with water which needs to be drawn from the pit to the surface in order to keep mines dry and suitable for working. In the early eighteenth century, water was drained by horse-turned 'gins', connected by shaft and pulley to a chain of buckets which scooped up the water and brought it to the surface.[40] Quite apart from the expense of maintaining teams of horses to operate the gins, the machinery was only effective at depths of up to 150 feet. Without a new solution to the problem of mines drainage, Britain's coal reserves would have remained where they were, buried deep underground.

The invention of Newcomen's steam pump in 1712 made it possible to sink deeper shafts, and thereby to extract this deep coal. Not only was Newcomen's pump more economical to run than were the horse gins, it could also pump water in much larger quantities and from far greater depths.[41] Once the advantages of the steam pump became apparent, it began to spread: in the following 20 years, 78 pumps were installed in coal mines throughout England. And when the engine's patent rights expired in 1733, the new machinery spread yet more rapidly: well over 300 more Newcomen pumping engines were installed in the following 40 years.[42] With successive, piecemeal refinements the size, pumping capacity, efficiency and reliability of the engine were increased. The steam engine was critical to Britain's transition from an organic to an inorganic economy, as it enabled the coal industry to provide abundant and relatively cheap fuel throughout the eighteenth century and beyond (Illustrations 7.3 and 7.4).[43]

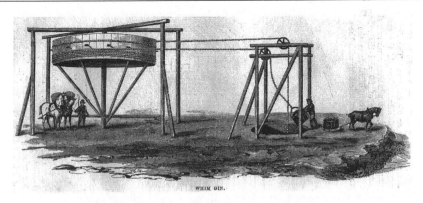

WHIM GIN.

Illustration 7.3 Whim Gin. Taylor, 'The archaeology of the coal trade'.

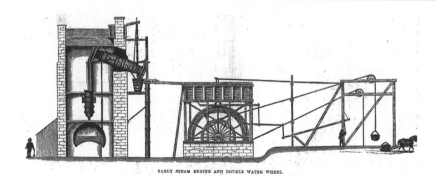

EARLY STEAM ENGINE AND DOUBLE WATER WHEEL.

Illustration 7.4 Early Steam Engine and Double Water Wheel. Taylor, 'The archae-ology of the coal trade'.

These two engravings illustrate alternative ways of draining water from mines. The whim gin shows the use of a horse turning a horizontal wooden drum to raise and lower buckets in the mine shaft. The second illustration shows the use of a Newcomen steam engine to perform the same operation. The greater power of the steam engine enabled the sinking of a much deeper mine shaft, but notice that the engine does not entirely supersede the work of the horse, which remains employed carting the buckets of water away from the surface. Horses were to remain a common fixture of coalmining well into the twentieth century.

Equally, just as new technology was needed to extract coal from the ground, so was new technology often required in order to put that coal to effective use elsewhere in the economy. The substitution of coal for wood was not necessarily straightforward, and manufacturers usually needed to devise ways of modifying their industrial processes before the switch from timber, water or wind to coal could be completed. This process is illustrated clearly by the history of the iron industry. Raw coal is full of impurities, and when it is burnt in the furnace these impurities are released and absorbed into the molten iron; hence the industry's ongoing reliance on charcoal, despite the relative scarcity of this fuel. Iron producers had been search-ing for a way to smelt iron from coal rather than charcoal since the early seventeenth century at least, but it was not until the early eighteenth cen-tury that a satisfactory solution was found. In the 1700s Abraham Darby experimented with 'coking' the coal – treating it to remove impurities – and using this rather than coal in his furnaces at Coalbrookdale. His success in replacing charcoal with coke rested upon a series of further adjustments to the size of the furnace and the blast from the bellows.[44]

Likewise, in the sphere of iron refining the substitution of coal for char-coal was far from simple, and the developments in iron refining outlined in Chapter 6 were essentially innovations aimed at replacing a scarce and expensive fuel with one that was cheaper and more widely available. The 'potting' process designed by the Woods Brothers in the 1760s worked by using coal to melt the pig iron and remove its silicon and then reheating the desiliconised iron in small pots with a flux such as lime to remove the remaining sulphur and carbon and produce wrought iron. Cort's 'puddling' process removed the need for pots and lime by using a coal-fired reverberatory furnace instead. Both were effectively techniques that refined iron using coal rather than charcoal.[45] Key stages in the process of iron production depended, therefore, not simply upon coal, but also on a series of improvements that enabled manufacturers to switch from their old fuel source to the new. It is what one historian has described as a 'typical problem in substituting coal for wood: the coal introduced impurities, so new technology had to be invented to eliminate them.'[46]

A similar pattern is observable in the textile industry. Down to the end of the eighteenth century, power in the textile factories was largely supplied by waterwheels, which provided the smooth rotary motion needed to power the machines. Early steam engines only provided power on the down stroke, making them suitable for pumping, but for not a lot else; and Watt's improvements in the 1760s had enhanced the efficiency of the Newcomen steam engine, but did not modify its mode of operation. As a result, engines remained largely confined to pumping water out of mines and to keeping waterwheels turning. It was not until Watt patented his 'Double Acting Rotative Engine' in 1784, which could transmit power on both the down and the upstroke and convert it into circular motion, that coal could be used to power engines in the textiles industry. Even with this innovation, however, the spread of steam engines in the textile industry was relatively slow, as each different machine needed to be individually connected to its engine. As one historian has pointed out, 'one of the major problems that faced the early mill builder was the construction of the machinery of transmission from the source of power to the various machines.'[47] Hence the delay that occurred in industries such as cotton, wool and worsted, and paper between the mechanisation of key processes and the adoption of coal-fired steam engines. The coal was always there, but the means of using it to drive new machinery generally required technical ingenuity as well.

Once again, there are, as might be expected, some exceptions to this general pattern. The use of coal in the secondary metalworking industries dotted all over the Black Country, for example, owed little to the development of new technology. Coal was shovelled into small domestic forges in place of charcoal to provide heat energy; kinetic energy was largely supplied by human muscles. But the interest of such examples lies largely in the fact that they are so unusual. With relatively few exceptions, the adoption of coal in manufacturing depended heavily on technological innovations enabling the adaptation of existing procedures to the new source of fuel.

Many of these themes are illustrated by the history of transport. Between 1700 and 1870 goods and people were moved around the British Isles on a network of roads, waterways and (latterly) railways. Any improvements to the transport infrastructure were a potential catalyst for economic growth, as lower transport costs enabled agricultural and industrial goods to be exchanged more cheaply, and historians have consequently taken a considerable interest in the development of transport throughout this period. Much of this literature has sought to determine what contribution, if any, transport made to the industrial revolution.[48] But Britain's evolving transport system also exemplifies many of the themes explored in this chapter: the constrained nature of growth within an organic system; the switch from an organic to a mineral-based transport system; and the need for new technologies before this switch could occur.

In 1700, Britain's waterways – both inland and coastal – formed a cheap alternative to road transport and played a pivotal role in the movement of industrial goods.[49] They were used primarily for the transport of heavy and bulky goods that needed to be moved about in large quantities – iron, tin, copper, bricks, timber and, above all, coal. The growth of all of these industries, rested, in turn, upon continuous improvements to the existing network of waterways, improvements which in the early eighteenth century generally took the form of deepening, straightening and widening existing rivers at strategic points, and of the construction of locks.[50] By the 1720s, however, most of the potential for river improvements had been exhausted and engineers began looking towards the making of entirely new waterways: the canals.[51] The first purpose-built canal was cut in the early 1760s between Manchester and the Duke of Bridgewater's mines at Worsley.[52] Its success was such that it sparked a spate of canal-building: fifty-two canal acts were passed in the next 15 years alone. Nonetheless, the actual construction of the canal network proved to be a slow business and it took about 60 years to complete about 2200 miles of canal.[53] The capacity of water-borne transport was further enhanced by the use of coastal routes, and here too a number of improvements throughout the eighteenth century helped to increase capacity. The rebuilding of harbours and docks allowed vessels to turn round more quickly; the construction of ships with flat-bottomed hulls increased carrying capacity; and improvements to rigging allowed ships to sail closer to the wind and thereby increased their speeds.[54]

Yet although coastal shipping and inland waterways were substantially improved and extended during the eighteenth century and despite the advent of new technology in the building of canals, the entire network remained essentially organic in nature. Goods were towed along natural and man-made watercourses by horses, or sailed over the seas thanks to the power provided by winds and tides, and this set limits to the speeds that could be achieved. And although there was certainly the potential for growth within this matrix of transport provision, growth was slow and could not be extended indefinitely. In shipping, for example, total factor productivity improved by 0.7 per cent per year in the century 1676–1776, a creditable, but hardly spectacular, performance.[55] Canal-building, meanwhile, proceeded at such a leisurely pace that one historian has concluded that 'by conventional dating, the industrial revolution progressed substantially without canals.'[56] In any case, loads were still moved along the new canals by horses, and horses needed to be fed, and that meant setting aside valuable land for fodder – between 3 and 5 acres for each working horse.[57] Canals usefully extended the provision of inland waterways, but did not offer the potential of rapid or continuous growth.

The contrast with railways and steam-shipping is clear. Railways have their origins in the organic economy. As early as the seventeenth century, there is evidence of mine-owners and ironmasters building parallel rails to link their pits to rivers: the rails and the wagons were made of wood; men, horses and gravity performed the work of moving the wagons along.[58] This primitive system was improved in the eighteenth century with the laying of iron rails, but the most significant development came with the use of steam engines, rather than horses, to pull the wagons along the tracks. The transition from horses to steam took some decades to complete. The first coal-powered steam locomotive was constructed in 1804, yet the Stockton to Darlington Railway did not open until 1825, and even then used both a locomotive engine and horses to move the wagons along.[59] But once a truly effective steam locomotive – George Stephenson's 'Rocket' – was developed in the 1820s, its superiority over horses was quickly realised, and the railway era dawned. The railway network grew considerably more rapidly than the canal network had grown. In 1829, a mere 51 miles of track had been laid; fifteen years later, the length of railway track already reached that of the canals – 2200 miles.[60] By 1852, 7500 miles of track were in existence and by 1872 this had doubled again to 15,736 miles.[61] Yet these figures fail to do justice to the full extent of the change that had occurred, for steam locomotives and railway tracks permitted the moving of goods and people around the British Isles on a scale, and at a speed, that was hitherto unimaginable. The number of railway passengers trebled in just 8 years between 1842 and 1850, while freight tonnage increased sevenfold. Traffic volumes roughly doubled in the 1850s and then doubled again in the 1860s – growth rates that could never have been achieved by the horse-drawn alternatives.[62] Furthermore, the railways had far-reaching social, economic and cultural consequences that went beyond anything that is measured by traffic volumes. The rail network encouraged trade (by lowering the costs for long-distance bulk travel) and personal mobility (by offering cheaper passenger fares) and was also pivotal to the creation of a national postal service and telegraph service. It helped to lower the costs of many goods and services in countless areas of the economy not directly connected with the transport industry.

The revolution in shipping occurred somewhat later, yet was no less dramatic when it came. A series of innovations from the 1820s transformed the wind-powered wooden sailing boat into the modern coal-driven steam ship. Between the late 1830s and the late 1870s, the tonnage brought into British ports in the coastal trade doubled from around 12 million tons to 25.5 million tons, almost entirely as a consequence of the expansion of steam shipping. The tonnage for sailing vessels held steady at about 9 million tons, while that for steam rose from 3 million tons to 16.5 million tons.[63] The

Illustration 7.5 Bridgewater Canal, Manchester.

Illustration 7.6 Birmingham New Street Station. *Illustrated London News.*

These two images highlight some of the differences between organic and inorganic forms of transport. Both the volume and the speed of traffic along the canal are heavily restricted. The train, track and station are largely constructed from an inorganic material (iron) and the train is powered by an inorganic fuel (coal): the capacity of this new form of transport clearly vastly exceeds that of its organic forbear.

introduction of steam shipping not only greatly enhanced capacity, it also improved the industry's productivity. Total factor productivity was increasing by 3.5 per cent per year between 1814 and 1860, considerably above the 0.7 per cent per year achieved in the eighteenth century.[64]

Finally, the transport industry also demonstrates the key role played by technology in allowing the switch from horses, tides and winds to coal to occur. Railways and coal both existed in the eighteenth century, but simply piling coal onto wagons did not make them move: in essence, what was missing was a technology that enabled the latter to drive the former. Before coal could be used for locomotion, a series of exceptionally complex technological difficulties had to be overcome. First, the existing steam engine needed to be adapted to provide locomotive power, a feat first accomplished by Richard Trevithick in 1804. But Trevithick's engine broke the cast-iron tracks over which it ran, and these needed to be substituted with wrought iron and redesigned before a system of steam-driven engines and iron rails became feasible. Finally, the early locomotive steam engines ran too slowly to have wide use, and it was not until George Stephenson's work in the 1820s that a lighter locomotive capable of pulling at speed was developed.[65] His 'Rocket', it is worth recalling, was something like the seventieth railway engine to be built and was, in turn, soon superseded by new designs.[66] In shipping, iron ships, steam power and screw propellers were all part of the process that enabled coal to be used to power large ships at speed. As we have seen in other areas of the economy, coal certainly did offer the capacity for far greater growth than the earlier organic alternatives, but this potential was only unlocked through the use of new technology.

If it is accepted that British industrialisation involved a twin process of new fuel and new forms of technology, then a number of significant implications for our understanding of economic growth in the period 1700–1870 follow. In the pages of this book we have been loosely considering the 170 years following 1700, and it is certainly not difficult to find evidence of economic growth and change at any point during this period. Nonetheless, the evidence presented here, as well as von Tunzelmann's and Crafts' estimates for the significance of steam power summarised in Chapter 6, all suggest that despite early starts in the mining and iron industries, coal and new technologies to convert coal to mechanical energy, in reality, only started to come on stream in textiles and transport in the nineteenth century.[67] But if coal and steam engines only became a significant force in British industry at some point in the second quarter of the nineteenth century, where does that leave the manifold and well-documented changes that had occurred in the economy in the preceding 125 years?

An alternative interpretation of the evidence is that the period 1700–1870 encompassed at least two different phases of economic growth. During the eighteenth century, most improvements to manufacturing took place within the organic economy. In the textiles industry, cotton in particular, and in the paper industry, the mechanisation of key processes speeded up production times and led to significantly higher output. In the transport industry, the new science of canals opened up previously inaccessible parts of the country for commerce and trade. Yet these innovations used the existing organic resource base – wood, wind, water and horses – and despite the impressive rates of growth they were sometimes able to achieve, it is unlikely that these growth rates could have been sustained over the longer term. At the same time, the eighteenth century also witnessed the development of a new form of economic growth resting upon the exploitation of a new energy source: coal. At some point in the century after 1750, key industries – mining, iron-making, textiles and transport – abandoned their reliance on horses, charcoal and water and switched to coal instead. The switch usually depended on the development of new technologies and changes in existing working methods but moving over to an almost limitless energy source opened the possibility of ongoing output gains and a way out of the old cycle of growth, stagnation and decline that had forever characterised the organic economy.

There was, of course, considerable overlap between these two phases of growth. The mining industry switched to coal in the early eighteenth century; the iron industry moved over to the new resource base from the 1760s; textiles followed around the turn of the century; and transport from the 1830s. From 1830, coal-fired steam engines spread through the manufacturing sector more widely, though industries that continued to rely heavily on organic fuels continued until well after 1850. At any given moment, organic and inorganic industries existed side by side. The suggestion here, then, is not that the organic economy was entirely superseded by the mineral economy. Rather, it is that economic change over the period 1700 to 1870 is best understood as the outcome of two quite different forces: the growth of both the organic economy and the inorganic one and a change in the relative importance of each.

This interpretation has the advantage of dovetailing with most of the other measures of the economy presented in earlier chapters. We have seen here that energy consumption in Britain took over a century to double from approximately 30 GJ per capita to 60 GJ per capita between 1700 and 1820, but only 50 years to double again to 120 GJ per capita. Crafts and Harley's estimates for industrial production and for GDP per capita followed a similar pattern. We observed in Chapter 2 that these estimates revealed a long period of relatively slow growth throughout the eighteenth century, followed by a second phase of faster growth from about 1800. During the eighteenth century, industrial output failed to rise much above 1 per cent per year. After 1800, output grew at a rate of at least 2 per cent per year, and between about 1820 and 1850 output peaked at over 3 per cent per year. GDP per capita rather less than doubled between 1700 and 1820 and then almost doubled in the next half century. The population estimates that we considered in Chapter 3 are similar yet again, showing the population roughly doubling between 1700 and 1820 and then doubling again in the next 50 years. And in Chapter 5, Wrigley and Shaw-Taylor's recent study of occupational structure tells much the same story, with rapid changes in occupational structure being confined to the half century after 1815. In each of these measures a similar pattern emerges, with the long eighteenth century appearing as a period of respectable but relatively slow development, followed by a shorter period of more rapid change beginning at some point in the first few decades of the nineteenth century.

Crafts and Harley's estimates initially led historians to suggest that the industrial revolution was a more drawn-out process than was hitherto believed, but an alternative interpretation is clearly now possible. The steady gains achieved over the eighteenth century were not in fact the beginning of a slow industrial revolution that was to span the best part of 150 years: it was actually the continuation of an earlier cycle of growth under the old economic regime. Indeed, in the context of an organic economy, the eighteenth century emerges as a particularly buoyant and prosperous period.[68] Yet with relatively few exceptions this growth continued upon the old lines rather than the new and did not portend the dawning of a new era. By the end of the eighteenth century, it was as yet far from clear that British history was about to depart from the traditional script.

Dating the industrial revolution has recently been dubbed a 'pointless exercise' by two leading scholars of industrialisation, and it is certainly unlikely that unanimous agreement on this point will ever be reached.[69] Yet providing a chronology for the industrial revolution is far from pointless, as it helps to clarify exactly what was most critical to the process. Placing an emphasis on the transformative role played by coal forces us to look for the industrial revolution no earlier than the late eighteenth century and also suggests that a return to the idea of a short and rapid period of change may not be misplaced. From this perspective, the 50 years between about 1820 and 1870 assume critical importance as it was at this time that coal began to be put to a very wide range of uses throughout industry. Equally, however, this period of dynamic growth did not emerge from nowhere: it was firmly based upon developments in the previous 50 years between about 1770 and 1820. This half century now emerges as a period of critical transition during which many industries were restructured as manufacturers adapted existing processes to the new source of fuel. Finally, it is interesting to note that this periodisation returns us in some respects to the interpretations that were dominant in the 1960s and 1970s. It indicates that the industrial revolution was indeed a relatively short rather than a protracted affair, though it recasts the half century between about 1770 and 1820 as a period of transition and places the industrial revolution proper in the 50 years following instead.

Why Was Britain First? The Global Context for Industrialisation

In no way is the superiority of the British manufactures more strikingly shown than in the extent of the triumph it has gained over the cotton fabrics of India.... The British manufacturer brings the cotton of India from a distance of 12,000 miles, commits it to his spinning jennies and power-looms, carries back their products to the East, making them again to travel 12,000 miles; and in spite of the loss of time, and of the enormous expense incurred by this voyage of 24,000 miles, the cotton manufactured by his machinery becomes less costly than the cotton of India spun and woven by the hand near the field that produced it.

(Waterston, *A Cyclopædia of Commerce*, 1846)[1]

It is a commonplace of any history textbook that the world's first industrial revolution took place in Britain. Yet this simple assertion leads quickly to the more complex question: why? What was unique about Britain? What qualities – political, economic, cultural, geographical or ecological – did Britain possess that predisposed it towards early industrialisation? Or, to put the question another way: what was missing in other countries so that their industrialisation was either delayed until the second half of the nineteenth century or, indeed, had failed to occur by the century's end at all? Considering alternative pathways to industrialisation is of course interesting in its own right, but it is also invaluable to any discussion of British industrialisation. Understanding the course of economic development in other parts of the world helps us to isolate which features of the British economy were critical to industrialisation, and which merely occurred at around the same time. The following chapter provides a global context for the economic transition that occurred in Britain in the nineteenth century. In the first place we shall look at the course of economic growth in Europe and consider when and why some of Britain's neighbours underwent the transformation to industrial society. Then we shall look beyond Europe and ask why a number of highly developed Asian nations failed to make a similar leap to full-blown industrialisation before the end of the nineteenth century.

Let us begin by briefly summarising the pattern of industrialisation that occurred in Britain. In previous chapters we have identified two distinct stages of economic growth between 1700 and 1870. Throughout the eighteenth century population grew steadily and some parts of industry were revolutionised by technological innovations, particularly towards the century's end. Yet, for all this, the profile of the economy changed relatively little: national income improved modestly and the structure of the workforce remained remarkably stable. The economy performed well, but improvements took place along traditional, organic lines. At some point in the first quarter of the nineteenth century, however, a new phase of growth began, characterised by an increase in the use of fossil fuels – coal in particular – in industry. The result was a sharp upturn in national income per capita, in rates of population growth and urbanisation, as well as a more significant restructuring of the workforce. Furthermore, in contrast to earlier periods of economic growth, which had eventually petered out and been followed by stagnation and decline, this growth continued through the rest of the nineteenth century, and has continued largely uninterrupted to the present day. The switch from wood, water and wind to fossil fuels substantially increased the energy available within the economy and underpinned the British industrial revolution. To what extent can these events be regarded as a model that can be usefully applied to other parts of the world?

It should be stressed at the outset that most accounts of European industrialisation have not placed a heavy emphasis on fossil fuels.[2] Through most of the second half of the twentieth century, economic historians tended to regard the British industrial revolution as part of a broader movement of European industrialisation, the beginning of a larger process that soon extended to mainland Europe in 'a purely and deliberately imitative process'.[3] A particularly influential interpretation of this process was provided by the historian and economist Alexander Gerschenkron, who in the 1960s placed especial emphasis on the extent of each country's 'backwardness' when contrasted with Britain. He suggested that the entry costs for early industrialisers, in particular Britain, using relatively cheap and simple technology and with few competitors, were far lower than for those that industrialised later, who found themselves competing against nations with efficient industries using complex and expensive machinery. For this reason, Britain, as the industrial pioneer, was able to undergo a spontaneous economic transformation largely funded by the manufacturing sector. Other parts of Europe lacked this advantage, and the stimulus for industrialisation was provided by either banks or the state, depending on the extent of their 'backwardness'. Gerschenkron labelled one group of western European countries – France, Germany, Switzerland, Italy and the western parts of Austria–Hungary – as 'underdeveloped' and pointed to the role played by banks and bank finance in propelling each of these nations towards industrial status. A second group of 'backward' countries in eastern and south-eastern Europe lacked altogether the kind of banking structures that had facilitated industrialisation in the 'underdeveloped' countries, and here energetic state interference provided the stimulus instead. By these different mechanisms, Gerschenkron posited a pattern of development spreading across Europe from the north-west to the south and east, determined to a large degree by the extent of economic, industrial, agricultural and fiscal development that had been attained in each country prior to the onset of the process.[4]

It must be admitted that Gerschenkron's analysis, in particular his focus upon 'backwardness', or, more loosely, the pre-existing economic conditions, has proved a very fruitful framework for the investigation of European industrialisation, and his concept of relative backwardness continues to enjoy some limited support. At the same time, however, research in the past 50 years has also drawn attention to some of the limitations of this account. In the first instance, his ideas have contributed to a heavy focus on the role played by financial institutions and the state in promoting industrialisation and a corresponding neglect of other forces, such as population growth, technological change and energy. More generally, the trend in the last two decades has been to move away from viewing Europe as a single economic area undergoing one unitary process to focussing instead upon the many different routes taken by European nations, with each country fashioning its own distinct pathway to industrialisation according to local resources, and political and economic traditions. This emphasis upon the diversity of the industrialisation process has provided a useful corrective to the earlier tendency to gloss over differences and divergences in the search of a universal system, but it also risks splintering our appreciation of the forces underpinning industrialisation to the extent that it becomes difficult to discern any coherency in the process at all.

In this chapter we shall seek to find a middle way between viewing European industrialisation as a unitary process following a universal pattern and regarding the industrialisation of each nation as a discrete event unconnected to the manifold changes occurring in its neighbours. In order to do so, we shall shift the traditional terms of the debate, turning attention away from pre-existing conditions and the roles of capital, finance and the state towards the energy economy instead. This provides a flexible way of understanding the many and diverse pathways to industrialisation followed by different European countries, while at the same time providing an organising framework within which the economic transformation of not just one nation here and another there, but an entire continent, can be properly comprehended. Given the constraints of space, our discussion is inevitably restricted in scope – with just four countries, Belgium, Germany, France and Italy, receiving detailed attention. Nevertheless, these examples are sufficient to provide a clear sense of the pivotal, yet highly varied and unpredictable, ways in which the deployment of new sources of energy transformed the European economy.

Let us begin by considering the small north-western country of Belgium, the first continental country to undergo a process of industrial development recognisably similar to that of Britain.[5] Belgium, like Britain, had abundant coal reserves, as well as rich deposits of lead and iron ore. No doubt for much the same reason, economic development in Belgium also followed a fairly similar pattern to that in Britain, with coal and heavy industry playing a pivotal role.[6] Industrial growth during the eighteenth century had been slow but steady. In the east of the country, coalmining, iron and lead production and a domestic metalworking industry, producing mainly nails and armaments, grew respectably; towards the west of Belgium, the domestic woollen and linen industries, based in Flanders, also expanded. Yet this growth proceeded along familiar lines and did not portend the more significant economic restructuring that was about to occur. Around the turn of the century, however, a striking and fundamental shift in the structure of the economy began to take place. Change after 1800 was so rapid that by the 1840s Belgium had clearly emerged as the most industrialised nation on the continent.

As in Britain, industrialisation was accompanied by a realignment in the economic significance of the country's different regions. Towards the south of Belgium the Hainaut province emerged as the centre of a rapidly expanding heavy industrial sector based around the neighbouring towns of Mons and Charleroi. At Mons, the coalmining industry underwent substantial growth through the eighteenth century, a response in part to growing demand for coal and in part to improved transport in the region. Meanwhile, Charleroi experienced industrial expansion from the 1820s following the introduction of iron-ore smelting and iron-processing, using the new techniques recently developed in England. As a result, the domestic iron manufacturing industry which had flourished in the town during the eighteenth century was joined by successful enterprises in iron-production and glass-making – all fuel-intensive industries whose growth was made possible only by the abundant and accessible coal reserves in the region. The Mons-Charleroi region thus emerged from relative obscurity to become Belgium's most dynamic industrial area, supplying coal, wrought iron and steam engines to France and Germany.[7]

Industrialisation in the two more established industrial regions, Liège province in the east and Flanders in the west, took a rather different form. In Liège province, the existing wool industry was gradually mechanised. Five mechanised wool-spinning factories were built at Verviers at the turn of the century, and the weaving and finishing processes were partially mechanised from the 1810s and 1820s. By 1810, just 5 firms out of a total of 144 were mechanised, yet they alone produced more than 50 per cent of output.[8] No less significantly, however, this region also witnessed the rapid expansion of the coal and iron industries and the emergence of a machine-building industry in the town of Liège. In less than two decades the rise of heavy industry in Liège and its hinterland had, in the opinion of one writer, transformed it into 'one of the most dynamic industrial regions of Europe'.[9] In Flanders, however, the pace of industrialisation was considerably less impressive. Though Flanders had long been the centre of a thriving textile industry, the transition to modern, mechanised production proved uneven and was largely delayed until the second half of the nineteenth century. Cotton-spinning machinery was introduced around Ghent in eastern Flanders at the turn of the century, and from the 1820s, steam power and mechanised weaving were introduced as well, but manufacturers in the neighbouring towns and villages showed no interest in following this example. As wages were low and the modern machinery was expensive, employers had little incentive to invest in the modern, labour-saving machines. As a result, the region's textile industry declined in importance relative to the heavy industry emerging in Hainaut province.[10]

It would clearly be mistaken to suggest that industrialisation in Belgium took precisely the same form as it did in Britain, yet there is one unmistakable similarity: a steady rise in the amount of coal mined and used. As in Britain, this created a discernible shift in population and industry towards the country's coalfields. The availability of coal opened the way for significant industrial growth in these regions, with a corresponding decline of industry in areas removed from the coalfields. Low wages helped to hold back the process of change in Belgium, particularly in Flanders; nonetheless, the shift towards a new resource base is clearly discernible.

The only other European country to industrialise in a way that bore strong similarities to the British experience was Germany, though industrialisation here was largely delayed until after 1850.[11] In the first half of the century, the German economy was largely stagnant: real wages and national product per head had barely moved in the 70 years prior to 1850.[12] In the following 50 years, GNP more than doubled from 265 marks per capita to 593 marks per capita, and in the following 14 years, it continued to rise sharply, reaching 728 marks per capita.[13] The growth of industry was largely responsible for this impressive economic growth: the annual rate of growth of production was around 4.8 per cent in the period 1850–73, helping to transform Germany into one of the world's great industrial powers by the outbreak of the First World War. As in Britain, economic growth was accompanied by both extensive population growth and significant restructuring of the workforce. The population of Germany (within the borders of 1871) almost tripled in the century following 1816. During the same period, the proportion of the workforce employed in agriculture, forestry and fishing declined steadily while those employed in industry, manufacturing, mining and transport rose.[14]

As in Britain and Belgium, Germany possessed rich coal deposits, and the great surge in Germany's economic performance after 1850 can be closely tied to the exploitation of these deposits. The Ruhr Valley, situated in Westphalia and Rhineland (Prussia), possessed extensive deposits of high-grade coal. This coal had been extracted since the thirteenth century at least, but in such small quantities that the region remained strongly rural in character even as late as 1850. In the second half of the nineteenth century, however, the Ruhr Valley's minor coal industry entered a period of massive expansion, with coal output increasing by at least 33 times in just 50 years.[15] Within a few decades, the region's small rural mines, mostly employing primitive techniques and a few hundred men, had been transformed into very large establishments employing thousands of men and using expensive mining machinery. In a familiar pattern, the production of iron and steel moved into the area, using both the local iron ore and the ore imported from Sweden and Lorraine. Much of the coal was put to use powering steam engines. The number of steam-powered machines in Rhineland-Westphalia grew from 650, with a total of less than 19,000 horsepower to near 12,000 with a combined horsepower of 380,000 in the quarter century between 1849 and 1975 – a twentyfold increase in the power derived from steam.[16] And as industry expanded, so did population flood in. The population of the Ruhr Valley swelled from some 200,000 in 1831 to nearly 3,000,000 just 80 years later, and in the process some of the Ruhr's small towns – Duisburg, Dortmund, Bochum, Essen and Oberhausen – were transformed into large industrial cities.[17] The medieval town of Essen had a population of 5000 in 1831 which had grown modestly to 10,000 by mid-century; by 1910 it had nearly reached 300,000.[18] By the late nineteenth century, the region easily eclipsed Belgium as the most important industrial centre on the European continent. And as in Belgium, German industrialisation whilst departing from the British model in some key respects, nonetheless also bore strong continuities. The amount of energy available to German manufacturing was vastly increased by exploiting the nation's rich coal reserves, and this shift from organic to inorganic fuels largely underpinned Germany's rapid economic growth in the second half of the nineteenth century.

With their coal, steam engines and heavy industry, Britain, Belgium and Germany industrialised in a recognisably similar fashion. At the same time, however, it was clear by the early twentieth century that other countries without significant coal, steam engines or heavy industries were also undergoing the transition to modern society. As the largest and most populous western European country in the eighteenth century, the experience of France has long been of particular interest. Geological fate determined that the French did not have the large coal reserves of Britain, Belgium or Germany, and so it is perhaps inevitable that the French economy did not follow in the same tracks. Furthermore, the population of France followed a very different trajectory over the nineteenth century to that taken elsewhere in Europe. Population increased by rather less than a third in the first half of the nineteenth century, and in the second half of the century it was largely stagnant.[19] As a result, the occupational structure of the country changed only slowly and cities grew at a much more leisurely pace. So modest were the nation's accomplishments in manufacturing by 1914 that many scholars in the early twentieth century expressed doubt over whether an industrial revolution had even occurred at all.[20]

Revisionist historiography in the 1960s and 1970s, underpinned by research within the newly developing national accounts framework, suggested that these pessimistic interpretations were misplaced and argued that despite some undeniable differences in economic structure, it was evident by the end of the nineteenth century that France was undergoing a process of industrialisation. New estimates of GDP suggested that the rate of growth of product per capita in France was not very different from that achieved by other industrial leaders. The most recent estimates indicate that by 1910, French GDP per capita was 68 per cent of the UK figure and 92 per cent of that for Germany.[21] The strong growth in the economy, particularly when measured against slow population growth, led many scholars to argue that far from failing to industrialise, France had simply taken a different path.[22] Certainly, it is important to consider exactly how France had achieved such dynamic growth during the nineteenth century, and to question whether the history of France provides an example of a 'different path' to industrialisation, a path without coal.

The earliest evidence of industrialisation in France dates from the late eighteenth century. The Napoleonic period witnessed the introduction of mechanised spinning in the cotton and wool industries, of a small machine-building industry and of coke-smelted iron production; but industrial advance was limited throughout the Napoleonic Wars and substantial progress was delayed until the return of peace in 1815. After this date, France's industrial sector, led by the textile industry, underwent more significant innovation and expansion. Mechanised cotton spinning and printing were introduced and spread quickly; and cotton weaving, though it remained unmechanised, nonetheless expanded. The wool and linen industries performed strongly, also on the back of a mix of mechanised and unmechanised processes. With mechanisation came factories and the emergence of a recognisably modern industrial sector.[23]

But alongside this modern industrial growth, a much larger cottage industry co-existed, transformed by the introduction of new technologies and new fuels to a much lesser degree. France's largest industry remained the silk industry centred on the country's second city, Lyon, yet as one scholar has noted, 'The organisation of the [silk] trade and methods of production hardly changed between 1815 and 1870.'[24] Silk production expanded considerably between 1815 and the 1860s, largely on the back of the Jacquard loom, invented and perfected in the first quarter of the nineteenth century. The loom was operated by skilled weavers, usually in their own home, though sometimes in small workshops instead. Admittedly factory production was introduced in the winding and throwing stages of silk production which led in time to the construction of hundreds of small mills located on the waterways scattered around Lyon. Yet the numbers employed were relatively modest when contrasted with the much larger army of silk-weavers in Lyon and the surrounding countryside and did little to alter the overwhelmingly rural and domestic character of the silk industry as a whole.[25]

Not only was the mechanisation of the textile industry in France incomplete, such mechanisation as did occur was also less frequently accompanied by the introduction of powered machinery. The Jacquard loom, while a significant technological innovation in its own right, was hand-powered and did not require a fuel source at all. Much of the rest of France's textile manufacturing was powered by water rather than by steam. As we have seen, water power remained an important source of power in British industry down to 1850, yet France necessarily relied on it to a far greater extent, not only down to mid-century, but well beyond as well. In the early 1860s, about two-thirds of France's industrial establishments were using water power, while one-third used steam; and even as late as 1899, over half of the horsepower of newly installed engines came from hydraulic motors.[26] With water power remaining such a critical fuel resource in France, considerable effort was also inevitably devoted to improving its efficiency, and the French took the lead in improving water power technology throughout the nineteenth century. Rotative water engines driven by water pressure and column-of-water engines improved the efficiency with which watermills could harness the energy of rivers, and further significant improvements followed the invention of the water turbine by Benoît Fourneyron in the 1820s.[27] As ever, the organic economy should not be too glibly equated with technological stagnation. Technological progress could – and in nineteenth-century France certainly was – achieved within the context of the organic economy.

This ongoing dependence on water power helps to explain some of the peculiarities of nineteenth-century French economic development. In contrast to Britain, where factory production tended to move to large cities placed close to coalfields, in France production remained scattered in much smaller, often rural, settlements situated on fast-flowing rivers, and this in turn underpinned the growth of small craft workshops rather than large factories.[28] Indeed, only the Nord-Pas-de-Calais region in the northern tip of France, which diversified from agriculture into coalmining, textiles, iron and food-processing, bore any resemblance to the English industrial counties of Lancashire and the West Riding of Yorkshire. Yet rather than viewing the craft and cottage economy of France as a different pathway to industrialisation, it is arguably more helpful to view it as economic growth taking place within the organic economy. With a series of significant improvements to technology, water power and industrial organisation, substantial growth in the French economy was achieved. At the same time, however, there were limits to the growth that could be reached along traditional organic lines. For all the improvements made to water power, for example, it nonetheless remained geographically restricted and irregular and unreliable, particularly during dry seasons. It also remained limited in the energy it could provide. It was rare for watermills to provide more than 20–30 HP and there was a cap to the number of watermills that could be squeezed onto one stretch of river.[29] How long could manufacturing have continued to grow on these lines? History teaches us that so long as any form of manufacturing enterprise was unable to increase its energy input, its output was likely to reach a ceiling to growth sooner or later.

Of course, growth in the organic economy did not preclude the emergence of an inorganic economy, and it is perhaps in this respect that the strongest case for a French 'industrial revolution' can be made. French coal reserves were small and expensive to mine; they also tended to be located far from centres of industry. The coal industry, nonetheless, underwent considerable expansion in the nineteenth century and it is clear that industrialists were endeavouring to exploit domestic coal deposits to the full. France was producing 1 million tons a year in 1820 which had risen to 8.3 million tons in 1860 – indeed the French were exploiting a higher percentage of their reserves than any other nation.[30] In addition, France imported coal – about one-third of the coal it used in the nineteenth century was imported from abroad.[31] While these quantities were relatively modest contrasted with those of some other European countries, they were nonetheless sufficient to open the possibility of further economic growth along new lines.

With a far smaller fuel resource base than its competitors, fuel had to be used somewhat differently, and so France followed that 'different path' that historians have identified. Owing to high fuel costs, French manufacturing did not travel far down the fuel-intensive heavy industry route taken in Britain, Belgium and Germany. French iron smelting from coal would never have been competitive on the global market, so despite some experimentation with coke-smelting and coke-refining techniques, the French continued to smelt iron from charcoal, a fuel which they possessed in relative abundance well into the nineteenth century.[32] Of course, the reliance on charcoal limited the expansion of the industry, and French iron production was outstripped after about 1800 by that of Britain, Belgium and, later, Germany. Rather than manufacture steel, France imported it where necessary, and reserved its coal for uses where the returns were higher. As a result, France industrialised without developing significant industries in mining, iron, steel and ship-building, and in this respect it did indeed follow a rather different path from other early industrialisers.

In the event, France industrialised not simply in the absence of a substantial heavy industry sector, but also without ever fully exploiting the power-systems that had been so central to industrialisation the other side of the Channel – coal and the steam engine. Towards the end of the nineteenth century, European and American scientists and engineers were developing a new power source – electricity – and in switching to this, France largely bypassed the coal-driven steam engine altogether.[33] Electricity can be generated by many means – coal, oil, tides, rivers, sunlight, wind or (more recently) nuclear reaction – and is therefore a potentially more accessible fuel source to coal-poor nations. It was certainly more attractive to France, and it underpinned the nation's steady acceleration in manufacturing output from the end of the nineteenth century until the outbreak of the First World War. Hydro-electricity provided cheap energy for the northern Alps, the Rhône valley and Lyon and promoted the growth of a number of new, energy-intensive industries: paper-making; the automobile and aeronautical industries; the chemical industry; and the electrical, electrochemistry and electrometallurgy industries.[34]

Framing France's economic development over the nineteenth century in this way helps to resolve one of the problems that generations of historians have puzzled over: how it was that industrialisation in France looked so different from the British experience, yet managed to achieve such impressive results. Much of the manufacturing growth that occurred in France in the nineteenth century was not modern industrial growth at all, but growth based upon improvements to the organic economy – similar indeed to Britain's economic growth during the eighteenth century. As such, it must be doubted that this growth could have continued long into the twentieth century. In fact, the French economy was spared the usual fate of growth within the organic economy, that is, growth followed by stagnation and decline, by turning first (though to a rather limited degree) to coal, and then (more emphatically) to electricity. France did indeed take a different path to industrialisation, but it nonetheless shared a core similarity with other industrialising nations: a fundamental shift in the ways in which energy was provided and used throughout the economy.

The flowering of industrial growth in late nineteenth-century France on the back of electricity generation also illustrates why linking industrialisation to new power sources is such a powerful concept. It provides a framework for understanding the broad processes at work in the transition from pre-industrial to industrial economy, yet is not prescriptive about the exact route that any given nation should take. There was nothing special or defining about the British pathway to industrialisation: it was based upon exploiting coal not because of any qualities intrinsic to coal, but simply because coal was relatively cheap and abundant in that country. Nations with a similar resource endowment followed a similar path, while those without necessarily took a different route. The key to industrialisation was not coal per se, but the untapping of new sources of energy.

This process can be illustrated more fully by one final example: that of Italy. In contrast to France, which throughout the nineteenth century was a relatively prosperous, trading nation, Italy remained a poor and largely agricultural nation down to the 1870s. Only the northern regions, Piedmont, Liguria and Lombardy, underwent much industrial development, with a successful silk industry, the introduction of mechanised spinning in the cotton and wool industries and the emergence of a metallurgical industry, producing primarily ships and weapons. This scattering of industrial enterprise in the north of Italy was too limited in extent to transform the Italian economy, and GDP grew slowly and real wages remained low.[35] Furthermore, Italy was a nation entirely lacking in coal reserves. The high price of importing coal – coal cost between 5 and 8 lire for one quintal in Italy compared to about 0.7 lira a quintal in England – rendered coal-powered technologies wholly uneconomic to Italian industrialists. Thus, in contrast to France, which made some inroads in exploring the advantages of working with new fuels, Italy remained largely committed to the old way of doing things.

Yet the absence of early experimentation with coal and steam engines did not ultimately hold back the Italian industrial revolution. In the century following unification in 1871, industrialisation spread decisively and rapidly, albeit unevenly, throughout the country, so that Italy had emerged as one of the richest manufacturing nations in Europe by the 1980s. As in France, electricity provided the key to this development. In 1890, the electricity industry provided 11 million kWh of energy; by the outbreak of the First World War, this had climbed to 2 billion and was on a par with the levels of electricity production in Britain and France.[36] Electricity provided the fuel needed for the nation's increasingly successful steel, transport, engineering and electromechanical industries. The use of electric motors, rather than steam engines, also helped to shape Italy's industrial landscape, encouraging the proliferation of small machines located in small, scattered factories and family workshops. Italian industrialisation was thus a world away from the German model, with its huge, vertically integrated industrial plants and very large urban conglomerations in the Ruhr Valley; yet time has proved it to be no less viable an alternative. In fine, the example of Italy provides yet another pathway to industrial status, underscoring both the diversity of the process and the central importance of harnessing new sources of energy if industrialisation is to succeed.

Before leaving European examples of industrialisation, it is important to note one other key difference between Britain and much of the rest of Europe. In the case of Britain, the switch to coal, as we noted in Chapter 7, invariably involved developing and investing in new technologies, and this was an expensive process. Many European countries were noticeably slower to shift towards new forms of powered production not simply because fuel was expensive, but also because local wages were low. We have already seen this in Belgium, where cotton producers in eastern Flanders took little interest in mechanised spinning for several decades because it remained cheaper to hire extra workers than to invest in the latest technology. A similar dynamic operated in Italy through most of the nineteenth century: with wages low and coal extremely expensive, there was no incentive to substitute workers with fuel-hungry machines. Robert Allen has recently demonstrated that many manufacturers across Europe found themselves in exactly the same situation: it was simply not cost effective to purchase labour-saving British technology at great expense when extra labour could be cheaply bought.[37] And this implies that the underlying structure of the economy, especially wage levels, was of particular importance in determining the alacrity (or otherwise) with which industrialists began to exploit novel sources of power. Industrialisation therefore occurred not only where there was power, but also where there was a strong incentive, usually in the form of high wages, to use that power.

The economic history of Europe in the nineteenth century broadly fits with the account of Britain's industrial revolution developed here, namely, that industrialisation involved a sharp increase in energy consumption. But how far can these ideas be applied to the rest of the world? How well can the global pattern of industrialisation be fitted to this European pattern? It is interesting to note that for much of the twentieth century, these questions received rather little scholarly attention. A generation of historians took it for granted that only western Europe possessed the economic, cultural and political qualities needed for successful and early industrialisation, so research into the global history of industrialisation turned upon questions such as whether Europe followed the British path, or why it was England (and not France, Belgium or Germany) that underwent the world's first industrial revolution. For many scholars, the possibility that any of the so-called Third World countries might have industrialised around the same time as, or even before, Europe and the United States seemed too remote to warrant serious investigation.

This belief was expressed with particular confidence in a series of influential books by the historian Eric Jones.[38] Jones argued that despite some episodes of significant economic growth outside Europe prior to Britain's industrial revolution, Europe enjoyed unique and superior political systems and cultural norms long before the onset of industrialisation. Europeans were 'peculiarly inventive', prudent in matters of family formation, and particularly blessed with 'special features of site, location and resource endowment': these qualities laid the necessary early foundations for the subsequent great economic and material advances associated with industrialisation.[39] And despite the criticisms that Jones' 'Eurocentric' position attracted in the years following publication, many writers have continued to find this account of long-standing differences between Europe and the rest of the world persuasive.[40] David Landes' successful *Wealth and Poverty of Nations,* published in 1998, for example, boldly declared that for 'the last thousand years Europe (the West) has been the prime mover of development and modernity'.[41]

In the past two decades, however, a new generation of world historians has begun to challenge this Eurocentric perspective and has forced us to contemplate the possibility that the European economy was not so unique in the eighteenth century as the older historiography would have us believe.[42] These revisionists have pointed to important parallels between parts of Europe and other parts of the world – the Yangtze Delta in China; the Kanto Plain in Japan; and Bengal and Gujarat in India – as late as about 1750. Far from being economically stagnant, or 'backward', it is suggested, these areas were undergoing extensive development during the period from roughly 1600–1800 and had economies that did not look very dissimilar from those of parts of Europe with free markets, a substantial manufacturing sector, commercialised agriculture and relatively high living standards.[43] Indeed, some historians have gone considerably further. Andre Gunder Frank, for example, has claimed that productivity was higher in parts of Asia than in Britain until the late eighteenth century and that owing largely to the economic might of India and China, Asia was at the centre of the world economy until at least that date. The world economy, he argues, remained 'dominated by Asian production, competitiveness, and trade' through the eighteenth century; Europe, by contrast, was only a 'marginal player'.[44] While some of these claims are hardly less controversial than the Eurocentric ones they seek to repudiate, it is nonetheless clear that this challenge from revisionist historians cannot be ignored. By stressing the extent of growth and the sophistication of the most advanced parts of Asia on the eve of Britain's industrial revolution, the inevitability of Britain's sudden and decisive economic lead begins to appear rather less certain, and extending our study of industrialisation beyond Europe's shores can only serve to deepen our understanding of the broad processes at work.

Whereas Eric Jones gloomily concluded that China, despite coming 'within a hair's breadth of industrialising in the fourteenth century', subsequently headed down a 'dead-end' path to economic stagnation, recent reassessments of the Chinese economy have reached considerably more upbeat conclusions.[45] R. Bin Wong, for example, has suggested that between the sixteenth and early nineteenth centuries the Chinese economy, far from stagnating, entered a period of sustained and significant expansion. The domestic cotton and silk industries in the lower Yangtze region near Shanghai grew particularly strongly, though the pottery and paper industries also underwent growth. In addition, this period witnessed the development of a commercialised agriculture, mainly of rice, but also of tobacco and indigo.[46] Furthermore, Wong stresses, while the market economy developed most rapidly along the Yangtze Delta, it was not confined to here. The eighteenth century also witnessed the expansion of commercial agriculture and domestic manufacture in many other parts of south and south-east China.

The evidence from population growth, living standards and life expectancy appears to confirm that the Chinese economy performed strongly throughout the eighteenth century. The population of China more than doubled between 1700 and 1800, rising from around 150 million souls to 320 million, thereby adding a population twice the total of Europe in 1700.[47] Yet despite this very substantial increase in numbers, Chinese living standards remained remarkably buoyant through the century. Kenneth Pomeranz has calculated that Chinese calorie consumption – obtained largely from rice, and supplemented with fruit and vegetables and a little protein from meat, fish and eggs – was broadly similar to that of eighteenth-century England.[48] Lack of data undermines attempts to measure wage levels, but Pomeranz argues that studies of material possessions lend further support to the claims of relatively high living standards in eighteenth-century China.[49] Studies of mortality are also bedevilled with inadequate data, yet one recent survey concludes that life expectancy for males in China was comparable with that of European males and that the case for deteriorating mortality is not compelling.[50] Whether measured as real wages, as calorie consumption or as life expectancy, the evidence appears to suggest that Chinese living standards were higher at the century's end than at its beginning. These results have led Wong and Pomeranz to conclude that the most advanced parts of China were on a par with Britain down to about 1800, and it was only thereafter that Britain followed a completely different trajectory.

The Indian example is different in several respects, but recent revisionist historiography points to the strength and sophistication of the early modern economy here as well. In the seventeenth century, India was a relatively urbanised and commercialised nation with a buoyant export trade, devoted largely to cotton textiles, but also including silk, spices and rice. By the end of the century, India was the world's main producer of cotton textiles and had a substantial export trade to Britain, as well as many other European countries, via the East India Company. The Indian cotton industry produced immensely popular and fashionable printed fabrics and had penetrated the British market so successfully by the late seventeenth century that domestic producers were arguing for protective legislation prohibiting the import of all printed calicos from India.[51] Indeed, cotton manufacture was so successful in eighteenth-century India that nationalist historians in the early twentieth century argued that India had been on the cusp of an industrial revolution of its own, a revolution that was only interrupted, prevented even, by the imposition of colonial rule.[52] Though few historians today accept the suggestion that India was on the brink of industrialisation prior to colonisation, the strength of India as a manufacturing and trading nation should not be underestimated.

Once again, wage levels have been used to support the claims of development. Prasannan Parthasarathi has argued that in the eighteenth century, the weekly wage of those employed in textiles and agriculture in the cotton-producing regions of southern India could purchase a roughly similar quantity of local grain (in this case, rice) as the wages that the equivalent British labourer could purchase. While conceding that money wages tended to be low, Parthasarathi argues that the cheapness of grain in south India ensured that the Indian worker enjoyed a comparable standard of living to his British counterpart. Nor, he stresses, should the cheapness of rice be too quickly dismissed, for this provides evidence of a highly efficient agricultural sector. He concludes, 'Agricultural productivity, not oppressed labourers, was the secret to South Asia's pre-eminent position in the world textile trade.'[53]

Of course, it is widely recognised that neither China nor India became industrialised nations in the course of the nineteenth century, but how far can our explanation of Britain's industrial revolution be used to explain the lack thereof in Asia? Is it convincing to suggest that China and India did not follow Britain and Europe down the path to industrialisation because they lacked the coal deposits necessary to sustain a switch from organic to inorganic fuels? The difficulty with this explanation is that both China and India, in fact, compared extremely favourably with many European nations in terms of their coal deposits. Both countries possess extensive coal reserves – they are the world's first and third coal producers in the present day. Much of this coal was admittedly located in regions far from their eighteenth-century centres of industry, yet these difficulties were hardly insurmountable.[54] France's far more meagre coal deposits were also inconveniently located, but producers worked around the coal shortage by mining what they could, improving transport infrastructure to facilitate its transportation, importing coal from abroad and developing hydro-electricity when the opportunity presented. Could not India and China have done likewise? In any case, the absence of coal need not have prevented industrialisation, which turns upon not coal, but upon increasing energy use, by whatever means appropriate. Either nation's power base might have been increased through a combination of different resources, different technologies and different industries. Given that Britain's resource endowment was hardly unique, her industrial revolution cannot be explained simply by gesturing to the fortuitous presence of generous coal deposits. The question of real interest therefore becomes: why did British industrialists go to the considerable expense and inconvenience of extracting coal from the ground and investigating ways of putting it to use in industry? And why did their Chinese and Indian counterparts not do likewise?

To understand the very different pathways taken by these three economies through the nineteenth century it is necessary to reconsider the claims that strong resemblances existed between them. Comparing pre-modern economies is fraught with problems. In Chapter 2, we rehearsed at length the difficulties surrounding Crafts' measurements of GDP in eighteenth-century Britain, yet Britain's statistical record for eighteenth-century industry is considerably more robust than that of either China or India. It is in part for this reason that much of the discussion about economic development turns upon the more indirect measure of real wages (though as we shall see in more detail in Chapter 9, the measurement of these is in fact far from straightforward). And the most recent studies of real wages suggest that the similarities between Europe and other core areas may not have been so great as the revisionists have argued. A recent comparison of real wages in China and Britain indicates that Pomeranz's optimism about wage levels in eighteenth-century China is unwarranted.[55] Robert Allen's research concludes that money wages in China's great eighteenth-century cities – Beijing, Suzhou and Canton – 'were certainly lower than wages in the advanced parts of western Europe' and much closer to those paid in the poorest parts of central and southern Europe.[56] They afforded peasants a basic subsistence diet, but left little in the way of disposable income.

The evidence for relatively low wages throughout most of China implies that some very real and significant differences between the Chinese and British economies existed. So long as labour was plentiful and cheap, two things followed. Firstly, as most of the population had very little disposable income, there was no mass market for consumer goods, and the stimulus for manufacturing growth that was present in Britain was therefore absent. Secondly, low wages gave manufacturers very little incentive to innovate, to look for alternative ways of structuring business or to explore the possible advantages of working with new fuels or new technologies. With cheap, plentiful labour, manufacturers could easily expand their production by simply employing more hands. Here then is a possible explanation for why the complex restructuring of industry that was required if coal was to replace wood and that occurred in Britain towards the end of the eighteenth century was not replicated in China until the late twentieth century.

Recent calculations of real wages in India also strongly reinforce this conclusion. Stephen Broadberry and Bishnupriya Gupta have revisited Parthasarathi's claim that wages in eighteenth-century Britain and India were broadly equivalent by distinguishing between 'grain wages' and 'silver wages' – the former being wages measured in terms of the amount of grain they could buy, and the latter being wages measured in terms of the silver content of the currency in which they were paid.[57] Broadberry and Gupta's analysis reveals that Indian workers did indeed enjoy relatively high grain wages, though this was not a consequence of a particularly developed agriculture sector. It was simply a consequence of large numbers working in agriculture and of the fact that yields in rice-growing regions are in any case higher than those of grain-growing ones. A high proportion of the population working in agriculture should not be taken as evidence of agricultural sophistication, but quite the reverse: it implies that agriculture depended upon relatively backward, labour-intensive techniques. The silver wages, meanwhile, provide a fairer indication of the state of development of the economy, and these, they suggest, were considerably lower in India than in Britain – about four times or less the British levels. They were low, they suggest, because the overall development of the economy was quite low, which indicates that the differences between the British and Indian economy were already firmly in place long before the onset of the eighteenth century. 'In short', they conclude, 'India was not on the same development level as Britain during the seventeenth and eighteenth centuries.'[58]

Broadberry and Gupta have also compared the consequences of a low-wage economy in India with Britain's high-wage one.[59] High labour costs, they argue, provided the spur for technological advances in the Lancashire cotton industry which, as we have seen, led to a sharp and dramatic improvement in labour productivity in the industry. This forms a stark contrast to the technology used in India, where poorly paid, highly skilled workers continued to spin and weave using very cheap and simple equipment. Once again, we encounter the obstacles to change that a low-wage economy presented: with low wages there was simply no incentive to innovate. Investing in expensive machinery made little sense when more hands could be employed at little extra cost, so manufacturers adhered to the same practices and processes that had worked for the generations before them (Illustration 8.1).

This discussion of Asia helps to clarify some of the forces at work when Britain began to industrialise at the turn of the nineteenth century. If the

Illustration 8.1 Indian Spinning and Weaving. *Illustrated London News.*

The low wages paid to cotton workers in nineteenth-century India provided manufacturers with little incentive to invest in expensive, labour-saving technologies. These engravings show elements of the spinning and weaving processes and illustrate the persistence of traditional techniques in the Indian cotton industry several decades after British manufacturers had started to replace workers with machines.

absence of Asian industrialisation cannot be explained by simple reference to the lack of coal, then so it follows that Britain's success was owing to more than the presence of coal. As we noted in Chapter 7, switching from wood to coal was far from straightforward. The two fuels are not interchangeable, and a series of complex technological innovations needed to be introduced if coal was to replace wood for industrial purposes. Britain, like many parts of the world, possessed the coal; more uniquely, however, it also had a very strong incentive, in the form of high wages, to experiment with ways of using that coal in novel contexts. This, in turn, suggests that in order to understand Britain's industrial revolution fully we need to look at the development that took place within the organic economy during the eighteenth century. Population growth, urbanisation, occupational change, agricultural improvement and technical advance had all helped to make the British economy look quite unique by the late eighteenth century; by this time Britain was, by world standards, an exceptionally prosperous nation. The avenues for further growth upon the existing organic lines, however, were also becoming constricted, and in order to realise further gains, manufacturers needed to look beyond the existing ways of doing things. This century of development provided a critical impetus for industrialisation and is central to understanding why the world's first industrial revolution took place in this small country, and at this particular point in time.[60]

More generally, the evidence for economic growth and change across the globe in the two centuries after 1700 that has been presented here provides broad support for the account of industrialisation that has been offered in previous chapters, namely, that Britain's industrial revolution was characterised above all by a sharp increase in the amount of energy used in the economy, itself the consequence of the switch to coal and the deployment of new technologies. Linking industrialisation to an increase in the amount of energy used in the economy is a powerful and flexible concept. Different nations, each with their own unique resource endowment, found different ways of tapping new sources of energy, hence the success with which some nations industrialised without coal and without steam engines. Nonetheless, linking industrialisation to energy use provides a way of connecting diverse pathways to industrialisation and offers a compelling framework for understanding the great economic and social transition that occurred across Europe between the nineteenth and twentieth centuries.

Winners and Losers: Living through the Industrial Revolution

> The poor might hope for good days; but, alas, they do not come this year, for meal and flour is high, and wages is low, and . . . work is very scarce, so the times is very bad for the poor.
>
> (William Varley, 'Diary', 16 July 1825)[1]

Few topics in British history have attracted so much research as the industrial revolution. But much of the attention that historians have paid to the industrial revolution over the past 100 years stems less from an interest in cotton, coal and the spinning jenny and more from a desire to establish how this event altered the life experiences of ordinary people. Who were the winners and who were the losers of this momentous event? And what benefits did industrialisation and mechanisation bring to the nameless men, women and children who worked in the factories and made it all happen? These are questions charged with political overtones, and they have polarised historians who have inevitably interpreted the disappearance of traditional society and the advent of capitalism in very different ways.

We have already noted that nineteenth-century English commentators did not use the expression the 'industrial revolution' in a clear and consistent manner. Nonetheless, they had a good sense that some fairly monumental social and economic changes were occurring at this time, and by the 1830s some commentators were starting to discuss what benefits, if any, the recent advances in manufacturing were bringing to the labouring poor. In 1839, the historian Thomas Carlyle coined the expression the 'Condition of England', and writers and thinkers from Charles Dickens, Elizabeth Gaskill, Benjamin Disraeli, Friedrich Engels to Karl Marx continued to debate the Condition of England throughout the 1840s and beyond.[2] These writers expressed a complex web of concerns about the ways in which rapid industrial and urban growth were changing the fabric of traditional society and tended to believe that the condition of the labouring poor was worsening as part of this process. Carlyle, for example, thought that the 'working body of this rich English Nation has sunk or is fast sinking

144

into a state, to which, all sides of it considered, there was literally never any parallel.'[3] Friedrich Engels, in his influential survey of the working class in Manchester, argued that not only were the workers' living and working conditions worse than ever before but their wages were lower-too: pre-industrial workers, he wrote, had lived a 'passably comfortable existence...and their material position was far better than that of their successors'.[4]

Of course, not everybody viewed the consequences of rapid industrialisation in such a negative light and others were considerably more sanguine. For example, Andrew Ure, the Scottish writer on factories, argued that factory employment was highly beneficial not simply to the nation in general, but in particular for those fortunate enough to be employed in them.[5] Workers in the cotton mills, he claimed, benefitted from high wages, easy labour and a healthy working environment; they were less susceptible to cholera; and they only suffered from deformity or accidents through their own careless misuse of the machines.[6] Indeed, even some of the great nineteenth-century social reformers believed that industrialisation was improving the living standards of the labouring poor. Edwin Chadwick, whose pioneering research into the conditions of urban slums formed the basis of the nation's earliest public health measures, nonetheless believed that 'wages, or the means of obtaining the necessaries of life for the whole mass of the labouring community, have advanced, and the comforts within the reach of the labouring classes have increased with the late increase of population.'[7]

And just as contemporaries were deeply divided over the relative gains for working people, so did historians continue to disagree throughout the twentieth century. It is perhaps significant that Arnold Toynbee, who first popularised the term 'industrial revolution' in the 1880s, was also the first historian to present a decisive argument about the impact of this revolution on working-class living standards. Toynbee was emphatic that industrialisation had been entirely deleterious for the men, women and children whose labour had underpinned it: 'The steam-engine, the spinning-jenny, the power-loom,' he wrote, 'had torn up the population by the roots...The effects of the Industrial Revolution prove that free competition may produce wealth without producing well-being.'[8] In this way, Toynbee provided a hugely influential interpretation of the industrial revolution as social catastrophe that informed writing about working-class living standards in Britain for several years.

In the decades following the publication of Toynbee's *Lectures*, historical opinion divided into two opposing camps, the 'optimists' and the 'pessimists', and this dichotomy continued to frame debate throughout the twentieth century. The 'optimists' argued that by raising incomes, the industrial revolution improved the lot of the labouring poor. For example, J. H. Clapham's *Economic History of Modern Britain*, published in three volumes between 1926 and 1928, argued that the period witnessed steady rises in the standard of living.[9] This view was strongly restated by

T. S. Ashton in the 1950s, by R. M. Hartwell, Phyllis Deane and W. A. Cole in the 1960s and Peter Lindert and Jeffrey Williamson in the early 1980s, as well as receiving more qualified support from a number of other historians.[10] On the other hand were the 'pessimists', who either denied that the working classes shared in the rising wealth of the nation or argued that whatever the paltry financial gains realised, they were more than outweighed by the disadvantages – the urban slums, the relentless discipline of the factory and the breaking of traditional family and community bonds – that the industrial revolution also brought in its wake. In the early twentieth century, the popular historians, Sidney and Beatrice Webb and J. L. and Barbara Hammond, writing for a public as well as an academic audience, echoed Toynbee's view of the industrial revolution as social disaster, bringing no immediate gains for the labouring poor.[11] In the 1960s, two highly influential Marxist historians, Eric Hobsbawm and E. P. Thompson, took a similarly bleak view of the impact of industrialisation on working-class living standards, and much of the writing in the past decade or so has also tilted towards the pessimist camp.[12] Establishing precisely what had happened to working-class living standards during the early years of industrialisation was far from straight forward given, on the one hand, the abundance and complexity of the surviving information about working people's wages and, on the other, the paucity of information about working hours and living costs. Added to this, there were inevitably differences over how the significance of qualitative changes in working patterns and domestic arrangements in the early nineteenth century should be interpreted. Little wonder, therefore, that historical consensus proved so elusive throughout the twentieth century.

In the past two decades, analyses of the social effects of industrialisation have become considerably more sophisticated as historians have moved away from measurements of real wages and explored new and innovative ways in which the people's living standards may be measured. Death rates; infant mortality; life expectancy; the consumption of 'luxuries', such as tea, coffee and tobacco; heights; and complex measures of 'well-being' incorporating mortality, heights as well as political rights and literacy levels have all been exploited to produce a detailed picture of the ways in which working people's lives changed during the industrial revolution. Yet despite the complex and varied literature that now exists, disagreements over whether living standards deteriorated, improved or remained unchanged still abound. It is the purpose of this chapter to explore this debate and to assess whether the plethora of recent studies provides the basis for any general conclusions on the impact of industrialisation on the labouring poor.

Real wages have long lain at the centre of historians' analyses of working-class living standards and we shall begin by looking at this most central of welfare measures. The 'real wage' is defined as wages that have been adjusted for inflation; it measures, in effect, the changing purchasing power of the worker's income. As such, it is a relative measure, contrasting the value of wages over time (or across space) rather than an absolute value measured in pounds, shillings and pence. Charting changes in the real wage requires knowledge of both the wages that workers received and their cost of living. During the nineteenth century, extensive information about the wages paid to different occupational groups was gathered, and the data have greatly assisted historians in calculating nominal wages rates.[13] Estimating the cost of living, however, is more complex, as it requires information about both the price of various essential items of working-class expenditure – food, fuel, rent and clothing – and the proportion of income spent on each item. Information on both prices and on the way in which workers' income was actually spent is considerably more sparse and this problem bedevils attempts to measure the real wage accurately.

The earliest attempts to calculate changes in the real wage date from the turn of the twentieth century, and estimates have been continually reworked and revised ever since.[14] In the 1980s, Lindert and Williamson offered an important addition to the literature when they replaced the existing cost-of-living indexes, mostly produced in the 1950s or earlier, with their own index based on extensive new research. This formed the basis for a fundamental revision to our understanding of the movements of real wages during the industrial revolution. Lindert and Williamson argued that the real wage had undergone very significant improvements during the nineteenth century, nearly doubling in just 30 years between 1820 and 1850. This rise was 'large enough', they concluded, 'to resolve most of the debate over whether real wages improved during the industrial revolution'.[15] In the event, however, their results did not 'resolve' the debate in the way they had envisaged. In little more than a decade new estimates, supporting considerably more pessimistic conclusions, were produced. Charles Feinstein's estimates, published in 1998, indicated a rise in real wages of no more than 15 per cent in the 70 years between 1780 and 1850. His verdict could hardly have been more different: 'For the majority of the working class the historical reality was that they had to endure almost a century of hard toil with little or no advance from a low base before they really began to share in any of the benefits of the economic transformation they had helped to create.'[16] Robert Allen's estimates of building wages in London published shortly thereafter pointed in a similarly pessimistic direction.[17] Not all the recent real wages estimates, however, have painted quite such a bleak picture. Gregory Clark's estimates for building labourers and farm labourers suggest that real wages rose by about 50 per cent between the mid-eighteenth and the mid-nineteenth century, a far more conservative improvement than the doubling of wages in three decades that Lindert and Williamson had reported, but a sizeable increase nonetheless.[18] Clearly, recent research into real wages has not yet resolved the standard of living debate.

While there is considerable disagreement over the direction of real wages in the century following 1750, it is important to note that most of this divergence in fact centres upon the movement of wages in the nineteenth century. There is unanimity among historians concerning the fate of wages during the eighteenth century, with all the recent studies concurring that real wages either stagnated or declined slightly. Turning to the nineteenth century, the discrepancies become more apparent. Feinstein's estimates, for example, have real wages rising by about 45 per cent between 1800 and 1870, with most of the rise occurring from the 1840s.[19] Allen has reported his results as 'welfare ratios' rather than real wages: his estimates suggest the welfare ratio for building craftsmen rose by about 44 per cent between the first and second halves of the nineteenth century.[20] Clark, by contrast, has the real wages of agricultural labourers increasing by 50 per cent between 1800 and 1870, and those of building craftsmen increasing by over 80 per cent – an improvement nearly double that reported by Feinstein.[21]

Not only is there some disagreement between historians over the movement of the real wage in the nineteenth century, there is also a significant conflict between these results for the real wage and what we already know about the growth of national income in Britain over this period. If we recall the macroeconomic estimates for national income considered in Chapter 2, it will be remembered that recent estimates suggest that economic growth was slow but steady down to about 1800 and then picked up speed considerably. The combined effect of this growth was that national income per head approximately doubled between 1760 and 1860, with the lion's share of growth occurring in the last 30 years.[22] This evidence poses something of a puzzle. How is it possible that there was an increase in wealth per person of around 100 per cent, yet that studies of the real wage show gains in the region of only 40 to 80 per cent?[23] Figure 9.1 plots the rise in GDP per capita and the rise in real wages according to Feinstein and clearly illustrates the difference between the two series.

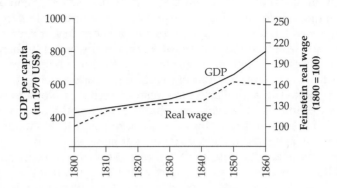

Figure 9.1 *Graph of gross domestic product (GDP) per capita and real wages in England, 1800–60.*

Sources: Crafts, 'Gross National Product in Europe', table 1, p. 389; Feinstein, 'Pessimism perpetuated' table 5, p. 648.

A number of solutions are possible. It may be that the newly created wealth was not shared equally among the population, with most of it settling in the pockets of those who did not work with their backs and hands to create it. This proposition is difficult to evaluate as historians have yet to devise convincing ways of measuring income inequality, though clearly if this explanation is correct this period must have seen the emergence of a very sharp increase in income inequality. Alternatively, it is possible that some of this extra wealth *was* filtering through to the labouring poor, but that they had to work longer hours in order to obtain it. One study of working hours in eighteenth-century London and the North of England certainly lends support for this suggestion; it is, however, confined to just these two areas, and it is not immediately clear how far the trends here were mirrored elsewhere in the country, or how long they were sustained into the nineteenth century.[24] Finally, it may be that these estimates of the real wages are simply wrong.

While challenging the accuracy of the recent real wage estimates is certainly a neat solution, all of the recent estimates are extremely careful studies and the variation between them and the national income accounts cannot be so easily dismissed. At the root of the problem lie not the errors of individual historians, but the more fundamental difficulties surrounding the conversion of the surviving data into information about the real wage. Measuring the real wage, it will be recalled, requires data about the movement of nominal wages on the one hand and the cost of living on the other. Recent real wage series have made considerable progress in addressing earlier criticisms of the measurement of nominal wages. Lindert and Williamson, for example, were criticised for not including women's wages and for assuming that *annual* income mirrored *weekly* wage rates, when in fact high rates of unemployment meant they were likely to be significantly lower. The more recent estimates have generally attempted to allow for both of these factors and do in fact largely agree over the movement of wages in the nineteenth century. The difficulties of accurately calculating the cost of living, however, are proving to be more intractable, and it is here that the divergences between the different series are greatest. Feinstein's cost-of-living index, for example, drops by 8 per cent between 1800 and 1860, whereas Allen's rises by about 10 per cent over roughly the same period.[25] Meanwhile, Clark's cost-of-living index dropped by a substantial 28 per cent in the first half of the nineteenth century.[26] In effect, the discrepancy between the different real wage estimates stems from disagreement over the direction of living costs in the nineteenth century, and in particular over whether the cost of living dropped following the Napoleonic Wars, and if so, by how much.

Nor is it clear exactly how further research will help us to decide which of these cost-of-living indexes is to be preferred. Although there are a relatively large number of estimates for prices, the difficulties of deciding how working-class families actually spent their wages still remain. In order to address this problem, Feinstein, Allen and Clark have turned to Sara Horrell and Jane Humphries' work on family budgets.[27] Horrell and Humphries analysed the breakdown of household expenditure in approximately 1350 family budgets between the 1780s and the 1860s. Each of these budgets provides detail about how much the family spent on bread, meat, potatoes, beer, clothing, rent and so forth. Yet in reality, Horrell and Humphries' sample of 1350 family budgets is not very large, particularly once it is recognised that well over half of all the budgets, 867 of the total, come from one county alone – Lancashire. We already know, of course, that the economic development of Lancashire was highly unusual, so the over-representation of this one, atypical county should give us pause for thought. On the other hand, some counties provide fewer than 10 separate budgets for the entire period.[28] Map 9.1 illustrates the geographical spread of the budgets that Horrell and Humphries amassed and reveals the uneven coverage of the surviving records. Similarly, some decades are quite poorly covered: for the 1820s, for example, fewer than 20 separate budgets have survived.[29] And in general, nineteenth-century investigators tended to research working-class budgets when times were hard, so the sample as a whole has a tendency to over-represent families in desperate poverty.

Even if this sample were to be improved and extended, a number of problems remain in converting the information from family budgets into estimates of the costs of living. The surviving information about how working-class families spent their income takes the form of one-off observations and does not, therefore, indicate how families responded when the economic climate changed. When, for example, the price of potatoes rose, did families continue to consume the same quantity as before, or did they begin to replace potatoes with a cheaper alternative? If rents rose, did they respond by moving to somewhere less costly? Feinstein and Allen have both assumed that families continued to consume the same quantity of each item, regardless of the relative movements in their prices. On the other hand, Clark assumes that if the price of an item increased, consumers responded by purchasing less of that item: consequently, the proportion of the income spent on each item remains constant in Clark's index although the relative quantities might change quite significantly. But how are we to decide who is right? It might seem fair to assume that many careful householders will cut back on potatoes if their price begins to rise, but how many would have actually moved to cheaper lodgings in response to rent rises? The answers to such questions do not lie in the sources, but are matters of judgement. Ultimately, the statistical techniques used do not allow for the fact that individuals will react to price rises in many different ways.

Using a cost-of-living index involves a gross simplification of spending habits that were in reality complex and highly varied. A brief glance at working-class budgets and autobiographies reveals the eye-watering variety of ways in which working-class families spent their meagre incomes. Consider, for example, expenditure on just one key item: clothing. Eight budgets from the 1830s and 1840s reveal families spending 0, 5, 7.5, 10.5, 11, 18.5 and 24 per cent of their annual income on clothing.[30] Autobiographers

Map 9.1 Distribution of household budgets by county. Adapted from S. Horrell and J. Humphries, 'Old questions, new data, and alternative perspectives: Families' living standards during the industrial revolution', *Journal of Economic History*, 52/4 (1992), pp. 849–80.

frequently remembered their parents' inability to provide them with adequate clothing during their childhood, yet at the same time reported spending fairly extravagant sums on clothes and boots as soon as they left home and were earning their own way.[31] Thomas Carter, for example, working as a tailor in London, fancied that his outward appearance would be 'greatly embellished' by some new footwear and spent no less than 36 shillings on a new pair of boots – a sum considerably in excess of that being spent in the family budgets.[32] So when economic historians declare that clothing formed 6 per cent or 12 per cent of working-class expenditure, they are guilty of an extreme simplification.[33] Some certainly did, but many did not. Nor is this an idle point. The decisions made concerning household expenditure are enough to determine whether real wages rose or fell during the nineteenth century, and by how much.

The difficulties of measuring the real wage are compounded by the fact that many at the lower end of society scraped together a living from a variety of sources, some not monetary, and in a way that varied from year to year and even from season to season. Historians of the labouring poor have recently deployed the concept of an 'economy of makeshift' to capture the diverse ways in which those at the bottom kept body and soul together. These might include taking on extra employment; accepting poor relief, charity or assistance from friends and family; taking out loans or selling or pawning furniture and clothing; exploiting common rights, gleaning, foraging on wastes or perhaps even resorting to a little illicit poaching; taking in washing, needlework or lodgers; or sending children out to work or to live with relatives better able to provide for them. When we look at the ways in which individuals on the margins of society managed to keep their precarious family economies afloat, it becomes clear that it is simply not possible to measure many of their strategies on any grand scale.[34]

How then may we summarise the complex literature on real wages? Certainly there are some points of agreement. All the recent studies concur that any improvements that occurred in the real wage in the eighteenth century were negligible. Likewise, all point to some improvement during the nineteenth century; the disagreement, in effect, is over the extent of the rise, not its existence. Beyond this, however, consensus is hard to find and it is far from evident that further research will bring us closer to one. The problems lie not in the inadequacy of the research to date, nor even in a scarcity of sources, but rather in the sheer complexity of calculating the real wage. There are clearly no easy answers, but one way forward is to contrast the evidence concerning real wages with some of the alternative indicators of living standards that historians have sought to measure.

At the same time as research into the real wage has advanced in the past two decades, historians have also been busy exploring different ways of measuring living standards. Much of this research has focussed upon the so-called 'biological' measures, that is, indicators that assess well-being in terms of nutrition, health and life-span. A particularly interesting and lively area of research in the past two decades has been the study of human heights. There are many factors that may influence stature, but the three forces of diet, work intensity and disease throughout childhood are widely regarded as critical determinants. Inadequate nutrition, heavy work or ill-health will all conspire to prevent an individual reaching his or her height potential. Clearly, genetics also affect growth, but as the genetic context did not change significantly in Britain during the period of industrialisation, we may safely assume that it was environmental, rather than genetic, factors that governed the trends in stature among the population at this time. The precise impact of these forces on adult stature is unknown, but modern studies have demonstrated that average heights are strongly correlated with per capita incomes in developed and developing countries, and this finding has reassured many historians that heights can indeed be used to provide a measure of the well-being of the population in industrialising Britain.[35]

The difficulty with using adult stature as a proxy for living standards, however, is that heights were not systematically measured at any point prior to the twentieth century, and the study of heights has consequently been confined to those subsets of the population whose height was, for one reason or another, measured and recorded. In effect, this restriction limits the study of heights to the following three groups: recruits to the army; boys joining the Marine Society; and those, male and female, who got caught up in the criminal justice system. Let us begin by considering what studies of these three groups have shown about changes in height during the period of industrialisation before evaluating the reliability of the research and its relevance to our analysis of living standards.

During the 1980s three historians – Roderick Floud, Kenneth Wachter and Annabel Gregory – together embarked on an ambitious project to analyse the heights of over 100,000 army recruits between the years 1750 and 1880 as well as the abundant data on the heights of adolescent boys joining the Marine Society of London. Their research suggested that heights rose steadily in the 70 years between 1750 and 1820, and then went into sharp decline, with adult heights dropping by more than 2 inches between the 1820s and the 1840s. Heights only started to rise once more in the 1860s. They concluded that prior to about 1820 industrialisation had had a largely benign effect on working-class living standards, but that these gains were interrupted by urbanisation and the French Wars in the early nineteenth century, and not recovered until after 1860.[36]

No sooner had these results been published, however, than John Komlos reworked the data and reached some startlingly different results.[37] Komlos was unhappy with the way the original researchers had analysed their data. He pointed out that the army operated a minimum height restriction: the smallest recruits were turned away and their heights never recorded. Consequently, the army data do not capture the full distribution of heights over time: the lower tail of the distribution is missing, so the original researchers used complex statistical techniques in order to try to correct for the truncation that is known to exist. Komlos argued they had applied inappropriate techniques to correct the truncation and adopted an alternative way of dealing with the problem. Whereas Floud, Wachter and Gregory had found that heights had risen over the second half of the eighteenth century, Komlos found they had been falling over the same period. His results for the nineteenth century did not differ significantly from those of the original research. These results led Komlos to reject their conclusion that the first phase of industrialisation had a positive impact on working-class living standards. 'In spite of the remarkable growth in GDP as a consequence of the industrial revolution', he wrote, 'the lowest segments of society apparently saw little or no improvement in their biological standard of living in the first century of the most momentous recorded expansion in industrial productivity.'[38]

The research into the heights of convicts and criminals is based on fresh datasets and looks at slightly different time periods, but taken together they broadly support Komlos' finding that heights were either stagnant or falling throughout the period 1750–1860. Nicholas and Steckel's study of the heights of men tried in the English courts and transported to New South Wales in Australia considers the early years of industrialisation, 1770 to 1815. Their research demonstrates a drop of about 1 inch in adult heights for those born between the 1780s and 1815, with urban heights falling more steeply than rural heights.[39] Nicholas and Oxley's work on female convicts also indicated a drop in heights, of about 0.75 inches, between 1800 and 1815.[40] Johnson and Nicholas' study of the heights of criminals between 1812 and 1857, likewise, reported a drop in stature, particularly pronounced in the two decades after 1830.[41] Male heights, they suggested, fell by about 1 inch over this period from about 65.5 inches to about 64.5. Female heights fell in roughly similar pattern, dropping in all by about 1 inch, from just over 61.5 inches to 60.5 inches.[42]

Most of the recent studies of human stature therefore suggest that heights either stagnated or deteriorated slightly in the second half of the eighteenth century, and all agree that heights continued to fall through much of the first half of the nineteenth century. The estimates differ over the degree and timing of falling stature, not over the existence of otherwise of a decline. Nonetheless, a very real disagreement does exist between these studies of heights and the estimates for real wages considered above. Most recent studies suggest that real wages rose, albeit modestly, in the first half of the nineteenth century, just at the time that heights appear to have fallen. Figure 9.2 plots the most pessimistic of the real wages series (the Feinstein index) against some recent estimates for male and female heights and clearly illustrates the divergence between the two sorts of evidence. So how, if at all, may these conflicting results be reconciled?

It is helpful to begin by considering in greater detail exactly what it is that heights measure. Human stature captures the balance between the nutrients that are consumed during the growing years and the claims on those nutrients, in terms of energy expended and disease. As heights are sensitive to food intake during childhood, we might reasonably expect that heights will rise during a period of rising real wages, as families living on the margins of a comfortable existence would presumably channel their extra income to an improved diet for themselves and their children in the first instance. That wages and heights were moving in opposite directions, therefore, poses something of a puzzle.[43] One possible reason for the divergence between

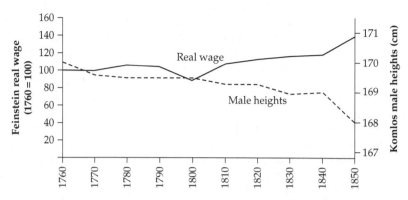

Figure 9.2 *Graph of real wages and male heights in England, 1760–1850.*
Source: Komlos, 'Secular trend in the biological standard of living', table 6, p. 136; Feinstein, 'Pessimism perpetuated', table 5, p. 648.

the two measures is that the studies of real wages and those of heights are in fact capturing the experiences of different sections of the population. It may be, for example, that the real wage data measure the experiences of the better-off working class, while the height data record that of the poorest in society, and that the former group did slightly better in the industrial revolution than the latter. On this point, the various scholars of human heights are emphatic: army recruits, convicts and criminals were *not* drawn from the bottom rungs of society, they insist, but accurately represent the working class as a whole. Thus write Nicholas and Steckel: 'the convicts transported to Australia were coincident with the broad skill-social class mix of the English working class.'[44] Or Nicholas and Oxley: criminals were 'broadly representative of the lower half of the English working class'.[45] Yet one might be sceptical of these claims. The great nineteenth-century General the Duke of Wellington declared that his army was composed of the 'scum of the earth'.[46] Unemployment, homelessness and desperate poverty were certainly great incentives for joining the army, as they always have been for turning to crime as well. This at least, offers one possible way of reconciling the difference between the evidence from income and the evidence from heights. If military recruits and criminals were largely drawn from the bottom tier of society, it may be that this social group did particularly badly during the industrial revolution and failed to share in the modestly increasing incomes that the rest of the working class enjoyed.

At the same time, however, it must be borne in mind that heights do not simply measure food intake. Heights will also vary according to the demands made on that nutrition, in terms of work performed and disease, and this provides an alternative way of reconciling the conflict that exists between the real wage data and the studies of human stature. It is quite possible that as a result of modestly rising incomes the nineteenth century did witness an improvement in food intake for all social groups, including those who would go on to become soldiers, convicts or criminals, but that these gains were entirely negated either by an increase in children's working hours or by a deterioration in the disease environment, or of course by some combination of the two. Let us consider each of these possibilities in greater detail.

The first suggestion is that although children were better nourished by the early nineteenth century, they were also working harder than previously with the result that better nutrition did not translate into height gains. While this is certainly plausible in principle, it is difficult to establish in practice. In the first instance, there is considerable uncertainly among historians over what happened to children's working hours during the industrial revolution.[47] Certainly, the children employed in factories did work very long hours, but most children were not employed in the factories, so this seems unable to account for the trends observed. Some historians have even suggested that high rates of unemployment provided a powerful check on the participation of children in paid work throughout this period, though agreement is far from unanimous on this point.[48] Evidence from working-class autobiographies makes the claim that children were working longer or harder in a period of rising wages slightly troubling. They reveal that most parents were happy to send their children to school so long as they could maintain a decent living standard without their children's wages, but took them from school and sent them to work when the need for extra income pressed harder. If adult wages were rising, why should parents have also increased the hours during which their children worked? Perhaps this is evidence of that 'industrious revolution' that Jan de Vries has described. He (it might be recalled) has argued that through the eighteenth and nineteenth centuries families worked ever longer hours in paid employment, trading their leisure time for a wider range of consumer goods. It may be that parents extended this new spirit of industriousness to their children's employment as well as their own – though it bears repeating that his suggestion that this period saw an increase in 'industriousness' has not received universal assent.[49] There are clearly too many unknowns regarding child labour for us to ascribe falling heights to increasing work intensity for children with any degree of confidence.

If the drop in adult stature in the first half of the nineteenth century cannot be pinned on increasing work intensity, perhaps that final factor – a deteriorating disease environment – was responsible. Once again, however, the evidence is complex and agreement among historians is hard to find. Certainly, it is widely accepted that the first half of the nineteenth century was a period of rapid urbanisation and industrialisation, and that rates of disease and mortality were higher in fast-growing towns and industrial villages.

What is far more difficult to clarify, however, is how far the unhealthy urban environment was the primary reason for the drop in heights.

The evidence from the heights data is contradictory on this point, with the male and female data each pointing to different conclusions. Floud, Wachter and Gregory and Komlos all agreed that the further an army recruit was born from London and the industrialising midlands and south Lancashire, the taller he was likely to be.[50] Nicholas and Steckel's study of convicts echoed this finding. Male adult heights, they concluded, were about half an inch greater for the rural-born: those from Ireland were slightly taller still – on average a quarter-inch so.[51] This would appear to imply that growing up in the unhealthiest urban environment had a detrimental impact on adult height. The evidence for female heights, however, poses some difficulties for this interpretation. For women the data suggest that although heights fell across the country from around the turn of the century, the fall was in fact greatest not in urban areas, but in rural areas.[52] This result cautions against placing too much emphasis on the role of disease in reducing adult heights as there are no strong grounds for suspecting that the worsening of the disease environment was particularly severe for women living in rural areas.

The problem, then, lies in determining the exact nature of the relationship between urbanisation and disease and the evolution of human heights. It is a difficult matter to resolve as no one is entirely sure how ill-health during childhood influenced adult stature. Some of the problems here are demonstrated by recent attempts by historians to determine what impact, if any, one single disease – smallpox – had on human heights. This question led to no fewer than ten exchanges in one history journal in the space of a decade, though little agreement over the precise connection between smallpox and height was finally reached.[53] No doubt there is confusion among historians about the impact of disease on heights because the relationship is both extremely complex and imperfectly understood. And without greater certainty on this point, it is difficult to sustain the argument that it was the unhealthy urban environment that caused falling heights in the nineteenth century (Illustration 9.1).

Finally, it should be noted that the drop in height that various scholars have observed between the 1790s and the mid-nineteenth century is relatively small in magnitude – most studies have observed falls in the region of about an inch. By contrast, in the first 50 years of the twentieth century, when all are agreed that incomes and living standards underwent sustained improvement, heights rose by an average of 3 inches. In this context, drops of an inch or less do not seem so significant, and it has even been rather gloomily noted by one historian that 'the magnitudes involved are too small to inspire much confidence in any conclusions based on anthropometric data.'[54]

Where then does this leave the material on heights? It is notable there is considerable accord between the different estimates for heights over the trends for the late eighteenth and the first half of the nineteenth century:

Illustration 9.1 Close, No. 80 High Street, plate 13 in Annan, *Old Closes and Streets of Glasgow*.

In the 1860s, Glasgow city council commissioned the photographer, Thomas Annan, to document the old town prior to its slum clearance project. This photograph of a close off the High Street gives a sense of the cramped and unsanitary living conditions that many city dwellers endured. The city's slums had attracted the attention of Engels two decades earlier. Quoting the government commissioner, J. C. Symons, he wrote: 'Until I visited the wynds of Glasgow I did not believe that so much crime, misery, and disease could exist in any civilised country . . . These dwellings are usually so damp, filthy, and ruinous, that no one could wish to keep his horse in one of them' (Engels, *Condition of the Working Class*, p. 79).

all point to stagnating or falling heights over this period. At the same time, however, it as yet remains unclear what exactly was responsible for this drop, and one can at present do scarcely more than gesture vaguely at some combination of a deteriorating diet, increased workload and worsening environment affecting some, if not all, sections of the labouring poor.

Once again, it may be possible to reach greater certainty on these issues by turning to alternative measures of working-class living standards. The great nineteenth-century demographer John Rickman considered that 'Human comfort is to be estimated by human health, and that by the length of human life,' and many historians have echoed his belief that the death rate provides a rough proxy for living standards.[55] Two local studies of mortality, the comprehensive work of the Cambridge Group on all aspects of population and Robert Woods' work on nineteenth-century civil registration data, shed valuable light on changes in mortality during the industrial revolution, and considered together with the evidence on real wages and heights, they help to build a rounded picture of the evolution of working-class living standards.

The two local studies are concerned with changing mortality patterns in Britain's industrialising regions, and both paint a broadly similar picture of deteriorating mortality in the first half of the nineteenth century. Paul Huck's study of nine urban parishes in the Black Country, the West Riding and south Lancashire revealed infant mortality rising by 14 per cent between 1813 and 1836 and continuing to creep upwards thereafter until mid-century.[56] Simon Szreter and Graham Mooney's research considered changes in expectation of life at birth in Britain's largest cities and reached broadly similar conclusions. They estimated that average life expectancy dropped by perhaps as much as 6 years between the 1820s and 1830s (from 35 years to 29 years) and gradually returned to its 1820 level by the 1850s: further improvements were delayed until the 1870s.[57] Both studies, it should be pointed out, have a relatively narrow geographical focus. Huck's study is based on just nine parishes, a small proportion of both the national total (there were over 10,000 English parishes in all) and of urban-industrial parishes. While Szreter and Mooney's research on life expectancy in large towns and cities reflects the experience of a significant proportion of the population (around a quarter of the population lived in towns with populations over 100,000 by 1851), most of their data for the period prior to 1851 are in fact extrapolated from the bills of mortality of just one city – Glasgow – which may, or may not, have been typical of large towns elsewhere in Britain. Nonetheless, while these researchers have not proved that mortality was universally higher in Britain's industrialising towns and villages, they have certainly demonstrated that mortality, whether measured by infant mortality or by expectation of life at birth, was elevated in some, at least, of Britain's new urban centres.

The evidence for deteriorating mortality in Britain's urban and industrial areas prior to about 1850 also receives some backing from the combined researches of the Cambridge Group and Robert Woods. Back-projection has showed a steady improvement in adult life expectancy from the 1750s to the end of the century, followed by a period of stagnation down to the middle of the nineteenth century. The child mortality rate fluctuated over the period 1750–1850, dipping slightly in the 1810s and 1820s and then rising again: in the 1850s it still remained about 3 per cent higher than it had been at the start of the century.[58] These general trends obscure some improvements. Child mortality actually dropped among certain age groups, and mortality was also falling in many rural areas, a fact that becomes obscured when aggregated with the urban areas. Nevertheless, considered in conjunction with the other studies of mortality, these studies confirm that the unhealthy living conditions of the urban environment served as a brake on any real improvement in the death rate prior to 1850. Furthermore, studies of mortality once again largely concur with the alternative indicators of living standards – real wages and heights – that have been considered here, strongly implying that gains for most of the working population were extremely limited prior to 1850 and decisive improvements were delayed until the 1870s.

Let us in conclusion relate the evidence for living standards presented here with the broader conclusions about the nature and pace of the British industrial revolution developed in previous chapters. As has been noted, there were two distinct phases of economic change over the period 1700–1870. The long eighteenth century saw steady population growth, some important technological developments and a slow but discernible rise in GDP, but little fundamental change in the way in which the British people provided for themselves. The same period witnessed no upward movement in living standards, as indeed we might expect given the underlying economic continuities. After about 1820, the British economy entered a period of far more dynamic change, the 'industrial revolution'. It was after 1820 that industry and transport were transformed by the advent of coal-using technologies, which substantially raised the economy's productive capacity and ushered in a new era of sustained growth. Yet despite the economic transformation that occurred during these years, the gains for the labouring poor appear to have been extremely modest. Real wages were moving along an upward bending curve, but even so late as 1870, the rise remained relatively slight. Furthermore, a range of indicators measuring the quality of life suggest that these gains were largely cancelled by the concurrent worsening of living conditions. Life expectancy remained depressingly low in the cities; infant mortality remained high, even rising in some places; and heights were stagnant or falling, reinforcing the suggestion that living conditions were deteriorating, although it remains impossible to pinpoint what exactly was deteriorating. Considered in this light, modestly rising real wages appear a very small compensation for the high price extracted in terms of health, longevity and well-being.

The long-term material gains of industrialisation are unmistakable. Throughout the world, industrialisation has been strongly associated with rising living standards and its absence still goes hand in hand with widespread poverty, high mortality and poor nutrition. Yet the evidence presented here suggests, in Britain at least, that the industrial revolution, the precise historical moment when one small country finally broke free from the constraints of the organic economy, was not a time of rising prosperity for all, but a period of painful transition which brought few gains for the men, women and children whose back-breaking labour underpinned it. Measured in global terms, British living standards were relatively favourable both before and during the industrial revolution. Nonetheless, the slow pace at which the gains of economic growth in the nineteenth century were translated into tangible benefits for the labouring poor remains an enduring feature of the world's first industrial revolution.

Notes

Chapter 1: Introduction

1 *Guardian*, 30 May 2008, p. 22.

2 Joseph Arch, *Joseph Arch: The Story of His Life, Told by Himself*. Edited with a preface by The Countess of Warwick (London, 1966), p. 23. See also James Caird, *The Landed Interest and the Supply of Food* (London, 1878; repr. 1967), pp. 28–9, who considered 'thirty years ago [ie. 1848] probably not more than one-third of the people of this country consumed animal food more than once a week. Now nearly all of them eat it, in meat, or cheese, or butter, once a day.'

3 Robert Anderson, 'Memoir of the author, written by himself', in *The Poetical Works of Robert Anderson* (Carlisle, 1820), p. xvi.

4 Alexander Somerville, *The Autobiography of a Working Man* (London, 1848; repr. London, 1967), p. 16.

5 James Hawker, 'The life of a poacher', in Garth Christian, ed., *A Victorian Poacher. James Hawker's Journal* (Oxford, 1978), p. 76.

6 A similar example is given in Charles I. Jones, 'Was an industrial revolution inevitable? Economic growth over the very long run', *Advances in Macroeconomics*, 1/2 (2001). See also E. A. Wrigley, *People Cities, Wealth* (New York, 1987), esp. pp. 2–4, 21–2.

7 E. A. Wrigley, 'The transition to an advanced organic economy: Half a millennium of English agriculture', *Economic History Review*, 59/3 (2006), pp. 435–80.

8 Robert William Fogel, 'New sources and new techniques for the study of secular trends in nutritional status, health, mortality, and the process of aging', *Historical Methods*, 26/1 (1993), pp. 5–43. See also Idem, *The Escape from Hunger and Premature Death, 1700–2100: Europe, America, and the Third World* (Cambridge, 2004), pp. 1–19.

9 www.wfp.org/country_brief/indexcountry.asp?country=178

10 Massimo Livi Bacci, *The Population of Europe: A History*. Translated by Cynthia De Nardi Ipsen and Carl Ipsen (Oxford, 2000), table 6.4, p. 135.

11 World Fact Book at www.cia.gov/library/index.html

12 Jan de Vries and A. van der Woude, *The First Modern Economy: Success, Failure and Perseverance of the Dutch Economy, 1500–1815* (Cambridge, 1997).

13 Richard Cantillon, *Essai sur la nature du commerce en général* (London, 1755), p. 1.

14 For the origin of this idea, See: Friedrich Engels, *The Condition of the Working Class in England*. Edited with introduction Victor G. Kiernan (Harmondsworth, 1987), p. 51.

15 In 2008, life expectancy in Glasgow City, the lowest in Britain, stood at 68.7 years. See www.poverty.org.uk/s60/index.shtml

16 Two excellent surveys of changing interpretations of the industrial revolution are David Cannadine, 'The present and the past in the English industrial revolution, 1880–1980', *Past and Present*, 103 (1984), pp. 131–72; D. C. Coleman, 'Myth, history and the industrial revolution', in *Myth, History and the Industrial Revolution* (London, 1992), p. 24.

17 French examples may be found in Natalis Briavoinne, *De l'industrie en Belgique. Sa situation actuelle. Causes de décadence et de prospérité* (Brussels, 1839), pp. 185–210; J. J. Fazy, *Principes d'organisation industrielle pour le développement des richesses en France* (Paris, 1830), p. 271.

A highly influential German example can be found in Friedrich Engels, *The Condition of the Working Class*, pp. 50, 52, 61, 65.

18 Travers Twiss, *View of the Progress of Political Economy in Europe since the Sixteenth Century* (London, 1847), p. 226; John Stuart Mill, *Principles of Political Economy: With Some of Their Applications to Social Philosophy*, ii. (London, 3rd edn., 1852), p. 120.

19 Arnold Toynbee, *Lectures on the Industrial Revolution of the Eighteenth Century in England* (London, 1884; repr. 1920), esp. pp. 64–73, quote p. 64. J. L. Hammond and Barbara Hammond, *The Town Labourer, 1760–1832* (London, 1917); Idem, *The Skilled Labourer, 1760–1832* (London, 1919).

20 Joseph Schumpeter, *Business Cycles*, i. (New York, 1939; repr. Philadelphia, 1989), pp. 67–8. J. H. Clapham, *An Economic History of Modern Britain*, i. (Cambridge, 1926), p. 143–5; E. M. Carus-Wilson, 'An industrial revolution of the thirteenth century', *Economic History Review*, 11 (1941), pp. 39–60; J. U. Nef, *The Rise of the British Coal Industry*, i. (London, 1932), p. 165–89; Idem, 'The progress of technology and the growth of large-scale industry in Great Britain, 1540–1640', *Economic History Review*, 5/1 (1934), p. 24.

21 Walt Whitman Rostow, *The Stages of Economic Growth: A Non-Communist Manifesto* (Cambridge, 1960). See also David Milne, *America's Rasputin: Walt Rostow and the Vietnam War* (New York, 2008), pp. 59–68.

22 Phyllis Deane, *The First Industrial Revolution* (Cambridge, 1967), p. 117; Phyllis Deane and W. A. Cole, *British Economic Growth, 1688–1959: Trends and Structure* (Cambridge, 1962).

23 Eric Hobsbawm, *Industry and Empire, from 1750 to the Present Day* (Harmondsworth, 1968; repr. London, 1999), p. xi.

24 Peter Mathias, 'Preface', in R. M. Hartwell, ed., *The Causes of the Industrial Revolution in England* (London, 1967), p. vii; M. W. Flinn, *The Origins of the Industrial Revolution* (London, 1966), pp. 1–5; R. M. Hartwell, *The Industrial Revolution and Economic Growth* (London, 1971).

25 A. E. Musson, *The Growth of British Industry* (London, 1978), p. 61.

26 C. Knick Harley, 'British industrialisation before 1841: Evidence of slower growth during the industrial revolution', *Journal of Economic History*, 42/2 (1982), pp. 267–89.

27 N. F. R. Crafts, *British Economic Growth during the Industrial Revolution* (Oxford, 1985), ch. 1; Idem, 'British economic growth, 1700–1831: A review', *Economic History Review*, 36/2 (1983). See also N. F. R. Crafts and C. Knick Harley, 'Output growth and the British industrial revolution: A restatement of the Crafts-Harley view', *Economic History Review*, 45/4 (1992), pp. 703–30.

28 Patrick K. O'Brien, 'Introduction: Modern conceptions of the Industrial Revolution', in Idem and Roland Quinault, eds., *The Industrial Revolution and British Society* (Cambridge, 1993), p. 1.

29 Maxine Berg and Pat Hudson, 'Rehabilitating the industrial revolution', *Economic History Review*, 45/1 (1992), pp. 24–50, p. 25.

30 See, however, J. C. D. Clark, who described it as a 'fictitious entity'. See his *English Society, 1688–1832: Ideology, Social Structure and Political Practice during the Ancien Regime* (Cambridge, 1985), p. 4. See also M. Fores, 'The myth of a British industrial revolution', *History*, 66 (1981) and the response by A. Musson, *History*, 67 (1982).

31 Quoted in Mokyr, 'Editor's Introduction', p. 17.

32 See, in particular, Joel Mokyr, *The Lever of Riches: Technological Creativity and Economic Progress* (Oxford, 1990); Idem, 'Technological change, 1700–1830', in R. Floud and D. McCloskey, eds., *The Economic History of Britain since 1700* (Cambridge, 2nd edn., 1994), p. 13.

33 Mokyr, *Lever of Riches*, p. 82.

34 Margaret K. Jacob, *Scientific Culture and the Making of the Industrial West* (Oxford, 1997).

35 Patrick K. O'Brien, 'Political preconditions for the industrial revolution', in Idem and Quinault, eds., *The Industrial Revolution and British Society*, pp. 124–55.

36 William J. Ashworth, *Customs and Excise: Trade, Production, and Consumption in England, 1640–1845* (Oxford, 2003).
37 M. J. Daunton, *Progress and Poverty: An Economic and Social History of Britain, 1700–1850* (Oxford, 1995).
38 Gregory Clark, *A Farewell to Alms: A Brief Economic History of the World* (Princeton, 2007).
39 Ibid., p. 187.
40 Maxine Berg, *Age of Manufactures, 1700–1820: Industry, Innovation and Work in Britain* (London, 2nd edn., 1994), p. xiii.
41 Ibid., p. 281. See also Raphael Samuel, 'The workshop of the world: Steam power and hand technology in mid-Victorian Britain', *History Workshop Journal*, 3 (1977), pp. 6–72.
42 E. A. Wrigley, *Continuity, Chance and Change: The Character of the Industrial Revolution in England* (Cambridge, 1988).
43 Eric Williams, *Capitalism and the Slave Trade* (London, 1944; 2nd edn., 1964).
44 Robin Blackburn, *The Making of New World Slavery: From the Baroque to the Modern, 1492–1800* (London, 1997).
45 Joseph E. Inikori, *Africans and the Industrial Revolution in England: A Study in International Trade and Economic Development* (Cambridge, 2002), p. 7.
46 Neil McKendrick, 'The consumer revolution of eighteenth-century England', in Idem, John Brewer and J. H. Plumb, eds., *The Birth of a Consumer Society: The Commercialisation of Eighteenth-Century England* (Bloomington, 1982), pp. 9–33, quote p. 9.
47 The most accessible introductions to de Vries' ideas are J. de Vries, 'The industrial revolution and the industrious revolution', *Journal of Economic History*, 54/2 (1994), pp. 249–70. See also Idem, 'The industrious revolution and economic growth, 1650–1830', in Paul A. David and Mark Thomas, eds., *The Economic Future in Historical Perspective* (Oxford, 2006), pp. 43–71. For more detail see Idem, *The Industrious Revolution: Consumer Behaviour and the Household Economy* (Cambridge, 2008).
48 De Vries, 'The industrial revolution', p. 256. Support for this view also comes from Hans-Joachim Voth, *Time and work in England 1750–1830* (Oxford, 2000); and Idem, 'Time and work in 18th century London.' *Journal of Economic History*, 58/1 (1998), pp. 29–58.

Chapter 2: Counting Growth: Measuring the Economy

1 Charles Dickens, *Hard Times: A Novel* (New York, 1854), p. 14.
2 Walther G. Hoffmann, *British Industry, 1700–1950* (Oxford, 1955); Phyllis M. Deane and W. A. Cole, *British Economic Growth, 1688–1959* (Cambridge, 1962).
3 C. Knick Harley, 'British industrialisation before 1841: Evidence of slower growth during the industrial revolution', *Journal of Economic History*, 42/2 (1982), pp. 267–89.
4 N. F. R. Crafts, 'British economic growth, 1700–1831: A review', *Economic History Review*, 36/2 (1983); Idem, *British Economic Growth during the Industrial Revolution* (Oxford, 1985), ch. 1.
5 N. F. R. Crafts and C. Knick Harley, 'Output growth and the British industrial revolution: A restatement of the Crafts-Harley view', *Economic History Review*, 45/4 (1992), pp. 703–30. See also R. V. Jackson, 'Rates of industrial growth during the industrial revolution', *Economic History Review*, 45/1 (1992), pp. 1–23.
6 Deane and Cole, *British Economic Growth*, pp. 50–62; Crafts, 'British economic growth', table 4, p. 185.
7 Harley, 'British industrialisation', table 5, p. 276.
8 Crafts, 'British economic growth', table 4, p. 185. These figures were revised slightly downwards in 1992 to 1.29 per cent in the period 1760–80; 1.96 per cent in the period 1780–1800; and 2.78 per cent in the period 1801–31. See Crafts and Harley, 'Output growth', table 2, p. 711.
9 Charles More, *Understanding the Industrial Revolution* (London, 2000), p. 174.

10 Crafts, *British Economic Growth*, table 2.11, p. 45. See also the revised estimates for GDP, Crafts and Harley, 'Output growth', p. 715.

11 R. V. Jackson, 'What was the rate of economic growth during the industrial revolution', in Graeme Donald Snooks, ed., *Was the Industrial Revolution Necessary?* (London, 1994), p. 81.

12 Crafts, *British Economic Growth*, p. 2.

13 Ibid., p. 84.

14 Ibid., table 4.4, p. 86.

15 Ibid.

16 Deane and Cole, *British Economic Growth*, pp. 96–7.

17 Crafts, *British Economic Growth*, table 4.2, p. 81. The 1992 recalculation modified these figure slightly, suggesting TFP grew at 0.1 per cent per year during 1760–1801 and at 0.35 per cent per year in 1801–31. See Crafts and Harley, 'Output growth', table 5, p. 718.

18 C. Knick Harley, 'Reassessing the industrial revolution: A macro view', in J. Mokyr, ed., *The British Industrial Revolution: An Economic Perspective* (Boulder, Colorado, 1993), p. 200.

19 Crafts, *British Economic Growth*, pp. 78–83.

20 Crafts and Harley, 'Output growth', p. 705. See also figure 1, p. 712.

21 R. C. O. Matthews, C. H. Feinstein and J. C. Odling-Smee, *British Economic Growth, 1856–1973* (Stanford, 1982); C. H. Feinstein, 'Capital formation in Great Britain', in P. Mathias and M. M. Postan, eds., *The Cambridge Economic History of Europe*, i. (Cambridge, 1978), pp. 28–96.

22 With the passage of time, the controversy caused by the publication of Deane and Cole's *British Economic Growth* has been largely forgotten. In the opinion of one critic (Sidney Pollard), their work had 'attracted some of the most devastating reviews to appear in learned journals recently'. Idem in *American Economic Review*, 53/3 (1963), pp. 475–9.

23 Julian Hoppit, 'Counting the industrial revolution', *Economic History Review*, 43/2 (1990), pp. 173–93; Maxine Berg and Pat Hudson, 'Rehabilitating the industrial revolution', *Economic History Review*, 45/1 (1992), pp. 24–50; Patrick K. O'Brien, 'Introduction: Modern conceptions of the industrial revolution', in Idem and Roland Quinault, *The Industrial Revolution and British Society* (Cambridge, 1993), pp. 1–30; M. J. Daunton, *Progress and Poverty: An Economic and Social History of Britain* (Oxford, 1995), pp. 125–47.

24 See in particular, Hoppit, 'Counting', pp. 179–80; Daunton, *Progress and Poverty*, pp. 128–9.

25 C. Knick Harley and N. F. R. Crafts, 'Cotton textiles and industrial output during the industrial revolution', *Economic History Review*, 48/1 (1995), 134–44, p. 140–1.

26 S. D. Chapman, *The Cotton Industry in the Industrial Revolution* (London, 1972), p. 65.

27 Hoppit, 'Counting', pp. 180–2; Daunton, *Progress and Poverty*, pp. 129–30.

28 Crafts and Harley, 'Output growth', p. 708.

29 Daunton, *Progress and Poverty*, pp. 128–9; Berg and Hudson, 'Rehabilitating the industrial revolution', p. 29.

30 Peter H. Lindert, 'English occupations, 1670–1811', *Journal of Economic History*, 40/4 (1980), pp. 685–712, esp. 701–7. See also Peter H. Lindert and Jeffrey G. Williamson, 'Revising England's social tables, 1688–1812', *Explorations in Economic History*, 19/4 (1982), pp. 385–804.

31 Hoppit, 'Counting', p. 177.

32 In addition to Ibid., see also Berg and Hudson, 'Rehabilitating the industrial revolution', pp. 28, 35–8.

33 John Tough, *A Short Narrative of the Life of an Aberdonian, Nearly Eight Years of Age* (Aberdeen, 1848), pp. 4–6.

34 Maxine Berg, 'What difference did women's work make to the industrial revolution?', *History Workshop Journal*, 35/1 (1993), pp. 22–44.

35 Berg, *Age of Manufactures*, p. 138.

36 For more detail see Crafts, *British Economic Growth*, pp. 11–17.

37 J. Cuenca Esteban, 'British textile prices, 1770–1831: Are British growth rates worth revising once again?', *Economic History Review*, 47/1 (1994), pp. 6–105.

38 Roderick Floud and Paul Johnson, eds., *The Cambridge Economic History of Modern Britain: Industrialisation, 1700–1860*, i. (Cambridge, 2004).
39 Berg and Hudson, 'Rehabilitating the industrial revolution', p. 26.
40 Nick Crafts, 'The industrial revolution: Economic growth in Britain, 1700–1860', *ReFRESH*, 4 (Spring 1987), p. 3 (available from the Economic History Society webpages).
41 Ibid.

Chapter 3: A Growing Population

1 Richard Cantillon, *Essai sur la nature du commerce en général* (London, 1755), p. 110.
2 Quoted in E. A. Wrigley, 'Growth of population in eighteenth-century England: A conundrum resolved', *Past and Present*, 98 (1983), pp. 121–50, p. 127.
3 E. A. Wrigley and R. S. Schofield, *Population History of England, 1541–1871: A Reconstruction* (Cambridge, 1981), table 7.15, pp. 230, 234–45; E. A. Wrigley, R. S. Smith, J. E. Oeppen and R. S. Schofield, *English Population History from Family Reconstitution, 1580–1837* (Cambridge, 1997), table A9.1, pp. 614–15.
4 See E. A. Wrigley, 'British population during the long eighteenth century', in Roderick Floud and Paul Johnson, eds., *The Cambridge Economic History of Modern Britain: Industrialisation, 1700–1860* (Cambridge, 2004), pp. 60–2.
5 Ibid., figure 3.1, p. 61. While this represented an unprecedented rate of growth for Britain, it is worth observing that it was nowhere near as rapid as some of the rates of population growth that were witnessed in the developing world in the twentieth century.
6 Andrew Hinde, *England's Population: A History since the Domesday Survey* (London, 2003), p. 2.
7 John Hatcher, 'England in the aftermath of the Black Death', *Past and Present*, 144 (1994), pp. 3–35, p. 3. See also Hinde, *England's Population*, pp. 39–52, esp. 44–7.
8 Wrigley et al., *English Population*, table A9.1, pp. 614–15; Wrigley et al., *Population History*, table A3.1, p. 207.
9 Wrigley, 'Growth of population', pp. 126, 129–31.
10 Wrigley et al., *Population History*, table 7.15, pp. 230, 234–45; Wrigley et al., *English Population*, table A9.1, pp. 614–15.
11 Wrigley et al., *Population History*, pp. 244–5.
12 Wrigley, 'Growth of population', pp. 129–31.
13 Wrigley, 'British population', p. 68.
14 See especially, Thomas McKeown, *The Modern Rise of Population* (London, 1976).
15 Useful summaries of the *Population History* may be found in M. W. Flinn, 'The population history of England, 1541–1871', *Economic History Review*, 35/3 (1982), pp. 443–57; Michael Anderson, 'Historical demography after the *Population History of England*', *Journal of Interdisciplinary History*, 15/4 (1985), pp. 595–607; David Levine, 'The population history of England', *Social History*, 8/2 (1983), p. 148–59.
16 Flinn, 'Population history', p. 448.
17 Anderson, 'Historical demography', p. 600.
18 For more on this problem, see in particular P. M. Kitson, 'Religious change and the timing of baptism in England, 1538–1750', *Historical Journal*, 52/2 (2009), pp. 269–94.
19 Levine, 'Population history', pp. 151–2. See also Wrigley, 'Demographic retrospective', in *Progress, Poverty and Population* (Cambridge, 2004), pp. 394–440.
20 Peter Laslett, *Family Life and Illicit Love in Earlier Generations* (Cambridge, 1977), pp. 102–55, esp. 102, 112–13.
21 R. Schofield, 'British population change, 1700–1871', in Roderick Floud and Donald McCloskey, eds., *The Economic History of Britain since 1700* (Cambridge, 2nd edn., 1994), pp. 60–95, p. 73.
22 Wrigley, 'British population', pp. 75–6.

23 Wrigley et al., *English Population*, pp. 221–2.
24 Wrigley, 'Population growth', p. 131.
25 E. A. Wrigley, 'Explaining the rise in marital fertility in England in the "long" eighteenth-century', *Economic History Review*, 51/3 (1998), pp. 435–64, p. 436.
26 Wrigley, 'British population', p. 71.
27 Wrigley, 'Growth of population', p. 131.
28 Ibid., p. 133.
29 D. R. Weir, 'Rather never than late: Celibacy and age at marriage in English cohort fertility', *Journal of Family History*, 9 (1984). Summarised in Schofield, 'British population growth', pp. 73–5.
30 J. A. Goldstone, 'The demographic revolution in England: A re-examination', *Population Studies*, 49 (1986), pp. 5–33, 19.
31 Wrigley et al., *English Population History*, esp. table 5.4.
32 Wrigley, 'British population', pp. 75–6.
33 Rickman, *Observations on the Results of the Population Act, 41 Geo. III*, p. 4. Quoted in E. A. Wrigley, 'English county populations in the later eighteenth century', *Economic History Review*, 60/1 (2007), pp. 35–69, 41.
34 E. A. Wrigley, 'Family limitation in pre-industrial England', *Economic History Review*, 19/1 (1966), pp. 82–109.
35 Schofield, 'British population', p. 73.
36 David Levine, 'Sampling history: The English population', *Journal of Interdisciplinary History*, 28/4 (1998), pp. 605–32.
37 Levine, 'Sampling history', p. 613.
38 Steven Ruggles, 'The limitations of English family reconstitution: English population history from family reconstitution, 1580–1837', *Continuity and Change*, 14/1 (1999), pp. 105–30, 108.
39 Levine, 'Sampling history', p. 614.
40 Ruggles, 'Limitations of family reconstitution', p. 107.
41 Levine, 'Sampling history', pp. 608, 613–14.
42 Ibid., pp. 611–12.
43 S. A. King, 'Migrants on the margin: Mobility, integration and occupation in the West Riding, 1650–1820', *Journal of Historical Geography*, 23/3 (1997), pp. 284–303, 284; Ruggles, 'Limitations of family reconstitution', p. 114.
44 See, for example, Wrigley et al., *English Population*, pp. 182–94, 501–7.
45 Pat Hudson and Steve King, 'Two textile townships, c. 1660–1820: A comparative demographic analysis', *Economic History Review*, 53/4 (2000), 706–41. See also Barry Reay's work on nineteenth-century Kent in Idem, *Microhistories: Demography, Society and Culture in Rural England, 1800–1930* (Cambridge, 1996), pp. 39–67.
46 Ibid., pp. 717–26.
47 Ibid.
48 Compare also with Reay's reconstitution of three parishes in rural Kent in Idem, *Microhistories*, pp. 41–8.
49 The key source for Scottish population history remains M. Flinn et al., *Scottish Population History from the Seventeenth Century to the 1930s* (Cambridge, 1977), pp. 203–97. Also useful are R. A Houston, 'The demographic regime, 1760–1830', in T. M. Devine and R. Mitchison, eds., *People and Society in Scotland*, i. (Edinburgh, 1988), pp. 9–26; Robert E. Tyson, 'Demographic change', in T. M. Devine and John R. Young, eds., *Eighteenth Century Scotland: New Perspectives* (East Linton, 1999), pp. 195–209.
50 Ibid., p. 195.
51 M. J. Daunton, *Progress and Poverty. An Economic and Social History of Britain* (Oxford, 1995), p. 406.
52 Tyson, 'Demographic change', pp. 198–9.

53 Houston, 'Demographic regime', pp. 17–18.
54 Ibid., pp. 19–20. Tyson, 'Demographic change', pp. 204–6.
55 Cantillon, *Essai sur la nature du commerce*, p. 102.
56 Ibid.
57 Ibid., p. 97.
58 Wrigley et al., *Population History*, p. 438; Wrigley, 'Growth of population', graph 5, p. 141.
59 For a good summary see Daunton, *Progress and Poverty*, pp. 396–402.
60 Peter H. Lindert and Jeffrey G. Williamson, 'English workers' living standards during the industrial revolution: A new look', *Economic History Review*, 36/1 (1983), pp. 1–25. These have since been revised again by Feinstein, and Wrigley has identified a correlation between this latest real wage index and the marriage rate. See Wrigley, 'British population', figure 3.7, pp. 77–9 and Charles H. Feinstein, 'Pessimism perpetuated: Real wages and the standard of living in Britain during and after the industrial revolution', *Journal of Economic History*, 58/3 (1998), pp. 625–58. As we shall see in Chapter 9, however, Feinstein's figures are not the only estimates for the real wage; so this procedure still remains open to criticism.
61 David Levine, *Family Formation in the Age of Nascent Capitalism* (New York, 1977), pp. 58–87; Idem, 'The Demographic implications of rural industrialization: A family reconstitution study of Shepshed, Leicestershire, 1600–1851', *Social History*, 2 (1976), p. 178; Idem, 'Industrialisation and the proletarian family', *Past and Present*, 107 (1985), pp. 168–203, esp. 175–181.
62 Rab Houston and K. D. M. Snell, 'Proto-industrialisation? Cottage industry, social change, and industrial revolution', *Historical Journal*, 27/2 (1984), pp. 473–92, 482–3.
63 Goldstone, 'Demographic revolution', pp. 20–31.
64 For the rise of day labour, see Ann Kussmaul, *Servants in Husbandry in Early Modern England* (Cambridge, 1981), esp. pp. 120–1. For proletarianisation, see Leigh Shaw-Taylor, 'Parliamentary enclosure and the emergence of an English agricultural proletariat', *Economic History Review*, 61/3 (2001), pp. 640–62.
65 Schofield, 'British population', pp. 90–1; K. D. M. Snell, *Annals of the Labouring Poor: Social Change and Agrarian England, 1660–1900* (Cambridge, 1985), pp. 352–54.
66 Steven King, 'Chance encounters? Paths to household formation in early modern England', *International Review of Social History*, 44 (1999), pp. 23–46, 32. See also the responses: John R Gillis, ' "A triumph of hope over experience": Chance and choice in the history of marriage', *International Review of Social History*, 44 (1999), pp. 47–54; Richard Wall, 'Beyond the household: Marriage, household formation, and the role of kin and neighbours', *International Review of Social History*, 44 (1999), pp. 55–67. For earlier work exploring the connection between marriage and household formation, see Richard M. Smith, 'Fertility, economy, and household formation in England over three centuries', *Population and Development Review*, 7/4 (1981), pp. 595–622; J. Hajnal, 'Two kinds of pre-industrial household formation system', *Population and Development Review*, 8/3, pp. 449–84.
67 William Thomas Swan, 'Journal', in *The Journals of Two Poor Dissenters, 1786–1880*. Edited with a preface by Guida Swan and an introduction by John Holloway (London, 1970), p. 6.
68 John Bates, *John Bates, the Veteran Reformer: A Sketch of His Life* (Queensbury, 1895; facs. repr. London, 1986), p. 10.
69 Joseph Arch, *Joseph Arch: The Story of His Life, Told by Himself*. Edited with a preface by The Countess of Warwick (London, 1966), p. 36.
70 John Green, *Vicissitudes of a Soldier's Life* (London, 1827), p. 223.
71 Leicestershire, Leicester & Rutland Record Office, 'Memoirs of Arnold Goodliffe', DE7196.
72 Jacques, 'Glimpses of a chequered life', *The Commonwealth*, 1 November 1856, p. 3.

73 Samuel Nye, *A Small Account of My Travels through the Wilderness*. ed. Vic Gammon (Brighton, 1981), p. 14.

74 James Bowd, 'The life of a farm worker', *The Countryman*, 51/2 (1955), pp. 293–300, 296.

75 Benjamin Shaw, *The Family Records of Benjamin Shaw, Mechanic of Dent, Dolphinholme and Preston, 1772–1841*. Ed. Alan G. Crosby. Record Society of Lancashire and Cheshire, 13 (1991), p. 30.

76 Ibid., p. 31.

77 Wrigley et al., *English Population*, table A9.1, pp. 614–15. See also Wrigley et al., *Population History*, table A3.1, pp. 531–5.

78 Tyson, 'Demographic change', p. 199.

79 Wrigley, 'British population', tables 3.5–3.7, pp. 80–2.

80 Ibid., table 3.6, p. 81.

81 Ibid., table 3.7, p. 82.

82 Hinde, *England's Population*, pp. 196–7.

83 Ibid., pp. 195–6.

84 Robert Woods, *The Demography of Victorian England and Wales, 1811–1911* (Cambridge, 2000) and summarised in Hinde, *England's Population*, pp. 196–7.

85 Wrigley et al., *English Population*, table 6.16, pp. 270–1 and table 6.17, p. 274. See also Hudson and King, 'Two textile townships', pp. 726–8.

86 Wrigley et al., *English Population*, p. 352.

87 Flinn, *Scottish Population*, pp. 100–1.

88 Houston, 'Demographic regime', pp. 14–17; Tyson, 'Demographic change', pp. 199–204.

89 Calculated from Flinn, *Scottish Population History*, table 4.4.5, p. 270, table 5.5.9, p. 386.

90 R. A. Houston, 'Writers to the Signet: Estimates of adult mortality in Scotland from the seventeenth to the nineteenth century', *Social History of Medicine*, 8 (1985), pp. 37–53; Idem, 'Mortality in early modern Scotland: The life expectancy of advocates', *Continuity and Change* (1992), pp. 47–69.

91 Tyson, 'Demographic change', 204.

92 Hudson and King, 'Two textile townships', pp. 726–8.

93 T. McKeown, R. G. Brown and R. G. Record, 'An interpretation of the modern rise of population in Europe', *Population Studies*, 26 (1972), pp. 345–82, esp. 350–7.

94 Wrigley et al., *English Population*, p. 206.

95 Cantillon, *Essai sur la nature du commerce*, pp. 109–10.

96 Office for National Statistics: www.statistics.gov.uk/CCI/nugget.asp?ID=6

Chapter 4: A Mobile Population

1 Charles Dickens, *Dombey and Son*, iii. (Cambridge, 1868), p. 70.

2 E. A. Wrigley, 'English county populations in the later eighteenth century', *Economic History Review*, 60/1 (2007), pp. 35–69, table 5, pp. 54–5.

3 Ibid.

4 Ibid., p. 66 and table 5, pp. 54–5.

5 Ibid.

6 Wrigley, 'English county populations', p. 59.

7 John Elliott, *The Industrial Development of the Ebbw Valleys, 1780–1914* (Cardiff, 2004), table 8.1, p. 165.

8 Ibid.

9 T. M. Devine, 'Industrialisation', in T. M. Devine, C. H. Lee and G. C Peden, eds., *The Transformation of Scotland. The Economy since 1700* (Edinburgh, 2005), pp. 40–1.

10 David Turnock, *The Historical Geography of Scotland since 1707: Geographical Aspects of Modernisation* (Cambridge, 1982), table 3.1, p. 40, table 1.1, p. 8.

11 Peter Kitson, 'The emergence of a mineral-based energy economy: the male occupational structure of Northumberland, 1762–1871', http://www.geog.cam.ac.uk/research/projects/occupations/abstracts/paper6.pdf, graph 1, p. 2. Compare with E. A. Wrigley et al, *English Population History from Family Reconstitution* (Cambridge, 1997), table A9.1, pp. 614–5.

12 Kitson, ''Emergence of a energy economy', p. 2.

13 Elliott, *Industrial Development*, table 8.1, p. 165; table 8.5, p. 181.

14 E. A. Wrigley, 'Urban growth and agricultural change: England and the continent in the early modern period', *Journal of Interdisciplinary History*, 15/4 (1985), pp. 683–728, 684, table 2, p. 628.

15 Ibid., p. 690.

16 John Langton, 'Urban growth and economic change from the seventeenth century to 1841', in Peter Clark, ed., *The Cambridge Urban History of Britain, 1540–1840*, ii. (Cambridge, 2000), pp. 453–90, 466.

17 C. M. Law, 'The growth of urban population in England and Wales, 1801–1911', *Transactions of the Institute of British Geographers*, 41 (1967), pp. 125–143, table 5, p. 130.

18 Wrigley, 'Urban growth', table 1, p. 686.

19 Alan Kidd, *Manchester* (Keele, 1993; 2nd edn., 1996), p. 22.

20 Ian D. Whyte, 'Urbanization in eighteenth-century Scotland', in T. M. Devine, Martin Thomas and John R. Young, eds., *Eighteenth Century Scotland: New Perspectives* (East Linton, 1999), pp. 176–94, table 1, p. 179.

21 Devine, 'Industrialisation', p. 39.

22 Jeffrey Williamson, 'Coping with city growth', in Roderick Floud and Donald McCloskey, eds., *The Economic History of Britain since 1700* (Cambridge, 2nd edn., 1994), pp. 332–56, 333.

23 Andrew Gibb, 'Industrialisation and demographic change: a case study of Glasgow, 1801–1914', in Richard Lawton and Robert Lee, eds., *Population and Society in Western European Port Cities, c.1650–1939* (Liverpool, 2002), table 2.3, p. 41. See also T. M, Devine, 'Urbanisation and the civic response: Glasgow, 1800–30', in A. J. G. Cummings and T. M. Devine, *Industry, Business and Society in Scotland since 1700* (Edinburgh, 1994), pp. 183–96.

24 Rosemary Sweet, *The English Town, 1660–1840* (Harlow, 1988), table 1, p. 3.

25 B. R. Mitchell & Phyllis Deane, *Abstract of British Historical Statistics* (Cambridge, 1962), pp. 24–7.

26 Ibid. See also R. J. Morris, 'Urbanisation', in Idem and Richard Rodger, eds., *The Victorian City: a reader in British Urban History, 1820–1914* (London, 1993), pp. 43–72.

27 Whyte, 'Urbanisation', pp. 183–4.

28 Wrigley, 'Urban growth ', table 1, p. 686.

29 Ibid. See also Langton, 'Urban growth and economic change', pp. 453–90.

30 William Page, ed., *Victoria History of the County of Staffordshire*, i. (London, 1908), p. 324 (Tipton and West Bromwich); Richard H. Trainor, *Black Country Elites: the Exercise of Authority in an Industrialized Area 1830–1900* (Oxford, 1993), p. 31 (Dudley).

31 Page, ed., *Victoria History*, p. 326 (Bilston, Rowley Regis, Sedgeley), p. 324 (Walsall and Wednesbury).

32 C. Roy Lewis, 'A stage in the development of the industrial town: A Case Study of Cardiff, 1845–75', *Transactions of the Institute of British Geographers*, 4/2 (1979), pp. 129–52, table 2, p. 134.

33 Williamson, 'Coping with city growth', pp. 332–56.

34 Whyte, 'Urbanisation', pp. 183, 187.

35 Robert C. Allen, 'Agriculture during the industrial revolution, 1700–1850', in Roderick Floud and Paul Johnson, eds., *The Cambridge economic history of England* (Cambridge, 2004), pp. 96–116. See also E. A. Wrigley, 'The transition to an advanced organic economy: half a millennium of English agriculture', *Economic History Review*, 59/3 (2006), pp. 435–80;

M. Overton and B. M. S. Campbell, 'Statistics of production and productivity in English agriculture 1086–1871', in B. J. P. van Bavel, and E. Thoen, eds., *Land Productivity and Agro-Systems in the North Sea Area* (Turnhout, 1999), pp. 189–208; G. Clark, 'Yields per acre in English agriculture, 1250–1860: evidence from labour inputs', *Economic History Review*, 44/2 (1991), pp. 445–60.

36 For a good overview of this debate see; M. Overton, 'Agricultural revolution? England, 1540–1850', in A Digby and C. Feinstein, eds., *New Directions in Economic and Social History* (London, 1989), pp. 9–21. See also M. Overton, *Agricultural Revolution in England: The Transformation of the Agrarian Economy 1500–1850* (Cambridge, 1996).

37 Allen, 'Agriculture during the industrial revolution', pp. 103–4.

38 Mark Overton and Bruce M. S. Campbell, 'Productivity change in European agricultural development', in B. M. S. Campbell, and M. Overton, eds., *Land, Labour and Livestock: Historical Studies in European Agricultural Productivity* (Manchester, 1991), pp. 7–17.

39 Robert C. Allen, 'Enclosure, farming methods, and the growth of productivity in the south Midlands', in G. Grantham and S. Leonard, eds., *Agrarian Organisation in the Century of Industrialisation* (Greenwich, 1989), pp. 69–88; Robert C. Allen, *Enclosure and the Yeoman* (Cambridge, 1992).

40 Overton, *Agricultural Revolution*, pp. 2–3.

41 Robert C. Allen, 'The two English agricultural revolutions', in Campbell and Overton, eds., *Land, Labour and Livestock*, pp. 236–54.

42 A. K. Copus, 'Changing markets and the development of sheep breeds in southern England, 1750–1900', *Agricultural History Review*, 37 (1989), pp. 36–51; M. Overton and B. M. S. Campbell, 'Norfolk livestock farming 1250–1740: A comparative study of manorial accounts and probate inventories', *Journal of Historical Geography*, 18 (1992), pp. 377–96.

43 Allen, 'Agriculture during the industrial revolution', p. 105.

44 G. Clark, 'Labour productivity in English agriculture, 1300–1860', in Campbell and Overton, eds., *Land, Labour and Livestock*, pp. 211–35; K. D. M. Snell, *Annals of the Labouring Poor* (Cambridge, 1985); Nicola Verdon, *Rural Women Workers in Nineteenth-Century England: Gender, Work and Wages* (Woodbridge, 2002).

45 Wrigley, 'Transition to advanced organic economy', pp. 447–53, p. 456.

46 Liam Brunt, 'Mechanical innovation in the industrial revolution: the case of Plough Design', *Economic History Review*, 56/3 (2003), pp. 444–77.

47 Patrick K. O'Brien, 'Agriculture and the home market for English industry 1660–1820', *English Historical Review*, 344 (1985), pp. 773–800.

48 Allen, 'Agriculture during the industrial revolution', pp. 114–15.

49 Wrigley, 'Urban growth', table 4, p. 700; Overton, *Agricultural Revolution in England*, p. 8.

50 A. Wadsworth and J. de Lacy Mann, *The Cotton Trade and Industrial Lancashire* (Manchester, 1931), p. 311.

51 Colin G. Pooley and Shani D'Cruz, 'Migration and urbanisation in north-west England, c.1760–1830', *Social History*, 19/3 (1994), 339–58.

52 Ibid., p. 348.

53 Steven King, 'Migrants on the margin: mobility, integration and occupation in the West Riding, 1650–1820', *Journal of Historical Geography*, 23/3 (1997), pp. 284–303.

54 Thomas Langdale, *A Topographical Dictionary of Yorkshire: Containing the Names of All the Towns, Villages, Hamlets, Gentlemen's Seats, &c. in the County of York* (Northallerton, 2nd edn., 1822), pp. 379, 324, 251.

55 Peter Laslett, *Family Life and Illicit Love in Earlier Generations* (Cambridge, 1977), pp. 50–101. See also, for example, J. Cornwall, 'Evidence of population mobility in the seventeenth century', *Bulletin of the Institute of Historical Research*, 40 (1967); David Cressy, 'Occupations, migration and literacy in East London, 1580–1740', *Local Population Studies*, 5 (1970).

56 C. Pooley and J. Turnball, *Migration and Mobility in Britain since the Eighteenth Century* (London, 1998); B. Stapleton, 'Migration in pre-industrial southern England: the example

of Odiham', *Southern History*, 10 (1988), pp. 47–93; King, 'Migrants on the margin', pp. 290, 291–2.

57 Charles W. J. Withers, *Urban Highlanders: Highland-Lowland Migration and Urban Gaelic Culture, 1700–1900* (East Linton, 1998), pp. 29–30. See also Eric Richard, 'Margins of the industrial revolution', in P. O'Brien and Roland Quinault, eds., *The Industrial Revolution and British Society* (Cambridge, 1993), pp. 203–28, esp. 215–20.

58 Steven King and Geoffrey Timmins, *Making Sense of the British Industrial Revolution* (Manchester, 2001), pp. 224–5.

59 T. M. Devine, 'Temporary migration and the Scottish Highlands in the nineteenth century', *Economic History Review*, 32/3 (1979), pp. 344–59.

60 King, 'Migrants on the margin', pp. 90–1.

61 *Bristol Mercury*, 15 August 1840. Also quoted in Elliott, *Industrial Development*, p. 181.

62 G. Turnbull, 'Canals, coal and regional growth during the industrial revolution', *Economic History Review*, 40/4 (1987), pp. 537–60, 539.

63 Ibid., p. 556.

64 G. E. Fussell, 'High farming in the East Midlands and East Anglia, 1840–1880', *Economic Geography*, 27/1 (1951), pp. 72–89. E. H. Hunt & S. J. Pam, 'Essex agriculture in the "Golden Age" ', *Agricultural History Review*, 43 (1995), pp. 160–77.

65 Wrigley, 'Urban growth', table 1, p. 686.

66 D. C. Coleman, 'Growth and decay during the industrial revolution: the case of East Anglia', *Scandinavian Economic History Review*, 10 (1962), 115–27, reprinted in his *Myth, History and the Industrial Revolution* (London, 1992), p. 93–106.

67 Wrigley, 'County populations', table 5.

68 Coleman, 'Growth and decay', pp. 94–101.

69 Julia Lacey De Mann, *The Cloth Industry in the West of England from 1640 to 1880* (Oxford, 1971). See also Adrian Randall, *Before the Luddites: Custom, Community and Machinery in the English Woollen Industry, 1770–1809* (Cambridge, 1991).

70 Bristol Record Office, 'John Bennett, Untitled T.S.', 36907, p. 4.

71 Ibid., p. 4.

72 Ibid., p. 7

73 Leicestershire, Leicester and Rutland Record Office, 'Memoirs of Arnold Goodliffe', DE7196.

Chapter 5: Worlds of Work

1 *London Saturday Journal*, 13 February 1841, p. 74.

2 D. V. Glass, 'Two papers on Gregory King', in D. V. Glass and D. E. C. Eversley, eds., *Population in History: Essays in Historical Demography* (London, 1965); G. S. Holmes, 'Gregory King and the social structure of pre-industrial England', *Transactions of the Royal Historical Society*, 5th ser., 27 (1977), pp. 41–68; Peter Laslett, 'Natural and political observations on the population of late seventeenth-century England: Reflections on the work of Gregory King and John Graunt', in K. Schurer and T. Arkell, eds., *Surveying the People: The Interpretation and Use of Document Sources for the Study of Population in the Later Seventeenth Century* (Oxford, 1992), pp. 6–30; Richard Stone, *Some British Empiricists in the Social Sciences, 1650–1900* (Cambridge, 1997), pp. 71–115; Tom Arkell, 'Illuminations and distortions: Gregory King's Scheme calculated for the year 1688 and the social structure of later Stuart England', *Economic History Review*, 59/1 (2006), pp. 32–69.

3 From Holmes, 'Gregory King', p. 66–8.

4 Peter Mathias, 'The social structure in the eighteenth century: A calculation by Joseph Massie', *Economic History Review*, 10/1 (1957), pp. 30–45, 36.

5 Arkell, 'Illuminations', p. 34.

6 Glass, 'Gregory King', p. 63.

7 Arkell, 'Illuminations', p. 65.

8   Mathias, 'Social structure', p. 36.
9   Peter H. Lindert and Jeffrey G. Williamson, 'Revising England's social tables, 1688–1812', *Explorations in Economic History*, 19/4 (1982), pp. 385–804, 394.
10 Boyd Hilton, *A Mad, Bad, and Dangerous People? England, 1783–1846* (Oxford, 2006), pp. 126–9.
11 Quoted in Lindert and Williamson, 'Revising England's social tables', p. 404.
12 Mathias, 'Social structure', p. 32.
13 Lindert and Williamson, 'Revising England's social tables'. Peter H. Lindert, 'English occupations, 1670–1811', *Journal of Economic History*, 40/4 (1980), pp. 685–712.
14 Lindert and Williamson, 'Revising England's social tables', table 1, pp. 388–9.
15 See, in particular, Julian Hoppit, 'Counting the industrial revolution', *Economic History Review*, 43/2 (1990), pp. 173–193; Maxine Berg and Pat Hudson, 'Rehabilitating the industrial revolution', *Economic History Review*, 45/1 (1992), pp. 24–50.
16 Lindert, 'English occupations', p. 690.
17 Ibid., p. 701.
18 Hoppit, 'Counting', pp. 176–8; Lindert, 'English occupations', table 3, pp. 702–4.
19 Ann Kussmaul, *A General View of the Rural Economy of England, 1538–1840* (Cambridge, 1990).
20 L. Shaw-Taylor and E. A. Wrigley, 'The occupational structure of England c. 1750–1871. A preliminary report', www.hpss.geog.cam.ac.uk/research/projects/occupations/introduction/summary.pdf
21 Shaw-Taylor and Wrigley, 'The occupational structure'.
22 A small tertiary sector provided the final 10 per cent of employment.
23 Mining and the tertiary sector provided the remaining 13 per cent of employment.
24 These findings largely confirm Timmins' analysis of Lancashire. See Geoffrey Timmins, *Made in Lancashire. A History of Regional Industrialisation* (Manchester, 1998), pp. 70–1, 161–2.
25 S. Horrell and J. Humphries, 'Women's labour force participation and the transition to the male breadwinner family, 1790–1865', *Economic History Review*, 48/1 (1995), pp. 89–117; J. Lown, *Women and Industrialization: Gender at Work in Nineteenth Century England* (Oxford, 1990); J. McKay, 'Married women and work in nineteenth century Lancashire: The evidence of the 1851 and 1861 census reports', *Local Population Studies*, 61 (1998), pp. 25–37.
26 Female participation rates were highest in the hat- and lace-making districts of south Bedfordshire, reaching 72 per cent in Luton.
27 P. Kirby, 'How many children were "unemployed" in eighteenth and nineteenth century England?', *Past and Present*, 186 (2005), pp. 187–202; P. Kirby, *Child Labour in Britain, 1750–1870* (Basingstoke, 2003).
28 Maxine Berg, *Age of Manufactures, 1700–1820. Industry, Innovation and Work in Britain* (London, 2nd edn., 1994), p. 138.
29 'Life of a journeyman baker, written by himself', *The Commonwealth*, 13, 20 December 1856.
30 Ibid.

Chapter 6: The 'Mechanical Age': Technology, Innovation and Industrialisation

1   Thomas Carlyle, 'Signs of the times', *Edinburgh Review*, 49 (June 1829), pp. 438–59.
2   William Lawson, *Geography of the British Empire* (London, 1861; repr. 1866), p. 192.
3   T. S. Ashton, *The Industrial Revolution, 1760–1830* (Oxford, 1948; repr. 1996), pp. 13, 48.
4   David Landes, 'Technological change and development in western Europe, 1750–1914', in H. J. Habbakuk and M. Postan, eds., *The Cambridge Economic History of Europe*, vi. (Cambridge, 1965); Idem, *The Unbound Prometheus: Technological Change and Development in Western Europe from 1750 to the Present* (Cambridge, 1969), p. 41.

5　Joel Mokyr, *The Lever of Riches. Technological Creativity and Economic Progress* (Oxford, 1990), p. 81; Idem, 'Editor's introduction: The New economic history and the industrial revolution', in Mokyr (ed.), *The British Industrial Revolution: An Economic Perspective* (Boulder, 1993), p. 18.

6　See especially C. Knick Harley, 'Reassessing the industrial revolution: A macro view', in Mokyr, ed., *British Industrial Revolution*, pp. 171–226, pp. 197–200; N. F. R. Crafts, *British Economic Growth during the Industrial Revolution* (Oxford, 1985), pp. 84–6.

7　C. Knick Harley, 'Reassessing the industrial revolution', p. 200.

8　C. Knick Harley, 'British industrialisation before 1841: Evidence of slower growth during the industrial revolution', *Journal of Economic History*, 42/2 (1982), pp. 267–89; N. F. R. Crafts, *British Economic Growth*, pp. 17–25; N. F. R. Crafts and C. Knick Harley, 'Output growth and the British industrial revolution: A restatement of the Crafts-Harley view', *Economic History Review*, 45/4 (1992), pp. 703–30.

9　D. Greasley and L. Oxley, 'British industrialization, 1815–1860: A disaggregate time-series perspective', *Explorations in Economic History*, 37/1 (2000), pp. 98–119, 101.

10　See Maxine Berg and Pat Hudson, 'Rehabilitating the industrial revolution', *Economic History Review*, 45/1 (1992), pp. 24–50; Crafts and Harley, 'Output growth', p. 711.

11　Peter Temin, 'Two views of the British industrial revolution', *Journal of Economic History*, 57/1 (1997), pp. 63–82.

12　See, however, their response to Temin's analysis. C. Knick Harley and N. F. R. Crafts, 'Simulating the two views of the British industrial revolution', *Journal of Economic History*, 60/3 (2000), pp. 819–41.

13　The definitive history of patents remains Christine MacLeod, *Inventing the Industrial Revolution: The English Patent System, 1660–1800* (Cambridge, 1988). A useful summary may also be found in Kristine Bruland, 'Industrialisation and technological change', in Roderick Floud and Paul Johnson, eds., *The Cambridge Economic History of Modern Britain: Industrialisation, 1700–1860*, i. (Cambridge, 2004), pp. 117–46.

14　Hargreaves sold a number of jennies before taking out a patent, and for this reason his claim was later rejected in the courts. Crompton was unable to patent his mule, probably because Arkwright's patent on his 'throstle' or 'frame' barred the way. See Ashton, *The Industrial Revolution*, pp. 58–60.

15　Bruland, 'Industrialisation', pp. 122–3.

16　MacLeod, *Inventing the Industrial Revolution*, p. 157.

17　Richard J. Sullivan, 'England's "Age of Invention": The acceleration of patents and patentable invention during the industrial revolution,' *Explorations in Economic History*, 26 (1989), pp. 424–52, 445, 447.

18　Ibid., p. 442.

19　MacLeod, *Inventing the Industrial Revolution*, p. 148. See also Trevor Griffiths, Philip A. Hunt and Patrick K. O'Brien, 'Inventive activity in the British textile industry, 1700–1800', *Journal of Economic History*, 52/4 (1992), pp. 881–906.

20　Michael W. Flinn, *The History of the British Coal Industry: 1700–1830: The Industrial Revolution*, ii. (Oxford, 1984), pp. 124–6; Steven King and Geoffrey Timmins, *Making Sense of the Industrial Revolution* (Manchester, 2001), pp. 84–5.

21　Geoffrey Timmins, *Made in Lancashire. A History of Regional Industrialisation* (Manchester, 1998), p. 85, table 6.1, p. 159.

22　Mokyr, *Lever of Riches*, p. 111. See also M. J. Daunton, *Progress and Poverty: An Economic and Social History of Britain* (Oxford, 1995), pp. 186–90 and 'Statistical appendix', table 3.d.i.–ii, pp. 586–7.

23　Good accounts of technological change in the spinning industry may be found in: Landes, *Unbound Prometheus*, pp. 82–6; Geoffrey Timmins, 'Technological change', in Mary B. Rose, ed., *The Lancashire Cotton Industry: A History since 1700* (Preston, 1996), pp. 29–62, 44–5; Mokyr, *Lever of Riches*, pp. 96–9; Bruland, 'Industrialisation', pp. 135–6.

24 Timmins, 'Technological change', pp. 44–5; and Mokyr, *Lever of Riches*, p. 99.

25 Timmins, *Made in Lancashire*, p. 127. See also G. N. von Tunzelmann, 'Time-saving technological change: The cotton industry in the English industrial revolution', *Explorations in Economic History*, 32 (1995), pp. 1–27, 11.

26 Timmins, *Made in Lancashire*, p. 128.

27 Roger Lloyd-Jones and M. J. Lewis, *British Industrial Capitalism since the Industrial Revolution* (London, 1998), p. 41.

28 Geoffrey Timmins, *The Last Shift: The Decline of Handloom Weaving in Nineteenth-Century Lancashire* (Manchester, 1993), pp. 157–9.

29 Ibid., p. 159 and Timmins, 'Technological change', pp. 45–7.

30 Timmins, *Made in Lancashire*, pp. 130, 170.

31 Ibid., p. 87.

32 Idem, *The Last Shift*, pp. 108–18.

33 Mokyr, 'Editor's introduction', p. 12.

34 Daunton, *Progress and Poverty*, pp. 211–19; Mokyr, *Lever of Riches*, pp. 93–5; J. R. Harris, *The British Iron Industry, 1700–1850* (London, 1988), pp. 30–40; Richard Hayman, *Ironmaking: The History and Archaeology of the Iron Industry* (Stroud, 2005), pp. 34–63.

35 Joel Mokyr, 'Technological change, 1700–1830', in R. Floud and D. McCloskey, eds., *The Economic History of Britain since 1700* (Cambridge, 2nd edn., 1994), pp. 25–7; Roger Burt, 'The extractive industries' in Floud and Johnson, eds., *Cambridge Economic History*, pp. 448–9.

36 Mokyr, 'Editor's introduction', p. 22.

37 Landes, *Unbound Prometheus*, p. 89.

38 P. Deane, *The First Industrial Revolution* (Cambridge, 1965), p. 130.

39 Mokyr, *Lever of Riches*.

40 Timmins, *Made in Lancashire*, p. 131.

41 See J. Kanefsky and J. Robey, 'Steam engines in eighteenth-century Britain: A quantitative assessment', *Technology and Culture*, 21 (1980), pp. 161–86, table 5, p. 176.

42 Marie Rowlands, *The West Midlands from AD 1000* (Harlow, 1987), p. 236.

43 G. N. Von Tunzelmann, *Steam Power and British Industrialisation to 1860* (Oxford, 1978), pp. 286–7.

44 N. F. R. Crafts, 'The first industrial revolution: Resolving the slow growth/rapid industrialization paradox', *Journal of the European Economic Association*, vol. 3, no. 2/3 (2005), pp. 525–34, 528.

45 Patrick K. O'Brien, 'The deconstruction of myths and reconstruction of metanarratives in global histories of material progress', in Benedikt Stuchtey and Eckhardt Fuchs, eds., *Writing World History* (Oxford, 2002).

46 A. E. Musson, *The Growth of British Industry* (London, 1978), p. 109.

47 The distinction is helpfully described in Mokyr, 'Editors introduction', pp. 17–24.

48 Quoted in King and Timmins, *Making Sense*, p. 75.

49 Raphael Samuel, 'Workshop of the world: Steam power and hand technology in mid Victorian Britain', *History Workshop Journal*, 3 (1977), pp. 6–72.

50 King and Timmins, *Making Sense*, pp. 71–2.

51 Griffiths, Hunt and O'Brien, 'Inventive activity', pp. 881–906, 892.

52 Maxine Berg, 'From imitation to invention: Creating commodities in eighteenth-century Britain', *Economic History Review*, 55/1 (2002), pp. 1–30.

53 Griffiths, Hunt and O'Brien, 'Inventive activity', p. 895; Berg, 'Imitation to invention', p. 23. See also, more generally, Maxine Berg, *Luxury and Pleasure in Eighteenth-Century Britain* (Oxford, 2005).

54 Wrigley, 'Urban growth', p. 686.

55 Eric Hopkins, *The Rise of the Manufacturing Town: Birmingham and the Industrial Revolution* (London, 1989; repr. Stroud 1998), pp. 3–4.

56 Ibid., p. 42.
57 Ibid., pp. 48–51.
58 Ibid., pp. 46–8.
59 Mokyr, 'Technological change', p. 28.
60 Stanley Chapman, *Hosiery and Knitwear: Four Centuries of Small-Scale Industry in Britain, c. 1589–2000* (Oxford, 2002), pp. 1–11, 65–71, 105–11.
61 Ibid., p. 52.

Chapter 7: Coal: The Key to the British Industrial Revolution?

1 Benjamin Disraeli, *Sybil Or the Two Nations* (London, 1853), p. 120.
2 E. A. Wrigley, 'The transition to an advanced organic economy: Half a millennium of English agriculture', *Economic History Review*, 59/3 (2006), pp. 435–80, 476.
3 Graeme Donald Snooks, 'Great waves of economic change: The industrial revolution in historical perspective', in Idem, ed., *Was the Industrial Revolution Necessary?* (London, 1994), figure 3.3, p. 65.
4 Richard Cantillon, *Essai sur la nature du commerce en général* (London, 1755), pp. 93–4, 113.
5 Ibid., p. 1.
6 E. A. Wrigley, *Continuity, Chance and Change: The Character of the Industrial Revolution in England* (Cambridge, 1990). See also, however, Rondo Cameron, 'A new view of European industrialisation', *Economic History Review*, 38/1 (1985), pp. 1–23; B. Thomas, 'Escaping from constraints: The industrial revolution in a Malthusian context', in R. I. Rotberg and Theodore Kwasnik Rabb, eds, *Population and Economy?: From the Traditional to the Modern World* (Cambridge, 1986), pp. 169–93; Arnold Pacey, *The Maze of Ingenuity: Ideas and Idealism in the Development of Technology* (New York, 1975; 2nd edn., 1992); Alfred D. Chandler, 'Anthracite coal', in Carlo Cipolla, ed., *The Economic History of World Population* (Harmondsworth, 5th edn., 1970), p. 57.
7 Cantillon, *Essai sur la nature du commerce*, p. 112.
8 Wrigley, *Continuity, Chance and Change*, p. 55.
9 See also K. Pomeranz, *The Great Divergence: China, Europe, and the Making of the Modern World Economy* (Princeton, 2000).
10 Michael W. Flinn, *The History of the British Coal Industry: 1700–1830: The Industrial Revolution*, ii. (Oxford, 1984), table 1.2, p. 26. S. Pollard, 'A new estimate of British coal production, 1750–1850', *Economic History Review*, 33/2 (1980), pp. 212–35, table 14, p. 229.
11 Flinn, *History of British Coal*, pp. 26, 121–8. R Church, *The History of the British Coal Industry: 1830–1913, Victorian Pre-eminence*, iii. (Oxford, 1986), table 1.1, p. 3, quote p. 758.
12 Paul Warde, *Energy Consumption in England and Wales, 1560–2000* (Naples: 2007), p. 61.
13 Ibid., appendix 2, pp. 123–30.
14 Ibid., appendix 3, pp. 131–8.
15 Wrigley, *Continuity, Chance, Change*, p. 80.
16 G. Hammersley, 'The charcoal iron industry and its fuel, 1540–1750', *Economic History Review*, 26/4 (1973), pp. 593–613; B. Thomas, 'Was there an energy crisis in Great Britain in the 17th century?', *Explorations in Economic History*, 23 (1986), pp. 124–52; M. W. Flinn, 'Technical change as an escape from resource scarcity: England in the seventeenth and eighteenth centuries', A. Maczak and W. N. Parker, *Natural Resources in European History* (Washington, 1978), pp. 139–59.
17 C. K. Hyde, *Technological Change and the British Iron Industry, 1700–1870* (Princeton, 1977), p. 67. See also, however, Richard Hayman, 'Charcoal ironmaking in nineteenth-century Shropshire', *Economic History Review*, 61/1 (2008), pp. 80–98.
18 M. J. Daunton, *Progress and Poverty: An Economic and Social History of Britain, 1700–1850* (Oxford, 1995), p. 212.

19 Philip Riden, 'The output of the British iron industry before 1870', *Economic History Review*, 30/3 (1977), pp. 442–59.

20 Ibid.

21 Roger Burt, 'The extractive industries', in Roderick Floud and Paul Johnson, eds., *The Cambridge Economic History of Modern Britain* (Cambridge, 2004), pp. 417–50, 419.

22 Flinn, *History of British Coal*, table 7.12, p. 243.

23 Marie Rowlands, *The West Midlands from AD 1000* (Harlow, 1987), p. 239; John Elliott, *The Industrial Development of the Ebbw Valleys, 1780–1914* (Cardiff, 2004), p. 80.

24 Flinn, *History of British Coal*, p. 252.

25 M. Berg, *The Age of Manufactures 1700–1820: Industry, Innovation and Work in Britain* (London, 2nd edn., 1994); M. B. Rowlands, 'Continuity and change in an industrializing society: The case of the West Midlands industries', in P. Hudson, ed., *Regions and Industries: A Perspective on the Industrial Revolution in Britain* (Cambridge, 1989), pp. 103–31.

26 Ibid., p. 124.

27 Geoffrey Timmins, *Made in Lancashire. A History of Regional Industrialisation* (Manchester, 1998), table 6.1, p. 159.

28 Ibid., p. 91.

29 Pacey, *Maze of Ingenuity*, p. 165.

30 Pomeranz, *Great Divergence*, pp. 66–8.

31 S. D. Chapman, *The Cotton Industry in the Industrial Revolution* (London, 1987), table 1, p. 19.

32 From C. Knick Harley, 'British industrialization before 1841: Evidence of slower growth during the industrial revolution', *Journal of Economic History*, 42/2 (1982), pp. 267–89, figures given on pp. 268–9.

33 Daunton, *Progress and Poverty*, table 3.d.i, 3.d.ii, pp. 585–7.

34 D. C. Coleman, 'Industrial growth and industrial revolutions', *Economica*, 23/89 (1956), pp. 1–22.

35 Harley, 'British industrialisation before 1841', table 1, p. 269.

36 C. Knick Harley, 'Reassessing the industrial revolution: A macro view', in Joel Mokyr, ed., *The British Industrial Revolution: An Economic Perspective* (Boulder, 1993), pp. 199–200.

37 G. Clark and D. Jacks, 'Coal and the industrial revolution, 1700–1869', *European Review of Economic History*, 11/1 (2007), pp. 39–72.

38 Jack A. Goldstone, 'Efflorescences and economic growth in world history: Rethinking the "rise of the West" and the British industrial revolution', *Journal of World History*, 13/2 (2002), pp. 323–89. See also R. C. Allen, 'The British industrial revolution in global perspective: How commerce created the industrial revolution and modern economic growth' (2006) University of Oxford. At: http://www.nuffield.ox.ac.uk/users/allen/unpublished/econinvent-3.pdf

39 Flinn, *History of British Coal*, pp. 69–145; Flinn, 'Technical change', pp. 147–50.

40 Flinn, *History of British Coal*, pp. 110–14.

41 Ibid., pp. 114–19.

42 Ibid., pp. 119–22.

43 See also, however, J. Kanefsky and J. Robey, 'Steam engines in eighteenth-century Britain: a quantitative assessment', *Technology and Culture*, 21 (1980), pp. 161–86.

44 T. S. Ashton, *Iron and Steel in the Industrial Revolution* (Manchester, 1951), pp. 24–39.

45 Charles K. Hyde, 'Technological change in the British wrought iron industry, 1750–1815: A reinterpretation', *Economic History Review*, 27/2 (1974), pp. 190–206.

46 Allen, 'British industrial revolution', p. 17.

47 Jenkins, *West Riding Wool Textile Industry*, p. 101. See also Jennifer Tann, 'The textile millwright in the early industrial revolution', *Textile History*, 5 (1974), pp. 88–8. pp. 80–89.

48 Simon Ville, 'Transport', in Floud and Johnson, eds., *Cambridge Economic History of Modern Britain*, pp. 295–331.

49 Daunton, *Progress and Poverty*, p. 287–8.

50 B. F. Duckham, 'Canals and river navigations', in D. H. Aldcroft and M. J. Freeman, eds., *Transport in the Industrial Revolution* (Manchester, 1983).
51 H. J. Dyos and D. H. Aldcroft, *British Transport: An Economic Survey from the Seventeenth Century to the Twentieth* (London, 1974), pp. 37–45.
52 G. Turnbull, 'Canals, coal and regional growth during the industrial revolution', *Economic History Review*, 40/4 (1987), pp. 537–60.
53 Ville, 'Transport', p. 299.
54 Daunton, *Progress and Poverty*, p. 290–7.
55 Ibid., p. 296.
56 Turnbull, 'Canals', p. 541. See also M. J. Freeman, 'Introduction', in Aldcroft and Freeman, eds., *Transport in the Industrial Revolution*, pp. 1–4.
57 Wrigley, *Continuity, Chance, Change*, p. 28.
58 Jack Simmons, *The Victorian Railway* (London, 1991); G. R. Hawke, *Railways and Economic Growth in England and Wales, 1840–70* (Oxford, 1970).
59 Jack Simmons, *The Railways of Britain* (London, 2nd edn., 1968), p. 3.
60 T. R. Gourvish, 'Railways 1830–70: The formative years', in Michael J. Freeman and Derek H. Aldcroft, eds., *Transport in Victorian Britain* (Manchester, 1988), p. 57.
61 Ibid.
62 Gourvish, 'Railways 1830–70', p. 73.
63 P. S. Bagwell and J. Armstrong, 'Coastal shipping', in Freeman and Aldcroft, eds., *Transport in Victorian Britain*, pp. 171–217.
64 Daunton, *Progress and Poverty*, p. 296.
65 M. J. Freeman, 'Introduction', in Freeman and Aldcroft, eds., *Transport in Victorian Britain*, p. 16.
66 Simmons, *Railways*, p. 110.
67 N. Crafts, 'Steam as a general purpose technology: A growth accounting perspective', *Economic Journal*, 114/495 (2004), pp. 338–51. See also A. E. Musson, 'Industrial motive power in the United Kingdom, 1800–1870', *Economic History Review*, 29/3 (1976), pp. 415–39; J. W. Kanefsky, 'Motive power in British industry and the accuracy of the 1870 factory return', *Economic History Review*, 32/3 (1979), pp. 360–75.
68 Wrigley, 'Transition to an advanced organic economy'; Goldstone, 'Efflorescences and economic growth'.
69 Stanley L. Engerman and Patrick K. O'Brien, 'The industrial revolution in global perspective', in Floud and Johnson, eds., *Cambridge Economic History of Modern Britain*, pp. 451–64, 451.

Chapter 8: Why Was Britain First? The Global Context for Industrialisation

1 William Waterston, *A Cyclopædia of Commerce, Mercantile Law, Finance, Commercial Geography* (London, 1846), p. 224.
2 Useful introductions to European industrialisation may be found in Colin Heywood, 'The challenge of industrialisation', in Pamela M. Pilbean, ed., *Themes in Modern European History, 1780–1830* (London, 1995), pp. 151–76; Clive Trebilcock, 'The industrialisation of modern Europe, 1750–1914', in T. C. W. Blanning, ed., *The Oxford Illustrated History of Modern Europe* (Oxford, 1996), pp. 40–68; Robert Lee, 'Industrial revolution, commerce and trade', in Stefan Berger, ed., *A Companion to Nineteenth Century Europe* (Oxford, 2000), pp. 44–55. See also, however, Rondo Cameron, 'A new view of European industrialisation', *Economic History Review*, 38/1 (1985), pp. 1–23.
3 Sidney Pollard, *Peaceful Conquest: The Industrialization of Europe, 1760–1970* (Oxford, 1981), p. vi.

4 A very helpful introduction to Gerschenkron's ideas may be found in Richard Sylla and Gianni Toniolo, eds., *Patterns of European Industrialisation: The Nineteenth Century* (London, 1991), pp. 1–28.

5 In fact, Belgium did not exist as a nation-state in the early nineteenth century and the territory corresponding to present-day Belgium was first under French, then Dutch, control. Belgium did not gain independence in the 1830s; nonetheless, we use the term 'Belgium' for convenience and refer to the nation recognised by the Treaty of London, signed in 1839.

6 Cameron, 'New view of European industrialisation', pp. 1–23.

7 Hilde Greefs, Bruno Blondí and Peter Clark, 'The growth of urban industrial regions: Belgian developments in comparative perspective, 1750–1850', in Jon Stobart and Neil Raven, eds., *Towns, Regions and Industries: Urban and Industrial Change in the Midlands, C. 1700–1840* (Manchester, 2005), pp. 210–27.

8 Ibid., p. 216.

9 Ibid., p. 217.

10 Herman van der Wee, 'The industrial revolution in Belgium', in Mikuláš Teich and Roy Porter, eds., *The Industrial Revolution in National Context: Europe and the USA* (Cambridge, 1996), pp. 64–77; Joel Mokyr, 'The Industrial revolution in the Low Countries in the first half of the nineteenth century: A comparative case study', *Journal of Economic History*, 34/2 (1974), pp. 365–91.

11 Germany, like Belgium, did not exist as a nation-state during much of the period under discussion here. It came into being with the creation of the Kaiserreich in 1871. Once again, we use the term here for convenience and refer to the state created in 1871.

12 Toni Pierenkemper and Richard Tilly, *The German Economy during the Nineteenth Century* (New York, 2004), graph 1, p. 14–15.

13 Richard Tilly, 'German industrialisation', in Sylla and Toniolo, eds., *Patterns of European Industrialisation*, table 5.1, p. 96.

14 Pierenkemper and Tilly, *The German Economy*, graph 4, pp. 18–20, 103–4.

15 Terry G. Jordan-Bychkov and Bella Bychkova Jordan, *European Culture Area: A Systematic Geography* (New York, 1973; 4th edn., Lanham, MD, 2002), pp. 292–4.

16 David Blackbourn, *The Fontana History of Germany, 1815–1918: The Long Nineteenth Century* (London, 1997), p. 178.

17 James H. Jackson, *Migration and Urbanization in the Ruhr Valley, 1821–1914* (Boston, MA, 1997), pp. 2–14.

18 Ibid., table 1.2, p. 7.

19 Georges Dupeux and Peter Wait, *French Society, 1789–1970* (London, 1976), pp. 1–2; Noël Bonneuil, *Transformation of the French Demographic Landscape, 1806–1906* (Oxford, 1997), pp. 85–7.

20 For a good survey of the historiography of French industrialisation, see, François Crouzet, 'The historiography of French economic growth in the nineteenth century', *Economic History Review*, 56/2 (2003), pp. 215–42. See also Robert Aldrich, 'Late-comer or early-starter? New views on French economic history', *Journal of European Economic History*, 16 (1987), pp. 85–100; Jeff Horn, *The Path Not Taken: French Industrialisation in the Age of Revolution, 1750–1830* (Cambridge, MA, 2006).

21 Calculated from N. F. R. Crafts, 'Economic growth in France and Britain, 1830–1910: A review of the evidence', *Journal of Economic History*, 44/1 (1984), pp. 49–67, table 1, p. 51.

22 Patrick K. O'Brien and C. Keyder, *Economic Growth in Britain and France, 1780–1914: Two Paths to the Twentieth Century* (London, 1978).

23 François Crouzet, *History of the European Economy, 1000–2000* (London, 2001), pp. 130–2.

24 Alan S. Milward and S. B. Saul, *The Economic Development of Continental Europe, 1780–1870*, i. (London, 1973).

25 Raymond A. Jonas, 'Peasants, population, and industry in France', *Journal of Interdisciplinary History*, 22/2 (1991), pp. 177–200. See also C. Sabel and J. Zeitlin, 'Historical alternatives to mass production', *Past and Present*, 108 (1985), pp. 133–76, esp. 144–5.

26 François Crouzet, 'France', in Teich and Porter, eds., *The Industrial Revolution*, p. 41; Cameron, 'New view of European industrialisation', p. 14.

27 Terry S. Reynolds, *Stronger than a Hundred Men: A History of the Vertical Water Wheel* (Baltimore, 1983), pp. 339–43.

28 Jonas, 'Peasants, population, and industry'; Crouzet, *History European Economy*, pp. 59–63.

29 Reynolds, *Stronger than a Hundred Men*, pp. 325–7.

30 Peter K. Stearns, *The Industrial Revolution in World History* (Boulder, 1993), p. 45.

31 Cameron, 'New view', figure 1.a, p. 12., pp. 13–14; F. Crouzet, *Britain Ascendant: Comparative Studies in Franco-British Economic History* (Cambridge, 1985), pp. 414–41.

32 Robert C. Allen, *The British Industrial Revolution in Global Perspective* (Cambridge, 2009), pp. 229–35.

33 See, in particular, Jordan Goodman and Katrina Honeyman, *Gainful Pursuits: The Making of Industrial Europe, 1600–1914* (London, 1992), pp. 196–202.

34 Ibid., pp. 198–200. See also François Caron and Barbara Bray, *An Economic History of Modern France* (London, 1979), 144–6; Alan S. Milward and S. B. Saul, *The Development of the Economies of Continental Europe, 1850–1914* (London, 1977); Xavier de Planhol, Paul Claval and Janet Lloyd, *An Historical Geography of France* (Cambridge, 1994), pp. 370–1; M. Henri Morsel, 'Les industries électrotechniques dans les Alpes françaises du Nord de 1869–1921' in Pierre Léon, *l'Industrialisation en Europe au XIXe siècle* (Lyon, 1972).

35 Vera Zamagni, *The Economic History of Italy, 1860–1990* (Oxford, 1993), pp. 36–43.

36 Ibid., pp. 92–4.

37 Allen, *The British Industrial Revolution*, pp. 203–12, 229–35.

38 Eric Jones, *European Miracle: Environment, Economies and Geopolitics in the History of Europe and Asia* (Cambridge, 3rd edn., 2003); Idem, *Growth Recurring: Economic Change in World History* (Oxford, 1988).

39 Jones, *European Miracle*, pp. 226–7.

40 See, for example, James M. Blaut, *Eight Eurocentric Historians* (New York, 2000), pp. 73–112.

41 D. S. Landes, *The Wealth and Poverty of Nations: Why Some Are So Rich and Some Are So Poor* (New York, 1998), p. xxi. See also the discussion in Jack Goody, *Capitalism and Modernity: the Great Debate* (Cambridge, 2004), pp. 27–49.

42 R. Bin Wong, *China Transformed: Historical Change and the Limits of European Experience* (Ithaca and London, 1997); K. Pomeranz, *The Great Divergence: China, Europe, and the Making of the Modern World Economy* (Princeton, 2000); Susan B. Hanley, *Everyday Things in Premodern Japan: The Hidden Legacy of Material Culture* (London, 1999); P. Parthasarathi, *The Transition to a Colonial Economy: Weavers, Merchants and Kings in South India, 1720–1800* (Cambridge, 2001).

43 Pomeranz, *Great Divergence*, p. 8.

44 A. G. Frank, *ReOrient: The Silver Age in Asia and the World Economy* (Berkeley, 1998), pp. 126–30, 179–97.

45 Jones, *Economic Miracle*, pp. 160, 202–22.

46 Wong, *China Transformed*, pp. 17–19.

47 Jack A. Goldstone, 'Efflorescences and economic growth in world history: Rethinking the "rise of the West" and the industrial revolution', *Journal of World History*, 13/2 (2002), pp. 323–89, 351.

48 Kenneth Pomeranz, 'Standards of living in eighteenth-century China: Regional differences, temporal trends, and incomplete evidence', in Robert C. Allen, Tommy Bengtsson and Martin Dribe, eds., *Living Standards in the Past: New Perspectives on Well-Being in Asia and Europe* (Oxford, 2005), pp. 23–54.

49 Ibid. See also James Z. Lee and Feng Wang. *One Quarter of Humanity: Malthusian Mythology and Chinese Realities, 1700–2000* (Cambridge, 1999), pp. 2–35.

50 William Lavely and R. Bin Wong, 'Revising the Malthusian narrative: The comparative study of population dynamics in late imperial China', *Journal of Asian Studies*, 57/3 (1998), pp. 714–48, esp. table 3A, pp. 720–4.

51 Stephen Broadberry and Bishnupriya Gupta, 'Lancashire, India and shifting competitive advantage in cotton textiles, 1700–1850: The neglected role of factor prices', *Economic History Review*, 62/2 (2009), pp. 279–305, pp. 282–4; Frank Perlin, 'Proto-industrialization and pre-colonial South Asia', *Past and Present*, 98 (1983), p. 98. Compare also with the quote at the head of this chapter from William Waterston, *A Cyclopædia of Commerce, Mercantile Law, Finance, Commercial Geography* (London, 1846), p. 224.

52 For a more recent example of historical research in the Indian nationalist tradition, see Amiya Bagchi, 'De-industrialisation in India in the nineteenth century: Some theoretical implications', *Journal of Development Studies*, 12 (1976), pp. 135–64. A far more benign interpretation of the impact of colonisation may be found in Irfan Habib, 'Potentialities of capitalistic development in the economy of Mughal India', *Journal of Economic History*, 29/1 (1969), pp. 32–78.

53 P. Parthasarathi, 'Rethinking wages and competitiveness in the eighteenth century: Britain and South India', *Past and Present*, 158 (1998), pp. 79–109.

54 P. H. H. Vries, 'Are coal and colonies really crucial? Kenneth Pomeranz and the great divergence,' *Journal of World History*, 12/2 (2001), pp. 407–46.

55 Robert C. Allen et al., 'Wages, prices, and living standards in China, Japan, and Europe, 1738–1925', unpublished paper (2005), http://personal.lse.ac.uk/mad1/ma_pdf_files/allen%20et%20al%202007.pdf

56 Ibid., p. 30.

57 S. N. Broadberry and B. Gupta, 'The early modern great divergence: Wages, prices and economic development in Europe and Asia, 1500–1800', *Economic History Review*, 59/1 (2006), pp. 2–31.

58 Ibid., p. 18.

59 Broadberry and Gupta, 'Lancashire, India', esp. pp. 295–302.

60 E. A. Wrigley, 'The transition to an advanced organic economy: Half a millennium of English agriculture', *Economic History Review*, 59/3 (2006), pp. 435–80.

Chapter 9: Winners and Losers: Living through the Industrial Revolution

1 William Varley, 'Diary of William Varley of Higham' in W. Bennett, ed., *The History of Burnley, 1650–1850* (Burnley, 1948).

2 Thomas Carlyle, *Past and Present* (London, 2nd edn., 1845).

3 Ibid., p. 4.

4 Friedrich Engels, *The Condition of the Working Class in England*. Edited with introduction Victor G. Kiernan (Harmondsworth, 1987), p. 51.

5 Andrew Ure, *The Philosophy of Manufactures, Or, An Exposition of the Scientific, Moral, and Commercial Economy of the Factory System of Great Britain* (London, 2nd edn., 1835), pp. 277–403.

6 Ibid., pp. 311, 309–13, 378, 380–4, 399, 379–402.

7 Quoted in T. S. Ashton, 'The standard of life of the workers of England, 1790–1830', *Journal of Economic History*, Supplement IX (1949), pp. 19–38, 20.

8 Arnold Toynbee, *Lectures on the Industrial Revolution of the Eighteenth Century in England* (London, 1884), p. 5.

9 J. H. Clapham, *An Economic History of Modern Britain*, i. (Cambridge, 1926), pp. 128, 561.

10 Ashton, 'Standard of life'; Phyllis Deane and W. A. Cole, *British Economic Growth, 1688–1959* (Cambridge, 1964), p. 27; R. M. Hartwell, 'The rising standard of living in England, 1800–1850', *Economic History Review*, 13/3 (1961), pp. 397–416; Peter H. Lindert and Jeffrey G. Williamson, 'English workers' living standards during the Industrial Revolution: A new look', *Economic History Review*, 36/1 (1983), pp. 1–25.

11 J. L. Hammond and Barbara Hammond, *The Town Labourer, 1760–1832* (London, 1917); Idem, *The Skilled Labourer, 1760–1832* (London, 1919); Sidney Webb and Beatrice Webb, *Industrial Democracy*, 2 vols (London, 1898).

12 E. J. Hobsbawm, 'The British standard of living, 1790–1850', *Economic History Review*, 10 (1957), pp. 46–68; E. P. Thompson, *The Making of the English Working Class* (London, 1963). See also A. J. Taylor, 'Progress and poverty in Britain', *History*, 45 (1960), pp. 16–31.

13 For a very useful discussion of the difficulties posed by this data, however, see Leonard Schwarz, 'Custom, wages, and workload in England during industrialisation', *Past and Present*, 197 (2007), pp. 143–75.

14 A. L. Bowley, 'The statistics of wages in the United Kingdom during the last hundred years', *Journal of the Royal Statistical Society*, 61 (1898).

15 Lindert and Williamson, 'English workers' living standards', pp. 11–12.

16 C. H. Feinstein, 'Pessimism perpetuated: Real wages and the standard of living in Britain during and after the industrial revolution', *Journal of Economic History*, 58/3 (1998), pp. 625–28, 652.

17 Robert C. Allen, 'The great divergence in European wages and prices from the middle ages to the First World War,' *Explorations in Economic History*, 38 (2001), pp. 411–47.

18 Gregory Clark, 'The condition of the working class in England, 1209–2004', *Journal of Political Economy*, 113/6 (2005), pp. 1307–40, taken from Table A2; Idem, 'Farm wages and living standards in the industrial revolution: England, 1670–1869', *Economic History Review*, 53/3 (2001), 477–505. See also Leonard Schwarz, 'Trends in real wages rates, 1750–1790', *Economic History Review*, 43/1 (1990), pp. 90–8.

19 Feinstein, 'Pessimism perpetuated', table 5, p. 648.

20 Allen, 'Great divergence', table 5, p. 428.

21 Clark, 'Wages and living standards', table 9, p. 496; Idem, 'Condition of the working class', table A2, p. 1325.

22 N. F. R. Crafts, 'Gross national product in Europe 1870–1910: Some new estimates', *Explorations in Economic History*, 20 (1983), 387–401, table 1, p. 389.

23 Luis Angeles, 'Making sense of conflicting views of pre-industrial Europe', *Explorations in Economic History*, 45 (2008), pp. 147–63.

24 Hans-Joachim Voth, *Time and Work in England 1750–1830* (Oxford, 2000); Idem, 'The longest years: New estimates of labor input in England, 1760–1830', *The Journal of Economic History*, 61/4 (2001), pp. 1065–82; E. Hopkins, 'Working hours and conditions during the industrial revolution: A reappraisal', *Economic History Review*, 35/1 (1982), pp. 52–66.

25 Feinstein, 'Pessimism perpetuated', table 2, p. 640; Allen, 'Great divergence', table 4, p. 326.

26 Clark, 'Condition of the working class', table A2, p. 1325; Idem, 'Wages and living standards', table A1, p. 503.

27 S. Horrell and J. Humphries, 'Old questions, new data, and alternative perspectives: Families' living standards during the industrial revolution', *Journal of Economic History*, 52/4 (1992), pp. 849–80.

28 The counties with fewer than ten observations are: North Riding of Yorkshire, Essex, Suffolk, Worcestershire, Nottinghamshire, Shropshire, Cambridgeshire, Huntingdonshire, Buckinghamshire and Oxfordshire.

29 All taken from Horrell and Humphries, 'Old questions, new data', figure 1, p. 874.

30 Henry Ashworth, 'Statistics of the present depression of trade at Bolton', *Journal of the Statistical Society of London*, 5/1 (1842), pp. 74–81, 78; William Charles Copperthwaite, 'Statistics of old and new Malton', *Journal of the Statistical Society of London*, 8/1 (1845), pp. 66–8, 68; W. H. Charlton, 'A statistical report from the Parish of Bellingham in the county of Northumberland', *Journal of the Statistical Society of London*, 1/7 (1838), pp. 420–6, 424–5; L. Hindmarsh, 'On the state of agriculture and condition of the agricultural labourers of the northern division of Northumberland', *Journal of the Statistical Society of London*, 1/7 (1838), pp. 397–414, 405.

31 For some examples of this, see James Nye, *A Small Account of My Travels through the Wilderness*, edited by Vic Gammon, (Brighton, 1981), p. 12; Robert Anderson, 'Memoir of the author, written by himself', in *The Poetical Works of Robert Anderson* (Carlisle, 1820), p. xvi; Joseph Jewell, 'Autobiographical memoir of Joseph Jewell, 1763–1846', ed. Arthur Walter Slater, *Camden Miscellany*, 22 (1964).

32 Thomas Carter, *Memoirs of a Working Man*, ed. Charles Knight (London, 1845), pp. 149–50.

33 Feinstein, 'Pessimism perpetuated', table 1, p. 635; Clark, 'Condition of the working class', table A3, p. 1327.

34 A good introduction to this literature is contained in S. King and A. Tomkins eds., *The Poor in England 1700–1850: An Economy of Makeshifts* (Manchester, 2003). See also Samantha Williams, 'Poor relief, labourers' households and living standards in rural England c. 1770–1834: A Bedfordshire case study', *Economic History Review*, 58/3 (2005), pp. 485–519; Idem, 'Earnings, poor relief and the economy of makeshifts: Bedfordshire in the early years of the New Poor Law', *Rural History*, 16/1 (2005), pp. 21–52; Jane Humphries, 'Enclosures, common rights, and women: The proletarianization of families in the late eighteenth and early nineteenth centuries', *Journal of Economic History*, 50/1 (1990); Penelope Lane, 'Work on the margins: Poor women and the informal economy of eighteenth and early nineteenth-century Leicestershire', *Midland History*, xxii (1997); Peter King, 'Customary rights and women's earnings: The importance of gleaning to the rural labouring poor, 1750–1850', *Economic History Review*, 44/3 (1991).

35 A useful introduction to the study of heights may be found in Stephen Nicholas and Richard H. Steckel, 'Heights and living standards of English workers during the early years of industrialization, 1770–1815', *Journal of Economic History*, 1/4 (1991), pp. 937–57, 940.

36 R. Floud, K. Wachter and A. Gregory, *Height, Health and History: Nutritional Status in the United Kingdom, 1750–1980* (Cambridge, 1990), pp. 275–306. Roderick Floud and Bernard Harris, 'Health, height, and welfare: Britain, 1700–1980', in Richard H. Steckel and Roderick Floud, eds., *Health and Welfare during Industrialization* (Chicago, 1997), pp. 91–126.

37 John Komlos, 'The secular trend in the biological standard of living in the United Kingdom', *Economic History Review*, 46/1 (1993), pp. 115–44.

38 Komlos, 'Secular trend', p. 142.

39 Nicholas and Steckel, 'Heights and living standards', figure 3, p. 948.

40 Stephen Nicholas and Deborah Oxley, 'The living standards of women during the industrial revolution, 1795–1820', *Economic History Review*, 46/4 (1993), pp. 723–49; Idem, 'The living standards of women in England and Wales, 1785–1815: New evidence from Newgate prison records', *Economic History Review*, 49/3 (1996), pp. 591–9.

41 Paul Johnson and Stephen Nicholas, 'Male and female living standards in England and Wales, 1812–1857: Evidence from criminal height records', *Economic History Review*, 48/3 (1995), pp. 470–81.

42 Johnson and Nicholas, 'Male and female living standards', figure 2, p. 477.

43 Gregory Clark, Michael Huberman and Peter Lindert, 'A British food puzzle, 1770–1850', *Economic History Review*, 48/2 (1995), pp. 215–37.

44 Nicholas and Steckel, 'English workers' living standards', p. 944; Nicholas and Oxley, 'Living standards of women', p. 730.

45 Johnson and Nicholas, 'Male and female living standards', p. 474.

46 Quoted in C. Barnett, *Britain and Her Army* (London, 1970), p. 280.

47 Jane Humphries, 'At what cost was preeminence purchased? Child labour and the first industrial revolution', in Scholliers and Leonard Schwarz, eds., *Experiencing Wages: Social and Cultural Aspects of Wage Forms in Europe since 1500* (New York, 2003), pp. 251–68; Carolyn Tuttle, *Hard at Work in Factories and Mines: The Economics of Child Labor during the British Industrial Revolution* (Boulder, 1999); Sara Horrell and Jane Humphries, ' "The exploitation of little children": Child labor and the family economy in the industrial

revolution', *Explorations in Economic History*, 32 (1995), pp. 485–516; Clark Nardinelli, *Child Labour and the Industrial Revolution* (Bloomington, 1990): C. Nardinelli, 'Child labour and the factory acts', *Journal of Economic History*, 40/4 (1980), pp. 739–55.

48 Peter Kirby, 'How many children were "unemployed" in eighteenth and nineteenth-century Britain?', *Past and Present*, 187 (2004), pp. 187–202; H. Cunningham, 'The employment and unemployment of children, 1680–1851', *Past and Present*, 126 (1990), pp. 115–50.

49 For a fuller description of de Vries' industrious revolution, see introduction, p. 11 and the references there. A good introduction is contained in J. de Vries, 'The industrial revolution and the industrious revolution', *Journal of Economic History*, 54/2 (1994).

50 Komlos, 'Secular trend', table 7, pp. 138–9. See also Paul Riggs, 'The standard of living in Scotland, 1800–1850', in John Komlos, ed., *Stature, Living Standards, and Economic Development* (Chicago, 1994), pp. 60–75.

51 Nicholas and Steckel, 'Heights and living standards', pp. 944, 947.

52 Nicholas and Oxley, 'Living standards of women'; Idem, 'Living standards of women in England and Wales'.

53 The debate on the effect of smallpox on heights may be followed in: H.-J. Voth and T. Leunig, 'Did smallpox reduce height? Stature and the standard of living in London, 1770–1873', *Economic History Review*, 49/3 (1996), pp. 541–60. Responses by Jackson; and Nicholas and Oxley in the same journal 49/3 (1996); by Razzell; Baten and Heintel; Voth and Leunig in 51/2 (1998); by Razzell; and Voth and Leunig in 54/1 (2001). See also Deborah Oxley, ' "Pitted but not pitied" or, does smallpox make you small?', *Economic History Review*, 59/3 (2006), pp. 617–35 and the response by Voth and Leunig in the same journal 59/3 (2006).

54 H.-J. Voth, 'Living standards and the urban environment', in Roderick Floud and Paul Johnson, eds., *The Cambridge Economic History of England* (Cambridge, 2004), p. 276.

55 Quoted in Ashton, 'Standard of life', p. 21.

56 P. Huck, 'Infant mortality and the living standards of English Workers during the industrial revolution', *Journal of Economic History*, 55/3 (1995), pp. 528–50.

57 Simon Szreter and Graham Mooney, 'Urbanisation, mortality, and the standard of living debate', *Economic History Review*, 51/1 (1998), table 6, p. 104.

58 Robert Woods, *The Demography of Victorian England and Wales* (Cambridge, 2000), table 9.3, p. 365.

Guide to Further Reading

The industrial revolution has generated a vast literature over the past century, and the following guide for further reading offers a brief outline of some of the key areas of historical debate. To keep the guide to manageable proportions, an effort has been made to confine it to seminal texts and more recent contributions to the field.

General. An excellent and very comprehensive survey of the British economy may be found in M. J. Daunton, *Progress and Poverty: An Economic and Social History of Britain* (Oxford, 1995). The recent *Cambridge Economic History* (Roderick Floud and Paul Johnson, eds., *The Cambridge Economic History of Modern Britain: Industrialisation, 1700–1860*, i. (Cambridge, 2004)) also provides a good starting point. The changing interpretations of industrialisation can be traced in Arnold Toynbee, *Lectures on the Industrial Revolution of the Eighteenth Century in England* (London, 1884; repr. 1920); J. L. Hammond and Barbara Hammond, *The Rise of Modern Industry* (London, 1925); Phyllis Deane, *The First Industrial Revolution* (Cambridge, 1967); Eric Hobsbawm, *Industry and Empire, from 1750 to the Present Day* (Harmondsworth, 1968; repr. London, 1999); and N. F. R. Crafts, *British Economic Growth during the Industrial Revolution* (Oxford, 1985). The constant revision of British industrialisation throughout the twentieth century has formed the focus of a number of studies: see, in particular, David Cannadine, 'The present and the past in the English industrial revolution, 1880–1980', *Past and Present*, 103 (1984), pp. 131–72; D. C. Coleman, 'Myth, history and the industrial revolution', in *Myth, History and the Industrial Revolution* (London, 1992); and Patrick K. O'Brien, 'Introduction: Modern conceptions of the Industrial Revolution', in Idem and Roland Quinault, eds., *The Industrial Revolution and British Society* (Cambridge, 1993).

Growth accounting. The new estimates for economic growth down to 1841 are outlined in C. Knick Harley, 'British industrialisation before 1841: Evidence of slower growth during the industrial revolution', *Journal of Economic History*, 42/2 (1982), pp. 267–89; N. F. R. Crafts, 'British economic growth, 1700–1831: A review', *Economic History Review*, 36/2 (1983), pp. 177–99 and Idem, *British Economic Growth*, ch. 1. A final set of estimates is contained in N. F. R. Crafts and C. Knick Harley, 'Output growth and the British industrial revolution: A restatement of the Crafts-Harley view', *Economic History Review*, 45/4 (1992), pp. 703–30. C. Knick Harley, 'Reassessing the industrial revolution: A macro view' in J. Mokyr, ed., *The British Industrial Revolution: An Economic Perspective* (Boulder, Colorado, 1993) provides a useful summary. The critiques by Hoppit and by Berg and Hudson still remain useful: Julian Hoppit, 'Counting the industrial revolution', *Economic History Review*, 43/2 (1990), pp. 173–93; and Maxine Berg and Pat Hudson, 'Rehabilitating the industrial revolution', *Economic History Review*, 45/1 (1992), pp. 24–50. For the period after 1830, see R. C. O. Matthews, C. H. Feinstein and J. C. Odling-Smee, *British Economic Growth, 1856–1973* (Stanford, 1982); C. H. Feinstein, 'Capital formation in Great Britain', in P. Mathias and M. M. Postan, eds., *The Cambridge Economic History of Europe*, i. (Cambridge, 1978), pp. 28–96. These estimates are rather old but they are all we have.

Population. The two key texts for the study of population history are E. A. Wrigley and R. S. Schofield, *Population History of England, 1541–1871: A Reconstruction* (Cambridge, 1981) and E. A. Wrigley, R. S. Smith, J. E. Oeppen and R. S. Schofield, *English Population History from Family Reconstitution, 1580–1837* (Cambridge, 1997). More accessible summaries of this research are contained in E. A. Wrigley, 'British population during the long eighteenth century', in Floud and Johnson, eds., *Cambridge Economic History of Modern Britain* and Andrew Hinde, *England's Population: A History since the Domesday Survey* (London, 2003). The following critiques of the methodology used by Wrigley and his team are also helpful: M. W. Flinn, 'The population history of England, 1541–1871', *Economic History Review*, 35/3 (1982), pp. 443–57; and Steven Ruggles, 'The limitations of English family reconstitution: English population history from family reconstitution, 1580–1837', *Continuity and Change*, 14/1 (1999), pp. 105–30. The debate about the causes of changing marriage patterns was kicked off in E. A. Wrigley, 'Growth of population in eighteenth-century England: A conundrum resolved', *Past and Present*, 98 (1983), pp. 121–50. By helping to refine exactly what needed to be explained, J. A. Goldstone, 'The demographic revolution in England: A re-examination', *Population Studies*, 49 (1986), pp. 5–33 made an important contribution. The recent family reconstitution by Hudson and King moves away from the generalising tendency of much demographic history and sheds valuable new light on the nature of demographic change during the period: Pat Hudson and Steve King, 'Two textile townships, c. 1660–1820: A comparative demographic analysis', *Economic History Review*, 53/4 (2000), pp. 706–41. For a discussion of marital fertility, see E. A. Wrigley, 'Explaining the rise in marital fertility in England in the "long" eighteenth-century', *Economic History Review*, 51/3 (1998), pp. 435–64. For mortality, see John Landers, *Death and the Metropolis: Studies in the Demographic History of London, 1670–1830* (Cambridge, 1993) and Mary Dobson, *Contours of Death and Disease in Early Modern England* (Cambridge, 1997). For the nineteenth century, see Robert Woods, *The Demography of Victorian England and Wales, 1811–1911* (Cambridge, 2000). The literature for Scotland is considerably less developed. M. Flinn et al., *Scottish Population History from the Seventeenth Century to the 1930s* (Cambridge, 1977) is old, but remains the most comprehensive study available.

Migration. A good overview of patterns of migration during this period may be found in Colin G. Pooley and Jean Turnball, *Migration and Mobility in Britain since the Eighteenth Century* (London, 1998). The following two essays provide more detailed local studies: Colin G. Pooley and Shani D'Cruz, 'Migration and urbanisation in north-west England, c.1760–1830', *Social History*, 19/3 (1994), pp. 339–58; S. King, 'Migrants on the margin: Mobility, integration and occupation in the West Riding, 1650–1820', *Journal of Historical Geography*, 23/3 (1997), pp. 284–303.

Urbanisation. For the eighteenth century, see E. A. Wrigley, 'Urban growth and agricultural change: England and the continent in the early modern period', *Journal of Interdisciplinary History*, 15/4 (1985), pp. 683–728. The story is continued into the nineteenth century in John Langton, 'Urban growth and economic change from the seventeenth century to 1841', in P. Clark, ed., *The Cambridge Urban History of Britain, 1540–1840*, ii. (Cambridge, 2000), pp. 453–90. For Scotland, see Ian D. Whyte,

'Urbanization in eighteenth-century Scotland', in T. M. Devine, Martin Thomas and John R. Young, eds., *Eighteenth-Century Scotland: New Perspectives* (East Linton, 1999), pp. 176–94.

Agriculture. Different interpretations of the agricultural revolution may be found in Mark Overton, 'Re-establishing the English agricultural revolution', *Agricultural History Review*, 44 (1996), pp. 1–20; and Robert Allen, 'Tracking the agricultural revolution in England', *Economic History Review*, 52/2 (1999), pp. 209–35. For the development of agriculture more generally, the following essays are useful: E. A. Wrigley, 'The transition to an advanced organic economy: Half a millennium of English agriculture', *Economic History Review*, 59/3 (2006), pp. 435–80; M. Overton and B. M. S. Campbell, 'Statistics of production and productivity in English agriculture 1086–1871', in B. J. P. van Bavel and E. Thoen, eds., *Land Productivity and Agro-Systems in the North Sea area* (Turnhout, 1999), pp. 189–208; G. Clark, 'Yields per acre in English agriculture, 1250–1860: Evidence from labour inputs', *Economic History Review*, 44/2 (1991), pp. 445–60. The impact of enclosure is considered in Robert Allen, *Enclosure and the Yeoman: The Agricultural Development of the South Midlands, 1450–1850* (Cambridge, 1992); Janette Neeson, *Commoners: Common Right, Enclosure and Social Change in England, 1700–1820* (Cambridge, 1993); and Leigh Shaw-Taylor, 'Labourers, cows, common rights and parliamentary enclosure: The evidence of contemporary comment c.1760–1810', *Past and Present*, 171 (2001), pp. 97–126.

Work. The most important research into occupational patterns is the research project run by Leigh Shaw-Taylor and E. A. Wrigley entitled 'The occupational structure of Britain 1379–1911'. At the time of writing, the project is still ongoing and working papers are added to the project's website (http://www.geog.cam.ac.uk/research/projects/occupations) as the results emerge. Also important are the earlier attempts to interpret the social tables devised by Gregory King and Joseph Massie: for these, see Tom Arkell, 'Illuminations and distortions: Gregory King's Scheme calculated for the year 1688 and the social structure of later Stuart England', *Economic History Review*, 59/1 (2006), pp. 32–69; and Peter Mathias, 'The social structure in the eighteenth century: A calculation by Joseph Massie', *Economic History Review*, 10/1 (1957), pp. 30–45. An early attempt to use baptism registers to study occupational structure was made in Peter H. Lindert and Jeffrey G. Williamson, 'Revising England's social tables, 1688–1812', *Explorations in Economic History*, 19/4 (1982), pp. 385–804. Kussmaul used marriage registers and the timing of weddings as an alternative way of gauging the distribution of the workforce. See Ann Kussmaul, *A General View of the Rural Economy of England, 1538–1840* (Cambridge, 1990). These overviews of occupational structure are based largely on material concerning male workers and they should be considered in conjunction with studies of female and child labour. The literature on women's work is vast: Katrina Honeyman, *Women, Gender and Industrialization in England, 1700–1870* (London, 2000) provides a useful overview and Pamela Sharpe, ed., *Women's Work: The English Experience, 1650–1914* (London, 1998) contains a number of important essays. Two detailed studies of women in industry and women in agriculture are Carol E. Morgan, *Women Workers and Gender Identities, 1835–1913: The Cotton and Metal Industries in England* (London, 2002) and Nicola Verdon, *Rural Women Workers in Nineteenth-Century England: Gender, Work and Wages* (Woodbridge, 2002). Other useful essays include Joyce Burnette, 'An investigation of the female–male wage gap during the industrial revolution in Britain', *Economic History Review*, 57/4 (1997), pp. 257–81; Sara Horrell and

Jane Humphries, 'Women's labour force participation and the transition to the male-breadwinner family, 1790–1865', *Economic History Review*, 48/1 (1995), pp. 89–117; Maxine Berg, 'What difference did women's work make to the industrial revolution?', *History Workshop Journal*, 35/1 (1993), pp. 22–44; and Deborah Valenze, 'The art of women and the business of men: Women's work and the dairy industry c.1740–1840', *Past and Present*, 130 (1991), pp. 142–69. For child labour, Peter Kirby, *Child Labour in Britain, 1750–1870* (Basingstoke, 2003) provides an excellent introduction. Hugh Cunningham, *Children and Childhood in Western Society since 1500* (London, 1995) and Eric Hopkins, *Childhood Transformed: Working-Class Children in Nineteenth-Century England* (Manchester, 1994) are older but still useful. An interesting collection of essays is to be found in Michael Lavalette, ed., *A Thing of the Past? Child Labour in Britain in the Nineteenth and Twentieth Centuries* (Liverpool, 1999). Also important are the following two essays: Sara Horrell and Jane Humphries, ' "The exploitation of little children": Child labor and the family economy in the industrial revolution', *Explorations in Economic History*, 32 (1995), pp. 485–516; and H. Cunningham, 'The employment and unemployment of children, 1680–1851', *Past and Present*, 126 (1990), pp. 115–50.

Technology. The development and significance of technological progress during the period of industrialisation has formed the focus of a number of studies. Important texts include David Landes, *The Unbound Prometheus: Technological Change and Development in Western Europe from 1750 to the Present* (Cambridge, 1969); Joel Mokyr, *The Lever of Riches: Technological Creativity and Economic Progress* (Oxford, 1990); and Margaret K. Jacob, *Scientific Culture and the Making of the Industrial West* (Oxford, 1997). A useful summary of the historiography may be found in Kristine Bruland, 'Industrialisation and technological change', in Floud and Johnson, eds., *Cambridge Economic History of Modern Britain*, pp. 117–46. Growth accounting has tended to underplay the significance of technology for British industrialisation and a recent restatement of this view may be found in N. F. R. Crafts, 'Steam as a general purpose technology: A growth accounting perspective', *Economic Journal*, 114/495 (2004), pp. 338–51. The study of particular industries and regions remains central to understanding the progress of technology during this period. For textiles, see S. D. Chapman, *The Cotton Industry in the Industrial Revolution* (London, 1972); Trevor Griffiths, Philip A. Hunt and Patrick K. O'Brien, 'Inventive activity in the British textile industry, 1700–1800', *Journal of Economic History*, 52/4 (1992), pp. 881–906; Adrian Randall, *Before the Luddites: Custom, Community and Machinery in the English Woollen Industry, 1770–1809* (Cambridge, 1991); Geoffrey Timmins, *The Last Shift: The Decline of Handloom Weaving in Nineteenth-century Lancashire* (Manchester, 1993); and Stanley Chapman, *Hosiery and Knitwear: Four Centuries of Small-Scale Industry in Britain, c.1589–2000* (Oxford, 2002). For metal-working, see Philip Riden, 'The output of the British iron industry before 1870', *Economic History Review*, 30/3 (1977), pp. 442–59; J. R. Harris, *The British Iron Industry, 1700–1850* (London, 1988); and R. Burt, 'The transformation of the non-ferrous metals industries in the seventeenth and eighteenth centuries', *Economic History Review*, 48/1 (1995), pp. 23–45. Industrial histories of Lancashire and Birmingham may be found in Geoffrey Timmins, *Made in Lancashire. A History of Regional Industrialisation* (Manchester, 1998) and Eric Hopkins, *The Rise of the Manufacturing town: Birmingham and the Industrial Revolution* (London, 1989; repr. Stroud, 1998). Finally, the following three works turn away from the great inventions and focus attention on the impact of improvements to hand technology (Steven King and Geoffrey Timmins, *Making Sense of the Industrial Revolution* (Manchester, 2001), ch. 3); to product design (M. Berg, 'From imitation to invention: Creating commodities in eighteenth-century Britain', *Economic History Review*, 55/1 (2002), pp. 1–30); and to smaller industries (Peter Temin, 'Two views of the British industrial revolution', *Journal of Economic History*, 57/1 (1997), pp. 63–82).

Transport. An excellent introduction to the history of transport may be found in Simon Ville, 'Transport', in Floud and Johnson, eds., *Cambridge Economic History of Modern Britain*, pp. 295–331. The topic has been somewhat neglected in recent years, but the following edited collection remains useful: Michael J. Freeman and Derek H. Aldcroft, eds., *Transport in Victorian Britain* (Manchester, 1988). Of enduring significance is Gerard Turnbull, 'Canals, coal and regional growth during the industrial revolution', *Economic History Review*, 40/4 (1987), pp. 537–60. Though ostensibly about canals, this essay also contains some important insights about the relationship between transport and economic change during this period.

Coal. Tony Wrigley provides a forceful argument for the centrality of coal to British industrialisation in E. A. Wrigley, *Continuity, Chance and Change: The Character of the Industrial Revolution in England* (Cambridge, 1990). The significance of coal is also highlighted in Rondo Cameron, 'A new view of European industrialisation', *Economic History Review*, 38/1 (1985), pp. 1–23; Jack A. Goldstone, 'Efflorescences and economic growth in world history: Rethinking the "rise of the West" and the industrial revolution', *Journal of World History*, 13/2 (2002), pp. 323–89; and Robert C. Allen, *The British Industrial Revolution in Global Perspective* (Cambridge, 2009). A more sceptical appraisal is contained in G. Clark and D. Jacks, 'Coal and the industrial revolution, 1700–1869', *European Review of Economic History*, 11/1 (2007), pp. 39–72. The following two histories of the coal industry between 1700 and 1913 provide important contextual detail on the development of the coal-mining and on coal output: Michael W. Flinn, *The History of the British Coal Industry: 1700–1830: The Industrial Revolution*, ii. (Oxford, 1984) and R. Church, *The History of the British Coal Industry: 1830–1913, Victorian Pre-eminence*, iii. (Oxford, 1986).

Global industrialisation. Useful overviews of European industrialisation may be found in Colin Heywood, 'The challenge of industrialisation', in Pamela M. Pilbean, ed., *Themes in Modern European History, 1780–1830* (London, 1995), pp. 151–76 and François Crouzet, *History of the European Economy, 1000–2000* (London, 2001), pp. 130–2. The following works provide greater detail and a useful departure point for the study of industrialisation across Europe: Hilde Greefs, Bruno Blondé and Peter Clark, 'The growth of urban industrial regions: Belgian developments in comparative perspective, 1750–1850', in Jon Stobart and Neil Raven, eds., *Towns, Regions and Industries: Urban and Industrial Change in the Midlands, C. 1700–1840* (Manchester, 2005), pp. 210–27; Jan de Vries and A. van der Woude, *The First Modern Economy: Success, Failure and Perseverance of the Dutch Economy, 1500–1815* (Cambridge, 1997); David Blackbourn, *The Fontana History of Germany, 1815–1918: The Long Nineteenth Century* (London, 1997); Toni Pierenkemper and Richard Tilly, *The German Economy during the Nineteenth Century* (New York, 2004); François Crouzet, 'The historiography of French economic growth in the nineteenth century', *Economic History Review*, 56/2 (2003), pp. 215–42; Jeff Horn, *The Path Not Taken: French Industrialisation in the Age of Revolution, 1750–1830* (Cambridge, MA, 2006); and Vera Zamagni, *The Economic History of Italy, 1860–1990* (Oxford, 1993). The significance of industrial change outside Europe has traditionally been discounted but the past decade has seen some important critiques of this view. See, in particular, A. G. Frank, *ReOrient: The Silver Age in Asia and the World Economy* (Berkeley, 1998) and Kenneth Pomeranz, *The Great Divergence: China, Europe, and the Making of the Modern World Economy* (Princeton, 2000). Economic progress in China, Japan and India is considered in R. Bin Wong, *China Transformed: Historical Change and the Limits of European Experience* (Ithaca and London, 1997); Susan B. Hanley, *Everyday Things in Premodern Japan: The Hidden Legacy of Material Culture* (London, 1999); P. Parthasarathi, *The Transition to a Colonial Economy: Weavers, Merchants and Kings in South India, 1720–1800* (Cambridge, 2001).

Living standards. A good and up-to-date overview of the very long-running debate over living standards during the industrial revolution may be found in Hans-Joachim Voth, 'Living standards and the urban environment', in Floud and Johnson, eds., *Cambridge Economic History of Modern Britain*, pp. 268–94. The most recent estimates for real wages are to be found in Charles H. Feinstein, 'Pessimism perpetuated: Real wages and the standard of living in Britain during and after the industrial revolution', *Journal of Economic History*, 58/3 (1998), pp. 625–58; G. Clark, 'The condition of the working class in England, 1209–2004', *Journal of Political Economy*, 113/6 (2005), pp. 1307–40; Idem., 'Farm wages and living standards in the industrial revolution: England, 1670–1869', *Economic History Review*, 54/3 (2001), pp. 477–505; Robert C. Allen, 'The great divergence in European wages and prices from the middle ages to the First World War,' *Explorations in Economic History*, 38 (2001), pp. 411–447. For heights, see Stephen Nicholas and Deborah Oxley, 'The living standards of women during the industrial revolution, 1795–1820', *Economic History Review*, 46/4 (1993), pp. 723–49; and Paul Johnson and Stephen Nicholas, 'Male and female living standards in England and Wales, 1812–1857: Evidence from criminal height records', *Economic History Review*, 48/3 (1995), pp. 470–81. For mortality, Wrigley et al., *English Population History* and E. A. Wrigley and R. S. Schofield, *Population History of England* are useful. In addition, the following two essays attempt to clarify the relationship between mortality and living standards: Paul Huck, 'Infant mortality and the living standards of English workers during the industrial revolution', *Journal of Economic History*, 55/3 (1995), pp. 528–50; and Simon Szreter and Graham Mooney, 'Urbanisation, mortality, and the standard of living debate', *Economic History Review*, 51/1, (1998), pp. 84–112. The following three essays offer some alternative approaches to the measurement of living standards: Joel Mokyr, 'Is there still life in the pessimist case? Consumption during the industrial revolution, 1790–1850', *Journal of Economic History*, 48 (1988), pp. 69–92; N. F. R. Crafts, 'Some dimensions of the "quality of life" during the British industrial revolution', *Economic History Review*, 50/4 (1997), pp. 617–39; Samantha Williams, 'Poor relief, labourers' households and living standards in rural England c. 1770–1834: A Bedfordshire case study', *Economic History Review*, 58/3 (2005), pp. 485–519. Finally, working-class autobiographies provide an excellent window into the social context of industrialisation. The following provides a selection of easily obtainable texts, available either as reprints or on Google Books: Joseph Arch, *Joseph Arch: The Story of His Life, Told by Himself.* Edited with a preface by The Countess of Warwick (London, 1966); Alexander Somerville, *The Autobiography of a Working Man* (London, 1848; repr. London, 1967); James Hawker, 'The life of a poacher', in Garth Christian, ed., *A Victorian Poacher. James Hawker's Journal* (Oxford, 1978); George Parkinson, *True Stories of Durham Pit-Life* (London, 1912); Samuel Bamford, *Early Days* (London, 1849); James R. Simmons and Janice Carlisle, eds., *Factory Lives: Four Nineteenth-Century Working-Class Autobiographies* (Ontario, 2007).

Index